NORMAN PORTER was born
his family emigrated to Austi
in Politics from Flinders U.
Politics from the University of Oxford. His book *Rethinking
Unionism* (Blackstaff Press, 1996), was a joint winner of the 1997
Christopher Ewart-Biggs Memorial Prize. He is currently a
Senior Visiting Research Fellow at the Institute of Irish Studies,
Queen's University Belfast.

Acclaim for *Rethinking Unionism: An Alternative Vision for
Northern Ireland* by Norman Porter (Blackstaff, 1996)

'One of the seminal books of the Troubles and the first genuinely
visionary statement to come from the unionist community . . .
an extremely daring, contemporaneous and inventive treatise in
political philosophy which discovers – virtually for the first time
– a concept of politics in a barren political terrain . . . A book that
deserves to be read well beyond the borders of Northern Ireland
for its contribution to the literature on conflict resolution.'

Paul Arthur, *Political Quarterly*

'Rich in ideas and generous in vision . . . a voice of prophetic
common sense which is sorely needed in a place where both
prophecy and common sense are rare commodities . . . the most
cheering blast of idealistic thinking to have come out of
Northern Ireland in some considerable time'

Andy Pollak, *Irish Times*

'In many ways this is a book we have been waiting for . . . a
scholarly, thoughtful, penetrating and very readable analysis of
the state of unionism, providing a philosophical basis for a new
departure.'

Maurice Hayes, *Belfast Telegraph*

'Norman Porter's surprising and iconoclastic book looks to the
future, equally asserting the need to recognise differences and
redefine traditional boundaries . . . a powerful and imaginative
contribution to the ideals represented by this Prize'

*Professor Roy Foster, speaking on behalf of the judges of the 1997
Christopher Ewart-Biggs Memorial Prize*

The Elusive Quest
Reconciliation in Northern Ireland

NORMAN PORTER

THE
BLACKSTAFF
PRESS

BELFAST

First published in 2003 by
Blackstaff Press Limited
Wildflower Way, Apollo Road
Belfast BT12 6TA

with the assistance of
INCORE and the financial support of NIVT

This book has received support from the NI Community Relations Council,
which aims to encourage acceptance and understanding of cultural diversity.
The views expressed do not necessarily reflect those of the
NI Community Relations Council.

Typeset by Techniset Typesetters, Newton-le-Willows, Merseyside

Printed in Ireland by Betaprint

A CIP catalogue record for this book is available
from the British Library

ISBN 0-85640-730-5

www.blackstaffpress.com

CONTENTS

To Shantala, Simon and Luke

ACKNOWLEDGEMENTS

This book has been much too long in coming. Most of the thinking about it, and some of the writing of it, were done while I had a research position at INCORE (Initiative on Conflict Resolution and Ethnicity) in the University of Ulster. The book was finally completed while I was a Senior Visiting Research Fellow at the Institute of Irish Studies, Queen's University Belfast. I am grateful for the space for thought and practical assistance that both institutions provided. I am also grateful for funding from the European Peace and Reconciliation Fund, the Ireland Funds, and Atlantic Philanthropies that facilitated the book's research and writing. Bits of the book were tried out on audiences in Adelaide, Belfast, Derry, Dublin, Melbourne, Nicosia and Vienna, and I benefited from the constructive comments and criticisms I received in each of these venues.

Given that political parties are sometimes seen as the bane of reconciliation in Northern society, not least by me, it is perhaps a little ironic that I owe a peculiar debt to so many of them. The motivation to write and the determination to persevere with the book came from my dealings with political representatives of the Alliance Party, Fianna Fáil, Fine Gael, the Progressive Unionist Party, the Social Democratic and Labour Party, Sinn Féin, the Ulster Democratic Party, the Ulster Unionist Party, the Northern Ireland Women's Coalition, and the Workers' Party. Whether any of them will be happy to learn that they were instrumental in inspiring me to write the sort of book that I have is, of course, another matter. As usual, I am indebted to the staff at Blackstaff Press, and particularly to Hilary Bell for her fine editorial skills. And my greatest debts are as ever to my family, to Helen, and to Shantala, Simon and Luke, and most of all to Lis.

INTRODUCTION

Reconciliation matters. And if it mattered enough to enough of us in Northern Ireland, then we would have it. Or at least we would have something tolerably close to it: citizens would not be alienated from their public institutions or from each other, sectarianism would no longer be our lot, and society's most serious divisions would be healed. So runs a dominant line of this book. Put so starkly, it probably sounds unduly cavalier. It is not, however, meant to signal an underestimation of the obstacles that stand in reconciliation's way. And it is not intended to trivialise the difficulties involved in trying to remove them. In fact, my line is not incompatible with the conclusion that the reality of Northern Ireland's circumstances is such that reconciliation is likely to prove elusive for quite some time. The point is to say that it need not be, that reconciliation's problems are not of such an order that they defy the powers of human wit, imagination and determination to resolve. As we shall see, this is a controversial argument.

It is, admittedly, an argument that is easier to make because conflict in Northern Ireland has lost its sharp, militaristic edge. Of course, violence has not vanished altogether and its persistence is a matter of consternation: paramilitary ceasefires notwithstanding, loyalists who have also murdered each other have murdered Catholics, republicans have settled scores within their own community, there remains a commitment to physical force within the ranks of the Continuity IRA and the Real IRA, and instances of intercommunal violence continue in flash point areas such as North Belfast. None the less, the scale of paramilitary activities has reduced dramatically. Despite strains in republican and loyalist ceasefires, and even despite the British government's judgement in October 2001 that the Ulster Defence Association's (UDA's) is no longer intact, the main point is that only a small minority still think that problems in the North can be sorted out through armed struggle. In addition, of course, the majority of Northern Ireland's political parties, subsequently backed by overwhelming majorities of the electorates North and South, ostensibly managed to settle enough of their differences to support the Agreement reached in Belfast on 10 April (Good Friday) 1998 (hereinafter referred to as the Agreement). Among other things, this has led to the formation of a power-sharing political Executive involving members from unionist, nationalist and republican parties. In short, peace and political initiatives since the mid-1990s, if not earlier, suggest very strongly that conflict in Northern Ireland was not, as Michael Ignatieff remarks of that in Kosovo, 'radical and unbridgeable'; that, unlike conflict there, conflict here did not witness the type of clash of irreconcilable 'interests, values and commitments'[1] that made the outbreak of full-scale war utterly unsurprising.

To a superficial glance, it might even seem odd that I am making an issue about reconciliation. The impression may be that conditions are now conducive to breaking down traditional barriers between Northern citizens, that reconciling processes are sufficiently established to enable citizens to set about the business of building a common civic and political life with a minimum of fuss. The contrast with Kosovo, the presence of relative peace, the existence of a formal political agreement between local parties and underwritten by the British and Irish governments, the inauguration of a power-sharing devolved government, not to mention the resources devoted to reconciliation at community levels for a generation and more, all combine to suggest that reconciliation is at hand, or certainly well on its way. Accordingly, to think it appropriate to make an argument for reconciliation, and a controversial one at that, may seem perverse.

Without doubt, achievements such as peace and political agreement are extremely significant, but it is premature to conclude that an argument for reconciliation is now redundant. For one thing, even if we take reconciliation's apparent achievements at face value, Northern Ireland remains a deeply divided society. The legacy of a generation of violence has left scars of bitterness and fear among citizens of all religious and political persuasions; cultural differences between unionists and nationalists are as pronounced as they have ever been and continue to create tense situations, especially during the marching season;[2] housing and educational segregation between Protestants and Catholics in working-class areas of Belfast, for example, is virtually complete and shows little sign of changing; and, in general, a climate of mistrust exists between large numbers of unionists and nationalists and stretches reconciliation's spirit to the limit.

Moreover, reconciliation's achievements are not easily taken at face value. Its political cornerstone, the Agreement, is opposed by so-called dissident republicans and, more worryingly, by a substantial number of unionists. Although it is still backed by a majority of Northern political parties and citizens, indications are that the slender majority support it initially enjoyed among unionists has been whittled away. Ian Paisley's Democratic Unionist Party (DUP), a number of other minor unionist parties, and the Orange Order actively denounce it. Commitment to it within the Ulster Unionist Party (UUP) has waned and, while formally entrusted to making it work, the party is seriously split over it. Disagreement over its meaning plagues pro-Agreement parties and is especially acute between the UUP and Sinn Féin. This disagreement has been serious enough to hinder the full implementation of the Agreement. It has prompted the British government to suspend the Northern Ireland Assembly on four occasions, and has made the experiment in power-sharing devolved government a difficult, some might say a crisis-ridden, experience. At the time of writing in October 2002, it is unclear what will become of the experiment, since a fourth, indefinite suspension is in place and direct rule from Westminster has returned. Clearly, political, let alone cultural, divisions in the North have not been eroded as a consequence of the Agreement and threats of its collapse, together with fears of a return to serious intercommunal paramilitary violence, are rarely far away.

Reconciliation's current achievements, then, are possibly precarious and definitely incomplete. The content of the Agreement may have reconciling intent, but, given the problems it has encountered, it is prudent to wonder whether its support among political parties reflects a reconciling ethos or simply calculations of tactical advantage. There is enough uncertainty about its future to give heart to reconciliation's detractors and to give pause to its backers, and enough ambiguity in Northern Ireland's contemporary cultural and political circumstances to undermine a commitment to reconciliation that, with honourable exceptions, has never been altogether convincing. Reconciliation's success clearly cannot be taken for granted and more progress than we have yet witnessed is needed to secure it. Reconciliation continues to require advocates.

In this book I want, above all else, to develop a case why reconciliation is a good thing, which should be pursued enthusiastically, even if it calls for a reordering of cultural and political priorities in the North. This involves questioning why support for reconciliation often seems lacklustre, refusing to be satisfied with much that passes under its name, confronting the arguments of its detractors, and advancing a stronger, and more demanding, understanding of reconciliation than many may think necessary or advisable. In addition, it involves reflecting on conditions in Northern Ireland in a manner that draws on larger cultural, political and philosophical analyses. By trying to show that reconciliation is desirable, and by stating what I think it consists in, I am also endeavouring to indicate that it is possible and need not remain elusive.

These attempts to vindicate reconciliation's project are, however, limited in scope. Not everything relevant to the project receives adequate treatment. Some may be disappointed by a lack of theological content, and others by a failure to explore reconciliation's prospects in terms of Northern Ireland's relationships with the

Republic of Ireland and Britain, if not also with Europe.[3] It is not that I think these wider political and theological dimensions of reconciliation are unimportant, and I do nod in their direction from time to time, but they very much play a secondary role to my pre-occupation with cultural and political relations within Northern Ireland. To Irish nationalists and republicans this may seem like loading the dice in unionism's favour, since it appears to preclude the possibility that reconciliation may be ultimately achieved only within an all-Ireland context. In truth, it is not my intention to rule out this possibility. It is more that I am taking my cue from the cir-cumstances that currently prevail in Northern society, especially as it is hard to understand how the divisions that characterise so much of them could be instantly transformed by the stroke of a constitu-tional pen. Accordingly, I am principally concerned here with existing relations within the North, which need to be sorted out whatever our view of Ireland's and Britain's future constitutional composition. A united Ireland may be eventually realised, or it may not, but for the moment we have to deal with political arrangements that formally recognise Northern Ireland's place within the United Kingdom, albeit under peculiar terms. It is in reference to these arrangements and the wider cultural and political issues they raise that I introduce questions of reconciliation's possibilities.

In Chapter 1, I outline a general context within which my particular discussion of reconciliation in Northern Ireland takes place. This is a context defined by what I call enthusiastic and cyni-cal responses to the idea of reconciliation. Reconciliation, I suggest, has increasingly become a buzz word for describing what is required in unstable situations of ongoing or recent conflict throughout the world and also in relatively stable situations of cul-tural contestation. A cynical attitude regards it as a misleading word, one used to assert power relations of some kind or another under a benign guise. An enthusiastic attitude, by contrast, thinks reconciliation is an entirely appropriate term, one that fuses tradi-tional religious and political concerns in a peculiarly modern form suited to address complex matters of cultural and political dispute.

My treatment of reconciliation in Northern Ireland operates mostly in an enthusiastic mode, although elements of a cynical attitude are also incorporated. This is not a recipe for an unproblematic discussion. Enthusiasm's appeal is complicated in the North and cynicism poses challenges to the entire project of reconciliation. In indicating some of these complications and challenges, I try to become clearer on the nature of the problems advocacy of reconciliation has to confront.

Four of these problems feature in Chapter 2, where I consider the possibility that reconciliation is not the positive thing that many of us presume. One problem focuses on the puzzle of why, given the resources devoted to it, Northern Ireland is not a model of reconciliation. Part of the answer, I propose, lies in understanding a second problem, namely that it is peace and not reconciliation that many of us in the North are keen on. Another part of the answer is that reconciliation and (cultural or political) difference are occasionally seen as incompatible alternatives. Here, a third problem emerges through the view that reconciliation really means assimilation and therefore entails an unwelcome, if not impossible, request that citizens consent to a political marginalisation of their differences. This is quickly followed by a fourth problem, which takes the form of implicit or explicit affirmations of difference at the expense of reconciliation. In dealing with these four problems, I am trying to explain why reconciliation is not always considered a good thing (even by some who say that it is), and I am indicating why I think that its alternatives in Northern Ireland are neither viable nor desirable. For example, I argue against attempts to separate peace from reconciliation, against a conception of reconciliation as assimilation, and against a prioritisation of difference. However, although I find all of these alternatives wanting, they bequeath further problems that have to be tackled before reconciliation can be unreservedly heralded as a positive thing.

In Chapter 3, I give a preliminary account of my understanding of reconciliation and assert that it faces general problems of a lack of civic virtue among citizens and of squaring concerns of commonality and difference. It also confronts entrenched cultural–political difficulties in Northern Ireland, which hinder resolution of these general problems. I consider whether such problems can be resolved by thinking of reconciliation as a balancing act. This is perhaps the most popular way of conceiving of it, and one that is prominent in government circles. It is a way that is encouraged by promotion of the concept of parity of esteem as a key to handling cultural and political conflicts in the North. And it has certain attractions. Among other things, it moves discussion beyond thinking of reconciliation and difference as either/or alternatives, it properly emphasises that a lot of give and take is required to achieve reconciliation, and it underscores that inclusion is one of reconciliation's necessary features. Undoubtedly, any successful attempt to reconcile opposing parties, traditions or communities does involve an act of balancing. Even so, only to think in terms of such an act does not suffice: it offers too weak a conception of reconciliation, and one that does not succeed in resolving the major problems I identified. Its failings reflect the inappropriateness of supposing that balancing acts can overcome the sort of obstacles that block reconciliation's path.

A typical mistake of equating reconciliation with balancing is to imagine that it always implies steering a middle path between competing claims. This gives rise to the familiar wisecrack, curiously appealing to a variety of government ministers, officials and international mediators, that a proposal that is equally unacceptable to two sides of a dispute is almost certainly the right one. No doubt the wisecrack has a point in emphasising the need for compromise if standoffs between traditional political enemies in the North are not to become intractable. But to make too much of it is counterproductive. Its difficulty is not merely that of cultivating allegiance to a solution nobody wants, it is also that of insinuating that questions of justice, say, are dispensable to the enterprise of reconciliation. What gets lost is the possibility that on a particular issue one side may be more right than another, and that reconciliation may involve trying to persuade the side that has least claim to justice to modify its stance. The relationship between reconciliation and justice is a delicate one, but to presume automatically that reconciliation infers taking a third or middle way on controversial questions sidelines any serious discussion of justice and risks becoming utterly vacuous. Another mistake of highlighting the benefits of balancing occurs when reconciliation is made hostage to the pragmatic calculations of unionist and nationalist interests. This happens when what I call parity of esteem's accommodating dimension – which I think has a lot to commend it – is weakened, and in practice overshadowed, by what I refer to as its extreme entitlement dimension. The result is that the quest for reconciliation becomes subservient to the pursuit of particular interests. When I say that I am concerned with affirming unreservedly that reconciliation is a good thing, this is not what I have in mind.

If the first three chapters endeavour to create a space within which we may think more clearly about reconciliation, the next four endeavour to fill it. Throughout Chapters 4–7, I consider what reconciliation requires in relation to questions of philosophy, politics and culture. My responses centre on teasing out an understanding of reconciliation briefly mooted in Chapter 3, which says that reconciliation entails embracing and engaging others who are different from us in a spirit of openness and with a view to expanding our horizons, healing our divisions and articulating common purposes. This understanding comprises the core of what I refer to as a strong conception of reconciliation, one that is capable in principle, I argue, of resolving the outstanding problems of virtue and the commonality–difference conundrum, and of showing what their resolution might mean in the particular circumstances of Northern Ireland. As my explanations and arguments make plain, reconciliation, far from being a soft option, appears here as a hard taskmaster. If taken seriously, it disturbs prejudices, disrupts practices and queries priorities. I specify its challenge in terms of three requirements.

Chapter 4 concentrates on one of these requirements, which I call that of fair interactions between citizens. Meeting it is a responsibility of us all and not just of our political representatives, and involves much more than adhering to a set of rules or procedures: it also involves cultivating civic virtues such as forgiveness, magnanimity and reasonableness, embracing those who are different from us by recognising the importance of mutual indebtedness and inclusion, and participating in practices of engagement such as dialogue. Among the forms of resistance the requirement of fair interactions encounters in Northern Ireland, those located in tendencies to privatise virtue and in anti-dialogical attitudes to language are particularly serious. Tendencies to privatisation pervade Northern culture and examples of anti-dialogical attitudes are evident within the tradition of physical force republicanism and, more diffusely, within unionism. If fair interactions are ever to be realised it is important to say why tendencies to reduce issues of virtue to the level of merely private concern should be challenged, as well as why anti-dialogical attitudes and practices should be transformed. There is, of course, no guarantee that the necessary challenges or cases for transformation will be successful, but in underscoring the obstacles to reconciliation posed by virtue's privatisation and by language's diminution in anti-dialogical approaches, I give reasons why they should be.

Chapter 5 takes up a second requirement of reconciliation, namely that we overcome our divisions in a way that enables us to occupy common ground without riding roughshod over our differences. Meeting this requirement initially means showing that it is not incoherent or impossible. Here I return in more detail to earlier criticisms of the very idea of reconciliation advanced in the name of protecting difference, and I also deal with others that dilute the strength and restrict the political reach of the idea I want to defend. Essentially, I try to show that the second requirement can be satisfied by conceiving of commonality (1) as a possible outcome of reasonable discussions of our differences, and (2) as a possibility that exists despite our differences. Conceiving of commonality in these ways provides a means of checking difference's excesses and a basis for anticipating the development of a common political life. Once again there is no attempt to pretend that appropriating such conceptions is easy in Northern Ireland, but suggesting why they (or something like them) should be appropriated is not entirely far-fetched either. For example, many of us believe that engaging in discussions with those who are culturally and politically different from us is not necessarily a futile exercise, and we are all committed to varying degrees to acknowledging that there are important things we share in common whatever our differences. In playing up the possibilities for commonality that are implied here, I am arguing that they should both concentrate our minds and shape our practices more firmly than they often appear to do.

A third requirement of reconciliation – that of inclusive citizen belonging – is foreshadowed in my treatment of the other two, but is dealt with explicitly in Chapters 6 and 7. It is a difficult requirement to satisfy because unionist and nationalist politics of belonging are attached to contrary cultural and political identities, which are rooted in different historical experiences and generate conflicting aspirations. The problem is that gains in one side's sense of belonging often appear as losses in the other's. As a consequence, attempts to resolve the question of belonging always appear vulnerable to charges of bias and exclusivity. A preliminary step in answering such charges is to frame the issues at stake in terms of our common entitlements to recognition as individual, cultural and political citizens. This enables us to identify the major block to inclusive citizen belonging in disputes at the level of cultural recognition, which occasionally impinge on the domain of individual recognition and almost always intrude negatively in the area of political recognition. I suggest that the Agreement keeps alive the prospect of reconciliation here by offering a creative way of handling these disputes, particularly in its endeavour to move beyond the constitutional impasse between unionism and nationalism. But the rejections of its opponents and the conflicting interpretations of its supporters make this way hard to pursue. Although the Agreement points to a new political dispensation in Northern society, it is hampered by old (divisive) practices, even among its supporters. The tactical manoeuvrings of local politicians cast doubt on just how seriously the reconciling ambitions of the Agreement are taken, especially since it is now typical to see pro-Agreement politicians making calculative political gambles with its future. There is plenty of cheer here for advocates of a cynical approach to politics, if not also for those who think it prudent to restrict aspirations in Northern Ireland to a very weak version of reconciliation. This is the grim note on which I end Chapter 6.

Nevertheless, since I do not believe such cheer is remotely gratifying, I move on in Chapter 7 to give reasons for not settling for it. For one thing, the claims of fair interactions on Northern politicians are not persuasively dodged by tactical or calculative manoeuvres, and neither are the claims of commonality, which persist despite various attempts to play up our differences and to exploit them for divisive intent. For another thing, the specific sticking points hindering reconciliation at the level of cultural recognition in post-Agreement Northern Ireland – different political priorities and views of legitimacy – do not have to be the obstacles they frequently prove to be. I try to show that there are serious problems with forms of unionist and republican reasoning here, and that these sticking points can be overcome. In doing so, I argue that the requirement of inclusive citizen belonging is not impossible to meet. But, as with the other requirements, it calls for a change of certain practices, attitudes and priorities.

It is perhaps worth remarking that the view that cultural resistance reinforces political opposition to reconciliation runs through the book. And political reconciliation is difficult to achieve, and even more difficult to sustain, if the agreements upon which it is based are perceived to upset deeply held cultural convictions. It is probably the case that cultural problems in Northern Ireland pose the stiffest challenges to the strong conception of reconciliation I am arguing for. During Chapters 4–7 especially, it becomes clear that the requirements of reconciliation which I argue can be met confront formidable hurdles: fair interactions (as already mentioned) entail attitudes to language that do not resonate across the North's cultural divisions; cultural differences are fiercely protected to the point where appeals to commonality are frequently seen as requiring unacceptable compromises; and a properly inclusive expression of citizen belonging runs foul of a cultural exclusivism that claims political privileges.

The underlying difficulty to which these hurdles attest is that reconciliation threatens certain types of cultural identities. It does, of course, call for respect of different identities, but in particular instances it also calls for their (partial) transformation. Or at least my version of strong reconciliation does, since without changes of a fundamental kind, it is fanciful to suppose we can ever overcome sectarianism. And that is why reconciliation is so hard to achieve. There is a temptation here to succumb to a variant of an assimilationist view, by simply bypassing the more taxing issues of cultural contestation and situating reconciliation on less controversial, albeit thinner, ground. This is a temptation I resist. Instead, I highlight instances of cultural difference that underpin many of our divisions in the North, and try to illustrate what it means to press for reconciliation and to face up to its requirements on matters of considerable controversy.

As should be already obvious, the argument of this book treats reconciliation, above all else, as a moral and political ideal. Like other ideals of this sort, such as justice, freedom and equality, it makes demands on how we live and think as social, political and cultural beings. In presenting reasons why reconciliation is a good thing, which should shape the priorities by which we share our collective lives in the North, I am not trying to disparage the value of other, less demanding (but some would say more realistic), attempts to indicate how we may live together in peace. But I am questioning their sufficiency. Reconciliation is integral to the process of making Northern Ireland a decent society. And, even though it does ask a lot of us, it need not be elusive.

1
CYNICISM
AND ENTHUSIASM

Reconciliation is a term that increasingly figures in our vocabularies, throughout the Western world and beyond. That reconciliation matters is no longer a verdict we expect to encounter merely in theological narratives of divine–human relations. It is also a verdict we cannot help but confront in a growing number of political narratives, as governments, international organisations, humanitarian agencies, and others comment on what is now required of relations between and within states. Most frequently, reconciliation appears as a priority in narratives of unstable regions or societies – the Middle East, the Balkans, various African nations, and so on – where sharp conflict is an ongoing or a recent reality. It may also loom large in narratives of certain stable societies – Australia, for instance – where governments face unfinished business in redressing the wrongs historically inflicted on indigenous peoples. And, of course, reconciliation features prominently in other narratives too, such as those concerned with harmonising relations within workplaces or even with healing relations within the self.

It is almost as though we live in an era of reconciliation, or at least in an era in which reconciliation is considered an important good. Politically speaking, the sources of so many conflicts between and within states – the distribution of power, alienation, division, marginalisation, humiliation, and the like – are being seen now as problems that cannot be left to fester, but that command the attention of governments and their agencies. And alongside the conventional terms in which these problems are typically discussed in the West – democracy, justice, equality, freedom, rights, stability, the rule of law, and so on – we also witness a resort to other terms – such as healing, repentance, forgiveness – that in their application to human relations were once largely restricted to a religious domain. The intermingling of conventional political and religious languages is one of the striking features of reconciliation's elevation to a political and cultural priority in recent times. And it is something of a curiosity. After all, various of the political problems considered ripe for treatment of a reconciling kind are nearly coeval with the political organisation of human society, besides being problems that certain Western nations in the heyday of their empire building and imperialism helped to exacerbate. And the language of reconciliation – certainly in its Judaic and Christian forms – has been available for millennia. So why is it now that these languages are intermingling, long after the eclipse of the idea of Christendom, long after the most important intellectual battles to separate the affairs of Church and State in the West have been fought and won? Why is reconciliation currently in vogue and considered applicable in political contexts that are largely secular or non-Christian?

TWO RESPONSES

These questions are too big to be dealt with in any depth here. But it is worth sketching two possible responses to them, which correspond roughly to contrasting attitudes to reconciliation. I will call these responses or attitudes the cynical and the enthusiastic respectively. Together they indicate a general backdrop against which my particular analysis of reconciliation in Northern Ireland is written.

CYNICAL

A cynical response is disinclined to ponder much over the intrinsic significance of the juxtaposition of political and religious languages. What counts instead is that through it we observe the growth of Western-sponsored interest in reconciliation serving as another device of control. Here reconciliation appears virtually as a tool of dominant strategic and economic interests. To illustrate, a cynical line might argue: burgeoning concern with reconciliation is a post-Cold War phenomenon and assumes a context of unrivalled Western, especially United States (US), military and technological superiority. When that superiority was not so assured and vital strategic interests were deemed to be at stake, there was precious little talk of reconciliation in the air of international relations. Prior to 1989, there were few suggestions that the US should conduct its relations with Eastern Europe in a reconciling mode, and attention was conspicuously diverted from the seriously unreconciled condition of various societies conscripted by the West in its fight to save the world from communism (as it continues to be in the current conscription of allies in the US-led war against terrorism). Besides, even with the demise of the Soviet Union, and the absence of any strategic threat on its doorstep, a vindictive rather than a reconciling spirit continues to characterise the US's attitude to Cuba.

As the Cuban example underscores, the West's current fascination with reconciliation is selective, occasionally for punitive reasons but mostly for economic and strategic reasons. That is why somewhere like Rwanda, however appalling its circumstances, is never going to attract the scale of peace building, conflict resolution and reconciliation resources devoted to more highly-valued trouble spots in the Middle East or Europe. And, anyway, current promotion of the idea of an increasingly reconciled world, particularly one indebted to Western beneficence, just happens to fit nicely with the interests of global capital in its quest to establish a world market free from trade barriers. Accordingly, the cynical response might conclude, reconciliation suits the US's agenda at the moment, but if it ever ceases to, it will be dropped rapidly. So let's not be hoodwinked: no grand moral conversion has occurred through the juxtaposition of political and religious languages, and no great transformation of Western *realpolitik* is afoot – the national, strategic and economic interests of the US remain sovereign.

ENTHUSIASTIC

An enthusiastic response takes a different tack. Value is discerned in the peculiarly modern form in which political and religious languages intermingle through the concept of reconciliation: it captures something important about cultural and political relations and taps into a contemporary mood that is difficult to ignore. And the hunch is that interest in reconciliation is not within the means even of a superpower to turn on and off at will, that once set in motion reconciliation's dynamic is difficult to derail.

Interestingly, the kind of case for reconciliation being hinted at here is broadly similar to that which may be made for rights. One of the central tasks performed by a modern language of rights is its affirmation of human dignity. Yet, in a sense, we did not need this language in order to make such an affirmation – notions of human dignity were already integral to earlier Greek and medieval systems of ethics – and some argue that we still do not.[1] In another sense, however, the language of rights now seems indispensable to how we express what we mean by human dignity, not least because of its universal scope. Thus it is commonplace for us to claim that all persons are equally worthy of respect simply by virtue of being persons, that equal respect or its equivalent is a right everyone is entitled to. And it is precisely such an idea of the inviolability of persons that is deemed necessary of protection in liberal societies, and that is at the core of various states' conventions and Bills of Rights, of the United Nations Universal Declaration of Human Rights, and so forth. In practice, of course, governments may fail miserably to recognise the rights of individuals, some of whom may even be treated as non-persons. And there are undoubtedly instances in liberal societies when interests and rights clash, often to the detriment of the latter. In these instances there is no question, however, of the language of rights being dispensed with, and it is not easy for proven rights violations to be cavalierly brushed aside. Instead, liberal governments more typically find themselves on the defensive as they are called to account by citizens or by various human rights monitoring groups. On occasions governments have to engage in fancy political footwork and special pleading to get off the hook. And this is the point: where the language of rights is culturally embedded and has acknowledged normative force, the onus is on governments to reflect the rights-respecting self-image of a liberal society. The language may be twisted and distorted at times but it still acts as a constraint on how governments may justifiably treat human beings.

Returning to reconciliation, the contention is not that the claims that may be made of it necessarily match the strength of those that may be made of rights, although in specific circumstances they might. It is more that an enthusiastic line on reconciliation invokes a similar pattern of reasoning, at least under certain conditions. Take the example of Australia, where reconciliation is concentrated on resolving the problem of the indigenous community's alienation from the mainstream life of society. In a sense, the language of reconciliation is unnecessary here. The problem of alienation is long-standing, and the language of justice, say, should be rich enough in itself to deal with the issues of cultural difference, land rights, and discriminatory laws, policies and practices it raises. Yet it is the language of reconciliation that is central to national debate on the problem, and that is functioning as the vehicle through which non-indigenous Australia is being shaken out of the collective amnesia that enabled it for so long to tolerate the intolerable. It is this language that is reflecting a contemporary mood to establish a fresh set of political and cultural relations. The language of justice alone – perhaps because of its propensity (in certain hands) to reduce to a clinical, overly procedural treatment of issues of communal division – is not perceived as capable of capturing all that is needed here. Concerns of justice remain central, of course, but they have been broadened out and grafted onto a language that goes beyond what justice strictly requires, when it speaks of healing divisions through forgiveness and apology. The language of reconciliation has come to seem indispensable, in short, because it expresses a spirit that gives promise of harmony replacing antagonism in relations between indigenous and non-indigenous Australians. And although there is resistance to this spirit, not least by the present federal government which thinks Australia is reconciled enough and refuses to offer an official apology for previous administrations' mistreatment of Aborigines, it is unlikely to carry the day. For instance, such resistance is explicitly dismissed by the main opposition parties and even (more quietly) by some members of the federal cabinet. Reconciliation marches have attracted hundreds of thousands of supporters in cities throughout Australia. And, strikingly, government resistance to the spirit of reconciliation was seriously rebuffed, and shown to be out of kilter with widespread public sentiment, during the 2000 Olympic Games in Sydney: there we witnessed themes of reconciliation being integrated into the opening and closing ceremonies in a manner that resonated with the Australian public and went well beyond current government thinking. There are strong grounds for claiming that it is present government attitudes and policies that will be eventually derailed and not reconciliation's dynamic.[2]

The example of Australia casts light on what it means for an enthusiastic line to welcome the peculiarly modern form in which political and religious languages come together through the concept of reconciliation. Crucially, no particular religious belief or content is presupposed, even if the borrowings from Christianity especially sometimes seem substantial. Some believers may regret this. And it may be thought that believers are already predisposed to embrace the language of reconciliation in a way that others are not. This may be true in some cases, but it certainly is not in others. It is a sorry indictment of much religion that it continues to serve as a major obstacle to political and cultural reconciliation between different groups in many parts of the world (though no longer in Australia). So often it is those who talk most fervently of forgiveness and repentance in describing their relationship with God who baulk at translating this talk into their relationships with other human beings, particularly with members of different religions, cultures and nationalities. And precisely because the concept of reconciliation, in the modern form I am considering, does not demand adherence to any faith, it is perfectly applicable to cultural and political relations in secular or non-Christian contexts. It does not betray some crafty ploy to smuggle back ideals of Christendom, or to win back any kind of clerical control over political affairs.

The significance of reconciliation's current prominence lies elsewhere. I think it has to do with at least two things, which in turn imply two others. First, *reconciliation* is a term that seems particularly apt in societies whose cohesion is at risk because of divisions created by cultural differences between citizens. To oversimplify wildly, it is a term that has come into vogue at a time when various Western nations – having convinced themselves (however oddly) that they had seen off the threat of divisions based on class – have found many of their complacently accepted cultural assumptions being called radically into question. Within their own societies, those of many of their former colonies, and others too, cultural minorities have pointed to the inherent injustice of being forced to conform to an alien ideal of cultural homogeneity, and to the arrogance of the assumption that Western military and technological superiority implies its cultural superiority. The Australian example is once again poignant, since it was precisely dubious notions of cultural homogeneity and superiority that underpinned White Australia's outrageous attempts to obliterate indigenous cultures. With the discrediting of these notions, the task of reconciling cultural differences has assumed a new importance, not least because the absence of cultural reconciliation has produced acute political conflict in many regions and societies. Second, there is growing appreciation of the delicacy of the task. This is a delicacy that suggests reconciliation must be conducted in a certain spirit, one that partly manifests itself through acts of forgiveness, repentance and apology, or through expressions of shame. These acts and expressions appear as necessary accompaniments to reconciling endeavours to extend justice's reach to include cultural disputes often excluded from its purview, and to heal wounds left open by countless instances of cultural injustice.

The disturbance of cultural complacency in the West and elsewhere, together with heightened awareness of a need to face up to culture-related divisions in a spirit capable of tackling the hostility they engender, lead easily to borrowing from the language of religion to enhance that of politics. And it is these factors that provide the clearest pointer to the significance of a modern convergence of the two languages through the concept of reconciliation. For an advocate of an enthusiastic response, this is not a contrived convergence; it is one that is suited to handling the issues at stake in frequently fractious cases of cultural–political conflict, and one that fits with serious attempts to resolve them in an appropriate spirit.

Two other things follow. One is that the ability of much conventional political language to deal with important matters of cultural concern is exposed as inadequate. This occurs even if lip service is paid to questions of reconciliation. And, to stick with the Australian example, it occurs not only when justice is defined too narrowly and procedurally, but also when the logic of market relations is allowed to invade most of public space. In a society where economic rationalism or market rationality has infiltrated almost every aspect of institutional life, politics itself frequently seems little more than a competitive game of calculation, interest-maximisation, and so on.[3] And a language that is tailored to the manoeuvres of this game may be one that can accommodate an obsession with rule following and procedures, but it is not one that can reflect much more than a wizened spirit. Racists aside, it is perhaps no accident that those politicians who have most difficulty tuning into the temper of the present mood for reconciliation are amongst economic rationalism's most bullish champions. Quite simply, a political language that has been stripped to fit market rationality is deprived of the resources to meet citizens' deeper needs. Even when such language includes reference to reconciliation, it has a hollow ring because its grasp of what reconciliation entails is too shallow. It is only the spiritually enriched political language of reconciliation which refuses to submit to procedural or economic reductionism, which discerns that more than applying (even impartial) rules is needed to heal rifts in cultural and political relations, and that a generous, forgiving and repentant spirit is required too. And it is this language that also conveys White Australia's sense of shame at the shabby, at times merciless, treatment the indigenous population has suffered.

The other thing that follows pertains to the hunch about reconciliation's dynamic implied by an enthusiastic response. Within certain societies, such as Australia, it appears considerably more than idle to think that, once awakened, concern with reconciliation cannot easily be brought back under control by a government that finds it inconvenient. There are occasions when a politics built on an image of *homo economicus* proves radically inadequate and has to give way to deeper and more complex images of human beings and of the purpose of politics. Current Australian interest in reconciliation represents just such an occasion.

NORTHERN IRELAND

The point of drawing on the example of Australia is not to suggest that it provides a model that can be duplicated elsewhere. Reconciliation's meanings and possibilities vary considerably. What they imply for relations between states is different from what they imply for relations within states. What they imply in Australia is different from what they imply in Northern Ireland. And what is easier to envisage in Australia is harder to envisage in Northern Ireland, but not as hard as it is to envisage in Kosovo. The Australian example simply serves to illustrate the credibility of an enthusiastic response to reconciliation under certain conditions, and to strike chords that may encourage playing to an enthusiastic tune in (some) other contexts too. Although its conditions are very different and more difficult, Northern Ireland is, I think, one of those other contexts. Enthusiasm's music is at times strange here, but not so exotic that it can be readily dismissed as a bizarre distraction.

It is within the ambit of the enthusiastic response that my discussion of reconciliation's prospects in the North is mostly located, although reference is also made to variants of the cynical response. To intimate what this means, let me give a preliminary sketch of how both responses relate to the central thesis of the book, namely that reconciliation may be an elusive quest in Northern Ireland, but that it need not be. In other words, the sorts of obstacles it confronts are serious, and may continue to prove their resilience for years to come, but they are not beyond the powers of human agents – or, more precisely, Northern Ireland's citizens – to overcome.

ENTHUSIASM AND ITS COMPLICATIONS

Given my basic thesis, it is hardly surprising that it is the enthusiastic response I wish to appropriate. But doing so is not straightforward. The conditions that facilitate receptiveness to an enthusiastic response to reconciliation are more easily obscured in Northern Ireland than they are, say, in Australia. Although the response entails a normative element equally applicable in both societies – reconciliation *should* be pursued because it is a good thing – more work is required of this element in Northern Ireland. For here there is less unambiguous agreement about reconciliation's desirability, and considerably less momentum to its quest. Whereas it is possible to be relatively confident that what counts as reconciliation in Australia will be eventually achieved, nothing comparable can be taken for granted in Northern Ireland. It is not that there are not encouraging signs or possibilities of reconciliation, it is just that it is harder to keep them to the fore. Pressing for reconciliation in the North is a more demanding task, as is playing up its possibilities to ensure that the normative argument appears as more than an abstract wish divorced from any practical realities.

Not surprisingly, then, the two major appeals of an enthusiastic response – that the concept of reconciliation enriches our political language, and that the process of reconciliation may develop a dynamic that its opponents find hard to successfully resist – are clouded by controversy in Northern Ireland. Preparing a path for their acceptance is a difficult business. Consider, for example, some of the complications attending specific and general aspects of the first appeal.

One of this appeal's specific claims is that forgiveness belongs to the grammar of reconciliation and plays a vital role in healing divisions between different cultural and political groups. Now, in Australia this may seem a pretty unexceptional claim, government mean-spiritedness notwithstanding, since the incontestable victims of Australian politics – Aborigines – have been by and large remarkably forthcoming in forgiving their non-indigenous victimisers. But in Northern Ireland the claim appears highly contentious: the relative absence of talk of forgiveness in politics suggests that it is either thought to muddy the waters of reconciliation or not to be relevant to political discourse. Besides, victimhood is a contestable issue and just who should be forgiving whom is a vexing question. When Ken Maginnis, a former UUP MP, remarks that 'unionists regard themselves as more sinned against than sinning',[4] he is both reflecting a majority view within his community and making a claim that most nationalists and republicans find incredible. In a society where forgiveness does not rate highly as a political good, where both unionists and nationalists consider themselves victims, and where few admit any responsibility for deepening and sustaining sectarian divisions, the specific claim about forgiveness has its work cut out to make an impression.

More generally, the gist of the first appeal – that the concept of reconciliation enlivens a jaded politics through a convergence of religious and political languages – also faces difficulties of translation into the context of Northern Ireland. For a start, it does not serve as a corrective to a political language that has been shrunk to fit the requirements of a narrow proceduralism or market rationality. These requirements have not yet become the fate of Northern politics, although there are narrow procedural tendencies in certain unionist uses of language, as I note in a later chapter, and it may be that in a so-called normalised society tendencies to shift in this direction would increase.

The real difficulty with the essence of the first appeal is that the concept of reconciliation is unsettling to a range of groups in Northern Ireland, either because they are uneasy with its political use, or because they are unconvinced that a political language already shot through with religious imagery needs further assistance from religious sources. For some, mainly Protestant fundamentalists, these two points come together in the objection that reconciliation is a politically misleading term for religious reasons. In their view, a robust, religiously inspired political language already exists and has no need of a supplement, especially one that is suspiciously ecumenical in tone. Rather than gesturing at political reconciliation, this language upholds political struggle and opposition as the legitimate offspring of religious conviction. Ian Paisley succinctly states the case when he proclaims, 'Christ did not come to reconcile man to man.'[5] And he reinforces it by maintaining that the root cause of conflict in the North is a war between 'Protestantism and popery', 'a war of survival between the opposing forces of Truth and Error'.[6] To talk of reconciliation in this context is, he thinks, not only to be politically misguided but also to be guilty of apostasy.

For others who recoil from Protestant fundamentalism, the objection may be that reconciliation is a misleading term for political reasons. The unionist historian A.T.Q. Stewart gives voice to this line when he pronounces in one place that 'all efforts to promote reconciliation are singularly futile',[7] and in another that reconciliation is 'hot air' and quite the wrong starting point for resolving conflict in the North. Instead of the sides coming together, he avers, 'one side or another has to surrender'.[8] This is not only a view found among unionists. It is hard not to believe that during the 1970s and 1980s it was the Provisional Irish Republican Army's (IRA's) view too, and it remains the view of those dissident republicans sympathetic to the Real IRA. For others still, including a range of liberal and socialist secularists, the objection is to any hint that politics should be indebted to religion. It is not so much the concept of reconciliation that is under fire here; it is, rather, any suggestion that there can be a benign marriage of religion and politics. Since religion in the North has fuelled the sectarianism that has poisoned political life, purging politics of its influence is taken to be the goal instead of, as it were, welcoming it back through a side entrance.

Openness to the core appeal of an enthusiastic response, then, cannot be assumed in Northern Ireland. There are enough doubts about the applicability of its specific and general connotations, as well as instances of antipathy to its very rationale, to indicate that reconciliation faces a rocky road. The presence of these kinds of doubts and antipathies also helps to explain the difficulty confronting an enthusiastic response's other appeal about reconciliation's dynamic, since concern for reconciliation has not developed such a head of steam that politicians ignore it at their peril. This is not to say that reconciliation's appeal falls entirely on deaf ears, or that it is incapable of building up a formidable momentum. Indeed, despite the sample of hesitations and objections I have mentioned, it is probably true to say that a majority of Northern citizens declare themselves in favour of reconciliation. The problem is that what is understood by it is often too vague or too weakly held to withstand the assaults of its detractors. This was effectively demonstrated by paramilitaries in the recent past. A conspicuous lack of majority support in either part of Ireland did not distract the Provisional IRA or its loyalist counterparts from prosecuting an armed struggle that deepened divisions and halted reconciliation in its tracks. And, currently, unionist politicians opposed to the Agreement are underscoring reconciliation's continuing vulnerability to determined spoiling tactics. The unrivalled prospects of political reconciliation suggested by the Agreement are easily made precarious by a minority of unionists who, in their self-absorbed mission of defending narrowly conceived unionist interests, are unperturbed by any thought of thwarting the will of the majority of citizens. It may be, of course, that this will has weakened, at least among unionists who, for reasons I discuss in Chapter 6, are susceptible to anti-Agreement overtures. But whether anti-Agreement activists will prove successful or whether a Northern mood for reconciliation will acquire a dynamic that overcomes their spoiling efforts remain open questions at the time of writing.

Predicting reconciliation's fate is not the purpose of the book. But this much at least may be said about it: reconciliation almost certainly will remain an elusive quest unless the convictions of the majority, who ostensibly support it, match the depth of those in the minority who evidently do not. Suggesting that there may be a significant difference of depth between the two sets of convictions, which more than nullifies the numerical advantage enjoyed by reconciliation's supporters, raises questions about the nature of commitment to reconciliation. I begin to take up these questions in the next chapter. The suggestion also anticipates an argument that runs through the book, namely that the single greatest obstacle blocking receptiveness to an enthusiastic response in Northern Ireland is that reconciliation is hugely demanding: it potentially disturbs any number of our prejudices, self-understandings, priorities and practices. That is why it is much easier to be against reconciliation in a divided society than it is to be for it. It is also why paying lip service to reconciling ideals is one thing, but facing up to what they ask of us is often quite another – which is why many of reconciliation's supporters are susceptible to the rationalisations of its detractors, even if they are reluctant to endorse everything associated with a full-blooded detracting stance. And this, in turn, is partly why the sorts of complications that temper reconciliation's appeal in Northern Ireland often assume a seemingly disproportionate importance.

This brief account indicates why I say that trying to remove the blocks that inhibit reception of an enthusiastic response to reconciliation in Northern Ireland is a difficult task. It also indicates much of what trying to remove them entails. For instance, the contrast I have gestured at between the resolution of reconciliation's opponents and the uncertainties of its supporters suggests that close attention needs to be devoted to its meanings and claims, and to the sorts of commitments they require. And this contrast, in conjunction with explicit rejections of reconciliation's political relevance, underlines why a serious case for reconciliation is unavoidably normative in kind. Reasons have to be given why reconciliation should be welcomed, why it should be regarded as a good thing. The bulk of this book amounts to an attempt to provide these reasons. Importantly, the reasons and the norms to which they relate are not abstract propositions. They are linked to existing, yet not properly realised, possibilities of reconciliation, such as majority support of the Agreement, even if they point to a stronger conception of reconciliation than many may find palatable. They are also intended to show why reconciliation's detractors are wrong, and why the complications that attend talk of reconciliation in Northern Ireland are not enough to render it implausible.

So, for example, in relation to the objections to reconciliation touched on earlier, I argue that forgiveness is a responsibility of all of us and must be incorporated in any worthwhile promotion of reconciliation in Northern Ireland. Needless to say, I dispute religiously and politically driven rejections of reconciliation partly because their alternatives are recipes for political disaster, and partly because they are morally suspect. The general point I made previously about religious faith being no guarantee of sympathy for reconciliation between different cultural groups has peculiar salience here: it is a curious irony that many who boast the purest Christian motives are among those most threatened by the possibility of political reconciliation in the North.

I am, however, less critical of secular opposition to an intermingling of political and religious languages. I broadly agree with its critique of how religion has been used to adverse political effect in Northern Ireland. But I have two reservations with it. First, its critique does not apply to a modern convergence of religious and political languages, which is different in kind from the religious–political mix typical in the North. As I have already clarified, such a convergence implies no theological content, no favouring of one faith over another, and therefore is not remotely guilty of stoking the fires of sectarianism, not even implicitly. Second, the problem with shunning an enthusiastic response on secular grounds is that it sells us short in our attempts to tackle the issue of division in Northern society. Or at least it does when it implies a tendency to shy away from the vocabulary of reconciliation, or to employ it too tamely, and therefore to downplay the significance of the role factors such as forgiveness, apology, shame, and so on, play in healing divisions. To regard these factors as soft or unnecessary is ultimately to leave out of politics a crucial dimension of relations between different groups and to end up with so-called solutions to our divisions that risk being overly procedural and too limited. An enthusiastic response, which in my understanding is compatible with much religious faith and with much secularism, deserves a comprehensive defence, not a truncated one. Or so I will argue.

CYNICISM AND ITS CHALLENGES

The cynical response to reconciliation also features in the following pages, although in quite a different way from the enthusiastic response. As I described it, the emphasis fell on international relations and the role of US foreign policy (see pp. 14–16). But it did so primarily for illustrative purposes. No doubt there are questions worth pursuing in relation to this emphasis, especially if we are trying to explain unprecedented American involvement in the Northern Ireland peace process under (former) US President Bill Clinton. These may include reference to unionist complaints that such involvement has been detrimental because it has significantly bolstered the cause of Irish nationalism, and to socialist suspicions that it has underwritten sectarian divisions by discouraging attempts to overcome them through fostering working-class unity. But these questions are left unexplored here. Whatever grounds there are for doubting American intentions, they are exaggerated to suggest that concern for reconciliation in Northern Ireland is a US-driven affair, or that it will only last for as long as it suits US interests. And, more importantly for my purposes, regardless of what may be said of the doubts, it is hard to see how they are capable of showing that an enthusiastic response is misplaced.

I am more interested in two variants of a cynical response, and in the challenges they pose. One is to think that what goes on at the micro-level of domestic politics is analogous to that which some think occurs at the macro-level of international relations. This is to say that just as reconciliation is used as a cover for superpower manoeuvrings, so too is it used as a cloak for securing advantageous political deals within particular societies. And here the challenge is to look behind the rhetoric of reconciliation to discern the interests that are being promoted through it. Responding to this challenge in the context of Northern Ireland, it is possible to push the following interpretation. (1) With so much international attention devoted to Northern Irish affairs, political parties which may not previously have cared about world opinion (and some still do not) are now more inclined to present an image of reasonableness to outsiders. (2) Certain of these parties support the Agreement, which the British and Irish governments worked assiduously to achieve to international acclaim. (3) But as difficulties in implementing the Agreement amply demonstrate, their support of it was more a reflection of tactical calculations than of deep commitment to political reconciliation. (4) These tactical calculations – which involve unionist parties trying to ensure that the British government remains sympathetic to their position, nationalist parties doing likewise with the Irish government, and all parties choreographing images agreeable to international opinion – dictate that no party wants to admit responsibility for the Agreement's difficulties. (5) Accordingly, there is reluctance to publicly express any misgivings about reconciliation, but a good deal of positioning to ensure that its failings are perceived as the fault of others. (6) The upshot is that much of reconciliation's rhetoric in the North is little more than humbug.

Now, I am not sure that this story tells the whole tale about political parties' attitudes to reconciliation, but there is enough uncomfortable truth in it to keep alive suspicions that much professed concern for reconciliation is really a tactic to strengthen the hand of particular interests. I incorporate parts of it in later chapters when criticising moves to reduce reconciliation to a balancing of interests, and when discussing the fortunes of the Agreement. In doing so, I am indicating that the enthusiastic and cynical responses to reconciliation are not in every respect incompatible alternatives. Contrary to a caricature, enthusiasm does not require gullibility.

Enthusiasm is, however, utterly at odds with another variant of a cynical response. This is one which treats *all* reconciling efforts as masks of other interests, as smokescreens for some power play or another. Its challenges come in a variety of forms, the most intellectually taxing of which appear as celebrations of difference and plurality. These challenges are potentially fatal to the thesis of this book, since pressed to their limit they conclude that any attempt at reconciliation is an exercise in illusion. Central to the arguments I develop in response is a refusal to accept cynicism's extraordinarily dim view of human agency and its capacity to make a difference to the quality of cultural and political relations.

Of course, this second type of cynical challenge also rejects the approach I am adopting to the issue of reconciliation in Northern Ireland and warrants a preliminary response now. To recall, at the heart of my approach lies a normative line – reconciliation should be pursued because it is a good thing – which I hope to support with adequate reasons. Of the range of cynical objections to this line, it is instructive here to pick out one that is accepted (implicitly or explicitly) by a number of academic and political commentators on Northern Ireland. This is a less philosophically encumbered objection than others and is close to the kind of political rejection of reconciliation I alluded to earlier. Its fundamental claim is that, whatever the rhetoric of reconciliation, it is naïve to suppose that either unionists or nationalists will ever act contrary to their perceived interests. And the problem with an approach such as mine is that, in calling a lot of current attitudes and practices into question and in pointing to alternative ways of seeing and doing things, it is inappropriate: it expects too much of people and becomes too abstract.

An example of how this objection may be teased out is provided by Arthur Aughey's articulation of it in his criticism of my (similar) approach to Northern politics in an earlier book, *Rethinking Unionism*.[9] In what I think is a caricature of this approach, he depicts me (1) as having a vision (which I called civic unionism), (2) as having a mission of political redemption, and (3) as having an 'object of ill-concealed contempt' which is to be redeemed (other unionists who I am said to think suffer from mental deficiencies or some 'Bourbonic stupidity').[10] Now, Aughey is evidently having fun and it is a little churlish to want to spoil it. But the issues at stake are too serious to ignore. For if he is right, then his depiction of my approach continues to tell against what I am proposing to do in this book: I still have a vision – that of a reconciled society – and I still want to persuade others to accept it and to criticise those beliefs and practices that stand in its way. But, contrary to what Aughey implies, the vision (whether of civic unionism or of a reconciled society) is not an abstract blueprint, but a tentative and provisional projection of normative and historical possibilities. Moreover, trying to persuade others is not quite the same as wanting to redeem them, that is, it has different connotations and is, I think, free of Messianic pretensions. Criticising other beliefs and practices does not mean holding their bearers and practitioners in contempt or regarding them as mentally deficient – quite the reverse actually. Giving reasons and leaving others to make what they will of them is at the core of what it means to treat other persons with respect. Or so argued Kant among others, and so I also argue.

Aughey's criticism and my response to it point towards a basic disagreement about the sorts of questions it is legitimate to ask of political actors in Northern Ireland. On Aughey's terms, our range of questions is circumscribed by having to accept unionists and nationalists as they are – as bundles of historical prejudices who are constrained by their history and their perceptions of it – and by accepting the limitations on political possibilities this imposes. On my terms, we have to take seriously how unionists and nationalists are, how they understand themselves, and so forth, but we also have to ask questions about their ways of life and conceptual frameworks, and about the practices and priorities these imply.

The cynical objection that to approach Northern politics with these kinds of questions in mind is too abstract and too idealistic is one I find odd. For a start, such questions open up a line of inquiry – pursued at length in *Rethinking Unionism* and in snatches here – that is not at all abstract, namely one that explores the possibility that various Northern Irish ways of life and conceptual frameworks may be internally contradictory and break down on their own terms. For another thing, the notion that idealism and expectation are inappropriate is in my view dubious. To accept it, and therefore to refuse to raise questions that might ruffle unionist or nationalist feathers, or (as frequently happens) merely to adopt the exclusive script of one tradition and use it to lampoon the other, comes close to ignoring problems such as sectarianism or to believing that they can be resolved without anybody having to change any of their practices or beliefs. In other words, where it is not irresponsible, cynicism of this type is incredible. And it skates on thin moral ice: its refusal to probe unionist and nationalist self-understandings is tantamount to exempting Northern political actors from a range of moral and normative requirements. Accordingly, we might anticipate being told it is inappropriate to make requests for forgiveness in politics because unionists (or nationalists) don't 'do' forgiveness. I won't buy this. And if the great flaw of my approach is that it entertains ideals associated with reconciliation and considers it reasonable to expect citizens in Northern Ireland to take them seriously, even if they go against the grain of some traditional ways of thinking and acting, then so be it. As I shall argue more than once in following chapters, its alternatives leave too much to be desired.

CONCLUSION

Reconciliation is worth fighting for (through non-violent words and deeds). And without fighting for it we will not get it. Given what I have said about enthusiasm's complications and cynicism's challenges, fighting for it involves considering whether we in the North really want reconciliation, and if we do, how badly. It also includes considering the prospect that it is impossible to have, although I do not think that it is (at least not in principle). If we want it and if what we want is not impossible, then we need to consider more closely what it is we do or should want, what it is we conceive reconciliation to be or not to be, and what it will take to overcome the obstacles that prevent us from having it. Taking up these considerations entails dealing with a range of cultural, political and philosophical questions, and defines the agenda of the remainder of the book.

2

IS RECONCILIATION
A GOOD THING?

Is reconciliation the good thing that many of us presume it is? Despite what I have already said about its detractors and cynics, this ought to be a startling question, given the elevated status accorded to the concept of reconciliation in our official public discourse. The political language of the British and Irish governments, the community language of the reconciliation industry, and the religious language of the mainline Churches – in spite of their different nuances – combine to invest the concept with virtual canonical privilege. And the singular message of these converging languages is clear: the malaise afflicting Northern society is curable if we allow the challenge of reconciliation to concentrate our minds and inspire us to common action.

The fact is, however, that many of us in the North, who do not think of ourselves as detractors or cynics, are expertly skilled in blocking out this message, or at least in dulling its impact, even as we protest our commitment to some version of it. After all, granted the message's powerful backing, it is doubtless politically imprudent to be expressly opposed to reconciliation in Northern Ireland, at least for parties that support the Agreement. Sure, many words and deeds even of pro-Agreement local politicians and their supporters suggest opposition, but rarely are these justified on the grounds that reconciliation is a bad thing. So, even in the face of troubling evidence to the contrary, there is a widespread tendency to persist with the officially endorsed presumption that reconciliation is a good thing, something most of us want. Whatever the dominant political, community and religious rhetoric, whatever the protestations of local politicians and activists, and, indeed, however much it captures the unreflective consciousness of many of us, this presumption increasingly strains credibility. It invites inspection.

Inspection uncovers a range of attitudes and approaches to reconciliation's cultural and political meanings in Northern Ireland. Some betray a decidedly weak commitment to reconciliation, and for a variety of reasons. Certain of these reasons are shabby, but others are not. Those, say, which encourage us to baulk at the inescapable difficulty of bridging our cultural and political divisions may even be thought to perform a salutary function: by subverting hazy assumptions about reconciliation's goodness and exposing much of our talk of reconciliation as sanctimonious cant; or by recommending that containing our differences, rather than trying to reconcile them, is an altogether more realistic ambition for Northern society.

Against the drift of such reasoning, I want to begin to develop a case why reconciliation remains a worthy goal for Northern Ireland that should not be forfeited lightly, however demanding its requirements. In this chapter, I do so principally by questioning the plausibility of reconciliation's alternatives, by disputing various descriptions of reconciliation's meaning, and by gesturing at better descriptions. In a sense, my argument serves to vindicate both the unreflective presumption about reconciliation's goodness I have suggested many of us share, but which many of our words and deeds belie, and the spirit of the message contained in our official public discourse. It does, however, already contain hints that risk upsetting both of these, by pointing to a conception of reconciliation which even some participants in our official public discourse might find too strong to be either welcome or necessary. But these only become clear in later chapters. I begin now with a quick and rather gloomy account of reconciliation's fate in Northern Ireland, which leads me to ask hard questions of its viability. I take up two of these questions that, respectively, query the appetite for, and the possibility of, reconciliation in Northern society. This involves dealing with tendencies to separate peace from reconciliation and with moves to depict reconciliation and difference as incompatible alternatives. I argue against both, and against the positions they reflect.

RECONCILIATION'S ABSENCE AND ITS PUZZLES

A prompt to reinspect reconciliation comes from the reality of its continuing absence from so much of the life of Northern society. Perhaps for those of us who are all too familiar with the North and its problems, this reality has lost its power to shock. More likely it is simply an unpleasant fact we have all become accustomed to, and, as such, something we merely shrug at as typical of the status quo in Northern Ireland. Maybe it is only in moments of intense piety that some of us even imagine how it could be otherwise. There is an irony here. As I hinted in the previous chapter, many of those who unreflectively accept that reconciliation is a good thing may also be among those who have very slender expectations of reconciliation's progress in Northern life; many who ostensibly value reconciliation may also lack faith in its efficacy. Or perhaps the sharper point is this: it is precisely because expectations are so slender, because trust in its efficacy is so low, that we are forced to question whether reconciliation is valued very highly at all, or whether it is in fact a good thing. Just as these questions ought to startle, so, observed from a certain angle, the reality of reconciliation's continuing absence ought to shock; or, if not shock, at least disconcert and puzzle.

DISCONCERTING PUZZLES

Prima facie, reconciliation's absence is a disconcerting and puzzling reality given the sheer number of attempts that have been made to heal rifts between unionists and nationalists, or between Protestants and Catholics. Consider the nature and scope of these attempts. They may be informal or very formal in character; they range from personal contacts to government-sponsored initiatives; they include low budget, locally run, cross-community social and cultural events, as well as high budget, officially backed economic and political partnerships. Promoting reconciliation consumes the energies of many community organisations, voluntary associations, and Church groups. The cause of reconciliation commands the attention and financial support of governments and their agencies in Britain and Ireland.

Reconciliation in Northern Ireland is also an international affair, economically and politically. Projects designed to enhance its prospects may receive funding from European Union (EU) and US sources. And, we are assured, the more signs of progress it shows the greater the chances are of securing job-creating, inward investments from international companies. Unprecedented political initiatives to encourage reconciliation run alongside international economic inducements. Four historic visits to Northern Ireland by Bill Clinton, for example, the pivotal role played by US Senator George Mitchell in chairing political talks at Stormont, and the duties assumed by the Canadian General John de Chastelain and his colleagues in overseeing the process of decommissioning weapons, attest to the type of commitments major international political players are prepared to make for the sake of reconciliation in the North.

And yet reconciliation continues to elude us. Its success manifestly cannot depend only on the time and effort spent on its behalf by local community, voluntary and religious activists, or on programmes devised by those employed in various capacities to promote it in Northern Ireland, or on intergovernmental initiatives and sponsorships, or on international concern, economic incentives and political commitments. If any, or some combination, of these factors were decisive, Northern Ireland would be by now a model of reconciliation. But it is not. It is a deeply divided, segregated and sectarian society. Gains for reconciliation no doubt have been chalked up at community, religious, and economic levels. The reconciliation industry's time, energy and money have not all been a waste. None the less, even in terms of cultivating an ethos of tolerance and respect that extends beyond certain sectors of civil society its results are pretty meagre. The issue of Orange marches, in particular, vividly illustrates the depth of cultural–political divisions in Northern Ireland – divisions exacerbated by segregated housing areas and the paucity of integrated educational opportunities.

And then, of course, there is the issue of reconciliation at the political level. Potential progress has been made here with the arrival of the Agreement in 1998. But, despite its potential, the Agreement has not ushered in a new dawn of political reconciliation. It is opposed by dissident republicans and, more significantly, by a substantial number of unionists. And among those political parties in favour of the Agreement, considerable tensions and discord are evident. Indeed, conflicting interpretations of the Agreement's meaning among its supporters have threatened to destroy the reconciling processes it intimates before they have barely begun. After two years of haggling over its meaning – especially in relation to the issue of decommissioning paramilitary weapons – and after a false start in December 1999, which ended abruptly with a suspension of the Northern Ireland Assembly, sufficient consensus was reached in May 2000 to give promise of its full implementation. During the summer and autumn of 2001 that consensus risked disintegration, with two further (temporary) suspensions of the Assembly, as a consequence of the bad faith that persists between rival parties. An initial act of weapons decommissioning by the Provisional IRA in October 2001, however, persuaded pro-Agreement unionists to withdraw their threat of resigning from ministerial office and a shaky consensus was re-established. Unfortunately by October 2002 this consensus had collapsed and the British government suspended the political institutions of devolution for a fourth time. Unionists are now refusing to work with Sinn Féin until the Provisional IRA is disbanded. It remains an open question whether the new, multi-party Executive will be restored and, if it is, whether it will be able to withstand the considerable challenges it faces and allow political reconciliation to proceed in spite of extremely deep-seated suspicions and hostilities.

HARD QUESTIONS

Such a disturbing state of affairs calls for analysis and questioning. We might want to ask, for instance, whether the reconciliation industry's priorities and targets have been the most appropriate of those available; whether time, effort and money could not have been better directed elsewhere and to greater effect. Or we might wish to ask questions of the strategies for political reconciliation pursued by the British and Irish governments: why they have delivered so little for so long; why we have had to wait for the Agreement before being given even a glimpse of realistic political hope; whether both governments could have done more to treat the sources of disaffection obvious in certain political circles. We might also wish to put local political parties in the dock and insist that they face some stiff interrogation: whether they have shown sufficient inclination to place the interests of all Northern Ireland's citizens above party – some might say sectarian – interests; whether they have genuinely tried to find common ground with their political adversaries; whether they have been prepared to show qualities of leadership aimed at breaking down barriers of mistrust between unionists and nationalists, between loyalists and republicans. And so on.

Pursuing questions such as these may make the absence of reconciliation in Northern Ireland less puzzling than it initially appears. But to focus on these alone may not force us to pose questions that disconcert even more. For example, perhaps we in the North also have to ask of ourselves, and not only of our politicians and bureaucrats, just how significant commitment to reconciliation really is. And perhaps we have to entertain the possibility that those things that ultimately separate and divide us are too deep and profound to be reconciled. It is these issues I would now like to begin to discuss.

PEACE WITHOUT RECONCILIATION?

Reconciliation is a word with strong connotations that demand a lot of give from all of us if our cultural and political divisions are to be healed. Perhaps they demand too much. Perhaps reconciliation is the wrong word to describe what many of us think is either desirable or feasible in Northern society today. Perhaps many would settle for peace – defined minimally as an absence of violent conflict – and take their chances on reconciliation. Perhaps, that is, uncoupling the terms peace and reconciliation would reveal a less edifying but truer picture of Northern sentiment: we can have minimalist peace without reconciliation and peace is what we really crave. Perhaps, then, since the quest for peace is hard enough and apparently cannot be won without concessions from all sides, the more exacting requirements of reconciliation should be set aside for another time, if not dropped altogether. Perhaps to insist upon them is to unduly burden the peace process.

Perhaps. I suspect that what I'll call *peace without reconciliation* is a position that resonates in parts of Northern society, even when it is not articulated in such terms. And arguably, one explanation why political reconciliation is in scarcer supply than it should be is because peace without reconciliation is the implicit position of more people in Northern Ireland than many of us care to admit. Maybe it is this position that feeds the political intransigence evident in various political parties and that is, in turn, reinforced by such intransigence. Whatever the case, it is a position that may derive from a number of sources, including those of indifference, fear, and bitterness.

INDIFFERENCE

Of the three sources of the peace without reconciliation formula I have just picked out, indifference – though perhaps interesting enough sociologically – is the least defensible. Indifference may be a reflection of political apathy shared by a cross-section of citizens, or a product of disillusionment with the manner in which Northern politics have been conducted. Although not restricted to any group or class, one of its more common expressions is found among those whose lives have been relatively unaffected by the conflict; those who are most seriously devoted to a life of cultivated consumption; those who have opted out of politics in any sense. The 'contented classes', as Colin Coulter refers to them, obviously fit into this category, namely those who have enjoyed the economic benefits of direct rule, without having had to incur any of the political costs.[1] The indifference frequently exhibited among such classes underwrites the peace without reconciliation formula by tacitly saying something like this: peace, minimally defined, is to be valued if for no other reason than that violence and the security measures necessary to counteract it are irritating inconveniences; but reconciliation has no comparable value since, if taken seriously, it promises only unwelcome intrusions into more or less settled lifestyles.

Now, even if we assume, as this line on indifference implicitly does, that the value of reconciliation is to be measured according to some cost-benefit calculus, it is not evident that the calculations being relied upon amount to much more than risky short-term gambles. In one scenario, for example, the political and economic conditions conducive to indifference may prove very transient: where, say, political agreement holds, direct rule definitively ends, and Westminster's subvention is reduced substantially. Or, in a quite different scenario, the immunity from conflict conditions conducive to indifference may prove exceptionally precarious: where, say, current attempts at political reconciliation fail miserably, republican and loyalist ceasefires collapse, and paramilitaries lay part of the blame for breakdown at the door of the contented classes. To push this scenario further, paramilitaries, unconstrained by official ceasefires, may decide even to unsettle the contented classes' complacency through inflicting upon them a bit of sharp suffering that is partly designed to put them in a better mood for reconciliation. Of course, if we do not assume – and I certainly do not – that the value of reconciliation is reducible to the vagaries of cost-benefit calculations, then there is little more to say about indifference than that it is morally and politically irresponsible.

FEAR

Fear as a source of the peace without reconciliation formula is a little harder to evaluate. Unlike indifference, it may be rooted in deep commitments to ways of life that are perceived to be under threat. And, rather than encourage political apathy, it may impel political action of a certain sort – invariably a defensive sort that stresses protecting one's patch as the principal rationale of political engagement. It is hard not to think of much of the North's politics as in part a reflection of fear: fear of the so-called 'other', fear of losing one's identity through too many concessions being granted to one's opponents, perhaps fear of losing power, influence and a position of dominance which 'our' kind consider their due. For those in the grip of such fears, peace, again minimally understood, has obvious attractions, but reconciliation demands too much: its request for openness is little more than a polite demand for surrender; its request for the recognition of both traditional identities typically overreaches itself politically and becomes, in effect, a demand for a diminution of 'our' identity and its political entitlements; and its request that we empathise with the other tradition in order to reach a mutually acceptable accommodation is, in truth, a demand that is existentially impossible to meet.

Such a fearful opposition to reconciliation is hard to ignore, given its prevalence in the politics of Northern Ireland. And it perhaps deserves sympathetic treatment inasmuch as it points to an acute edginess at the prospect – which many unionists claim to dread – of familiar practices being disrupted to the point where radical disorientation becomes a common experience. In other words, in certain circumstances it may be prudent to proceed cautiously rather than brashly when trying to implement some programme of reconciliation. It would be counterproductive if the promotion of reconciliation simply exacerbated the type of radical disorientation that made social and political instability more probable than not.

Being sympathetically alert to such a possibility should not mean, however, capitulating to the perceptions and analyses of the politics of fear. In the nature of things, these perceptions and analyses, though sincerely held, would be expected to involve seriously defective elements – as I think is unquestionably the case in Northern Ireland. Northern politics of fear, whether unionist or nationalist, typically entail jaundiced views of the British and Irish states, and of the intentions and nature of the other tradition. Of course, this is not to say there is never any substance to the fears that are evident in our politics. In Chapters 3 and 6 especially, I consider more closely the content of claims through which expressions of fear are typically conveyed in Northern society. But, for the moment, I am merely judging whether the presence of fear in itself should be sufficient to allow a case to be made for peace, while simultaneously applying a brake on larger aspirations for reconciliation. I do not think it should. To put matters sharply, to allow one's attitude to reconciliation to be dictated either by the apparent intractability of the politics of fear or by sensitivity to its existential plight of disorientation is ultimately to pay costs that should be too great to contemplate. It is to downplay the fact that distortions of others and their motives are unacceptable, and then to affect obliviousness of the consequences of such distortions for the rest of society. It is to turn a blind eye to the advocacy of differential treatment to the point of virtually tolerating the intolerable. It is to invite atavism and to close off responsible thinking about an alternative future. There is a danger, in other words, of allowing prudent caution to mask a lack of moral and political courage.

BITTERNESS

Bitterness as a source of the peace without reconciliation formula is in some respects the most difficult to deal with. This is because bitterness may be frequently a product of extremely traumatic experiences: of having been subjected to acts of injustice, humiliation or brutalisation that go against our most basic moral sensibilities. And in Northern Ireland too many such acts have been committed for the grossest sectarian reasons. A few victims of particularly horrendous crimes may be so damaged that they find acceptance even of minimalist peace difficult, such is their desire for revenge. But for many more it is reconciliation that is the problem and, in particular, its requirement of forgiveness. Forgiveness seems to some too exacting a request and too naïve a remedy. Too exacting as it demands more than the emotional and moral resources many victims are capable of mustering, because it seems to set an impossibly high standard of virtue. And too naïve because forgiveness, even if forthcoming, would not be the panacea some imagine. It would not constitute an adequate assault on the cultural–political conditions that cast some in the role of oppressors and others in the role of victims.

Three comments are in order. First, the request for forgiveness at the level of the individual has to be handled with the utmost sensitivity, but not relinquished altogether. Here it may seem heartless, if not downright callous, to make such a request of those individuals who have endured tragedies many others have escaped. This is indeed delicate territory upon which to tread. What is easier for some to entertain is harder for others, and different people deal differently with their hurt, grief and pain. At the very least, it is obvious that the request that victims forgive their oppressors – often enough without their oppressors asking for it or expressing remorse, let alone repentance – cannot be made in any homogeneous way. There is not some formula that all victims should be expected to adhere to. But does that mean it is unreasonable to request forgiveness at all? I do not think so. To explain why, let me allow the Croatian theologian Miroslav Volf to lay out the basic answer. Modifying his wording slightly, he reasons as follows:

> For a victim to [forgive] means not to allow the oppressors to determine the terms under which social conflict is carried out, the values around which the conflict is raging and the means by which it is fought. [Forgiveness] thus empowers victims and disempowers oppressors. It 'humanizes' the victims precisely by protecting them from either mimicking or dehumanizing the oppressors.[2]

Accordingly, those who cannot find it within themselves to forgive, however understandable their predicament, risk becoming like their oppressors: if not in deed, then in thought. They risk being warped by a twisted intent that succumbs to a dreadful logic of dehumanisation, which is ultimately why the request for forgiveness remains indispensable to reconciliation, however harrowing its granting may seem.

Second, if it is true to say that the request for forgiveness holds at an individual level, it is true to say with even greater force that it holds at a political level. This is not to advocate any cavalier dismissal of the political grounds on which both unionists and nationalists consider themselves victims. There is a point to unionist perceptions of themselves as victims of a sustained Provisional IRA campaign to rob them of their Britishness, as there is also to nationalist perceptions of themselves as victims of a type of state-sponsored violence and a regime of discrimination that have deprived them, among other things, of a sufficiently meaningful expression of their Irishness.

But there are exaggerations and blind spots in both sets of perceptions, which are particularly evident in the tendency of both to lay the bulk of blame for their woes on the other side. And it is precisely this tendency that inhibits acknowledgement of any shared responsibility for our difficulties in the North. Here one of our most poignant quandaries arises: how are we to break out of the (often vicious) cycle of mutually accusing definitions of political victimhood? Forgiveness seems a key to any adequate answer. That is why it is important to treat forgiveness as a political virtue and not merely as a private one. Hannah Arendt's remarks have a salience in this context, when she refers to forgiveness as a 'genuinely free act which does not merely re-act',[3] an act which 'breaks the power of the remembered past and transcends the claims of the affirmed justice, and so makes the spiral of vengeance grind to a halt'.[4]

Forgiveness, then, has the capacity to relieve us from the often onerous burden of our history. It has the capacity to break the cycle of perpetual victimhood – and its debilitating practice of recrimination – by not insisting that justice, as one side conceives of it, be done first. And that is why, again, forgiveness deserves to be thought of politically.

Third, to stress that forgiveness is central to reconciliation is not to sideline investigation of the cultural and political circumstances that make the quest for reconciliation so arduous. If forgiveness is regarded as a panacea then it is rightly to be ridiculed. But the points about forgiveness breaking 'the power of the remembered past' and transcending 'the claims of the affirmed justice' are not meant to imply some form of political acquiescence. They are not pious ruses for abandoning concerns of history or of justice. Forgiveness, rather, enables us to address these concerns in a less precious or self-righteous way. This is a way that opens up space for types of political exploration and interchange that would be otherwise closed off. Put simply, forgiveness is a necessary but not a sufficient condition of reconciliation. And the hope is not some absurd one that in embracing forgiveness the political and cultural obstacles to reconciliation will be instantly transformed, as if by magic, but that these obstacles can be tackled with a little more magnanimity and a little less obsessive rancour.

To summarise, peace without reconciliation, whether deriving from indifference, fear or bitterness, is a radically inadequate position, even if there are occasions when its claims need to be treated gently. In addition to the reasons I have already raised against it, I would like to add two others of a more general nature, which I return to at more length later from a slightly different angle. As a guide to political practice, it is not up to scratch, first, because its achievement would undoubtedly prove too fragile to work for long, and those who suppose otherwise – namely, that lasting peace is possible without reconciliation – seem to be in flight from political realities in the North. And second, because it entails a very miserly view of politics and of what is required to create and sustain a decent society for all citizens. To operate within its boundaries, in short, is to court escapism and to entertain a very narrow notion of political responsibility.

RECONCILIATION OR DIFFERENCE?

Now, it is one thing to maintain that the terms *peace* and *reconciliation* should not be uncoupled, that refusing to yield to indifference, fear, or bitterness opens us up to creative explorations of our differences, and that, being so unshackled, as it were, we may anticipate the development of a more generous and inclusive mode of politics. But it is another thing entirely to suppose that maintaining any of these things amounts to a sufficient guarantee that our differences are in fact reconcilable or that our politics can be transformed. It does not. And as soon as we admit this, we see that the idea of reconciliation confronts another set of challenges of a quite formidable kind, some of which I tackle directly in subsequent chapters.

For example, how are we to bridge our rudimentary constitutional divisions, especially if they are reinforced by a whole series of seemingly binary oppositions that bring into play cultural–political differences of ethnicity, religion, history, and so on? How is it possible realistically to imagine unionists and nationalists in the North working some mutually acceptable agreement, when so many of them plug into quite exclusive self-definitions which are shaped by such different historical memories and heritages? How is it possible even to imagine unionists and nationalists engaging in the sort of dialogue that gives promise of a thriving polity when they seem to have such utterly different understandings of what it means to conduct political talks, understandings which may, in turn, reflect underlying disagreements about language itself – whether words should always admit of strict literal meanings, for instance, or how much ambiguity and fudge should be allowed in our formulations? Or how can we envisage breaking out of the ethical impasse that creates such barriers between, say, the republican movement and mainstream unionism: where apparently different moral vocabularies are drawn upon and where the moral outrage expressed by one side has no effect whatsoever on the other?

ASSIMILATION

One response to questions of this kind is simply to ignore the challenges they imply by saying in effect that reconciliation means assimilation, and if assimilation is not forthcoming, then too bad for reconciliation. This is, ultimately, an unsatisfactory response to complex issues of social and political life, but one version of it has an appeal of sorts. To become embroiled in controversies between unionism and nationalism is to be distracted by little more than what Michael Ignatieff, following Freud, calls the 'narcissism of minor difference'.[5] And to be so distracted is to be blind to the drive to assimilation that runs deep in modern society. Or so it could be argued.

The argument goes something like this. As a consequence of the emergence of capitalism, modern societies are organised in terms of an economy based on growth and change. To function effectively, such societies need a centralised homogeneous culture, since the various practices involved in doing business, operating a legal system, or running a bureaucratic state presuppose the presence of a standardised language, a virtually context-free mode of communication. The modern state helps meet this need by inducting citizens into what Charles Taylor calls 'official languages, almost official cultures'.[6] And it does so because, as Ernest Gellner put it, homogeneity is an 'inescapable imperative' of modernity.[7] Accordingly, sources of, say, cultural difference between citizens must be deprived of any central role in public life, and pushed to the margins. On the terms of this argument, modern societies and the type of states they require for their successful functioning cannot allow their basic institutions to reflect the particular nuances of local customs and dialects or the context-specific traditions and languages of parochial identities. That is why the drive to assimilation runs deep.

To suggest that reconciliation means assimilation seems, then, to imply that those matters of difference between unionism and nationalism really are minor, if not indeed narcissistic, affairs. To leave these matters aside for the sake of pursuing priorities dictated by modernity may appear compelling because a properly functioning modern society requires nothing less. And the claim here is that pursuing such priorities makes possible not only the achievement of an efficient society, but reconciliation too. For doing so loosens us from the grip of particular historical allegiances, as we are assimilated into the (supposedly) neutral culture of modernity. This is precisely what hope of reconciliation consists in, according to this line on assimilation. On its terms, not to be released from the hold of historical allegiances is to be deprived of any meaningful prospect of our divisions being overcome, as it is these allegiances that are at the heart of the discord in Northern Ireland. Thus, it is possible to say that in the absence of assimilation it just is too bad for reconciliation. Put slightly differently, one rendering of the message on offer here boils down to contending that to be reconciled means transcending the sources of our differences through assimilation; that unionism, nationalism or any other local variant of cultural and political identification should be exchanged for a kind of modern cosmopolitanism; and that such acts of transcendence and exchange have the backing of rationality.

In a sense, this pattern of reasoning puts an intellectual gloss on a familiar enough response of incomprehension to the problems of Northern Ireland, especially from those living outside its borders. This response may come in the form of a genuine expression of bewilderment – conveyed, say, by sections of the international media – that the impact of modernity apparently has not been sufficiently strong to subvert our ancient prejudices; or in the form of a more exasperated, frequently patronising, disdain – common enough in Britain – at the seeming irrationality of allowing differences of culture and religion to hinder economic and political development. Even when indelicately articulated, there is a glimmer of truth in these forms of response, one that the reconciliation as assimilation argument draws out. Set against a global backdrop, our differences are relatively minor and there probably is a good deal of narcissism involved in our preoccupation with them. And it is pertinent to ask whether the economic and political costs incurred by concentrating on them – not least during the marching season – are worth paying.

There remain, however, two major problems with the reconciliation as assimilation argument. One concerns its strategy for overcoming obstacles caused by cultural difference in Northern Ireland. Although it is entirely commendable to seek common ground that draws citizens together, it is implausible to think that the best route to such ground lies in trying to transcend the obstacles that block its path. Sure, in the grand scheme of things, differences between people in the North may be minor and emphasis of them narcissistic, but that neither makes them any less real nor more amenable to quick fixes. If there is to be a reconciliation of differences and an occupation of common ground, then there is no short cut available: differences and the hurdles they create have to be tackled rather than avoided. What is also troubling about the strategy of transcendence are the assumptions upon which it relies: that it is always irrational not to prioritise interests of economic and political efficiency, that the culture of modernity is neutral, and that a cosmopolitan identity is all that modern citizens require for anything other than private purposes.[8] Each of these is controversial and deserves to be challenged, especially when used to underpin a strategy that cannot take seriously the importance Northern Ireland's people attach to their differences and to the priorities that follow from them.

To question such assumptions as neutrality and cosmopolitanism not only adds to doubts about the strategy of the reconciliation as assimilation argument, but also raises worries about the argument's very ideal. These worries may be grouped around a second major problem, namely the unacknowledged bias inherent in the ideal of a homogeneous culture into which we all should be assimilated. For example, even if we allow the supposition that homogeneity implies a kind of cosmopolitanism, we are not dealing with a strictly neutral ideal. Indeed, its sole stake in neutrality amounts to an indifference to disputes between competing local cultures. But this is hardly enough to immunise the ideal from other kinds of bias. Concisely, the homogeneous culture of modernity, which ostensibly privileges a cosmopolitan orientation at the expense of particular attachments, unavoidably entails a claim to superiority over local cultural variants. And this is a claim that may be judged convincing or unconvincing, but certainly not neutral.

The ideal's fate is even more precarious when we disallow the link between homogeneity and cosmopolitanism on account of its fictional status. The ideal of a homogeneous culture reflecting purely cosmopolitan sympathies continues to await realisation.

Even the USA, that most technologically advanced of modern societies, very much relies upon its own brand of patriotism for its cohesion. The point is that inasmuch as homogeneous cultures exist within specific societies, they depend upon particular forms of patriotism or nationalism rather than upon cosmopolitanism. And this is the point Gellner was driving at when he claimed that modernity has an 'inescapable imperative' to homogeneity: nationalism is a peculiarly modern phenomenon, rather than an atavistic throwback, equipped to provide the social cement required by a successfully functioning modern society. Whatever we make of Gellner's explanation of the emergence of modern nationalism, the salient issue here is that within any contemporary society the prevailing political culture is not neutral but invariably reflects a dominant or majority ethos. Assimilation means buying into it. Sacrificing the public ambitions of a minority culture is the price it exacts.

Concern with this price is evident throughout the Western world, not least in debates about multi-culturalism. In deeply divided societies, the question of whether it is even sensible to ask for such a price might be expected to acquire a particularly sharp edge. Yet this is precisely what is missed by the ideal of assimilation. As a consequence, it appears more than a little misconceived. For example, within the current context of Northern Ireland, to press for assimilation amounts to asking Northern nationalists to accept the sufficiency of a British identity and therefore to cease to be what they are. Or, alternatively, within the context of a projected united Ireland, it is tantamount to instructing unionists that they are victims of a quite extraordinary self-delusion, since they were only confused Irish nationalists all along. Either way, to adopt Claude Lévi-Strauss's terminology, thinking of reconciliation as assimilation involves saying, 'we [the majority] will refrain from vomiting you out if you let us swallow you up'.[9] Reconciliation is thus reduced to farce.

PRIORITISING DIFFERENCE

An opposite response to the challenge of bridging divisions ascribes primary value to our differences. Various reasons may motivate such a response: because these differences are believed to provide indispensable sources of identity, say, or because concentrating on them – especially given their cultural significance – is seen as necessary preparation for reconciliation, or because they are supposed to indicate stubborn realities of division – most notably political – which no amount of reconciling aspirations can spirit away. These different reasons for taking our differences seriously may overlap or not, but they share one common effect: a prioritisation of difference at the expense of reconciliation. My claim is not that this effect is always intentional, though in instances it manifestly is, but that it is integral to certain ways of approaching questions of difference and reconciliation. To back up the claim, let me highlight three ways that exemplify the reasons I have suggested why primary value is sometimes ascribed to our differences. For convenience, I refer to these ways as principled, practical, and realist.

A *principled* way of prioritising difference latches on to part of the argument already made against assimilation. The North American political philosopher Iris Marion Young neatly captures its core convictions:

> [The] norm of the homogeneous public is oppressive. Not only does it put unassimilated persons and groups at a severe disadvantage in the competition for scarce positions and resources, but it requires that persons transform their sense of identity in order to assimilate. Self-annihilation is an unreasonable and unjust requirement of citizenship.[10]

Accordingly, she maintains, we need to acknowledge group differences of nationality, ethnicity, and the like. And, as we do, we may come to see that in the late 'twentieth century the ideal state is composed of a plurality of nations or cultural groups'.[11]

The virtue of this principled way of prioritising difference is that it underscores precisely what the assimilation argument misses, namely the importance of doing justice to the particular sources of identity valued by members of society. Here there can be no justification for social or political domination of one group by another, or for trying to squeeze either unionists or nationalists into contrived and utterly unsuitable moulds. But what is bothering is that it is hard to see how concern with reconciliation can be other than side-lined as a consequence. Sure, it may be edifying, if not indeed liber-ating, within Northern Ireland, to talk of the plurality of difference, or of difference being encouraged to flourish, or, in Alan Finlay-son's playful suggestion with serious intent, of our received tradi-tions in the North being subjected 'to the cold winds of contemporary cultural confusion'.[12] The problem is that such talk may mean many very different things, none of which appears up to handling the crucial issue sustaining concern with reconciliation: how to overcome the divisiveness which our differences have helped to create.

This may seem a premature judgement given that there are at least three responses to the issue, open to advocates of a principled politics of difference. More than that, it probably appears unduly harsh when directed against one of these in particular, namely a response that, despite its prioritisation of difference, claims sensitiv-ity to problems of division and is compatible with a notion of reconciliation as a balancing of differences. I want to delay consid-eration of this response until discussing the view of reconciliation as a balancing act in Chapter 3. But, to anticipate part of that discus-sion, I should say that I stand by my negative judgement, since what is missing from this response is an adequate understanding of commonality. And it is just such an understanding, I shall argue, that is required if the promise of our divisions being healed is to have substance. In short, once difference is prioritised, the strength of reconciliation is necessarily diluted. Of course, for certain propo-nents of a politics of difference, this is scarcely a problem. It is, rather, reconciliation that is problematic. Let me take up two other responses to the issue of division that argue along such lines.

Another, philosophically inspired, response is to retort that reconciliation is an illusory goal, that our divisions do not admit of any grand solution, and that learning to live with difference with-out the aid of comforting myths is our sober lot. Reconciliation is said to be illusory because it 'depends upon a complete coincidence with the self' that 'by definition rules out any relation to another which prevents such self-completion'.[13] To unpack this response a little, we are being told that reconciliation's putative root aspiration – the possibility of complete self-coincidence – is both highly implausible and self-defeating. Highly implausible because it projects a possibility beyond human experience: the realisation of an undistorted self-identity that allows its possessors to stand in a transparent and perfectly harmonious relation to themselves, and that therefore promises relief from such common human burdens as doubt, uncertainty and self-conflict. Self-defeating because even imagining this unlikely possibility entails not reaching out to others, but denying, eliminating or, at the very least, shutting out all that seems different, foreign or threatening.

Accordingly, the argument goes, sidelining reconciliation should not be a matter of embarrassment, but one of honest necessity. At a general level, this means giving up reconciliation's anticipation of unity, since any attempt to realise it would ride roughshod over differences within the self and within society. At a political level, it means abandoning all dreams of cultural and political cohesion and acknowledging that there is no viable alternative to living in the face of 'the cold winds of contemporary cultural confusion', to use again Finlayson's phrase. Here reconciliation's hope of a unity that bridges differences is replaced by an expectation of finding enough social and political space to permit difference expression without fear of others, that is, of political circumstances that allow our differences to flourish even as they are managed in a manner that avoids us destroying each other.

Now, this argument is convincing only if we accept its very restricted understanding of reconciliation and if we ignore its political vacuity. There are good reasons for doing neither. Commitment to reconciliation, for example, does not necessarily involve adhering to a rigid ideal of perfect self-harmony, where everything within and without the self reassuringly reflects one's identity. Such an ideal, admittedly, may be a goal of various visions of reconciliation, especially some that are theologically motivated. But, even among visions that uphold the ideal, there is considerable variance about what it means and how it should be pursued. And certainly not all of them require the sort of closure to difference that is being suggested. Indeed, the charge that reconciliation relies upon an ideal that is highly implausible and self-defeating tells only against visions which are fundamentalist in kind, namely those which assume an individual or collective self immune to doubt or scrutiny, which prescribe an immutable set of truths and values, which demand conformity to a privileged way of life and reject everything that falls beyond its narrow parameters.

Fundamentalism aside, what emerges unscathed is a view of reconciliation as a dynamic quest in which openness to difference is seen as intrinsically valuable. Here there is no suggestion of a self-completion that denies others. On the contrary, respecting and engaging others are regarded as indispensable to reconciliation. Not only do respect and engagement disturb prejudices and broaden and deepen one's own self-understanding, but they also contribute to developing the trust required to overcome the divisiveness that an accentuation of difference very often increases. And what is held out is hope not in difference's elimination but in a reconciliation that takes difference seriously.

A crucial issue at stake between this approach to reconciliation and what I have called a philosophically inspired prioritisation of difference may now be recast as follows: the conviction of the former that searching for common ground in the midst of our differences is neither an inherently futile nor a subtly oppressive endeavour. I return to this issue in more detail in Chapter 5. For the moment, it is enough to note that disagreement over it matters, not least politically. Indeed, the abandonment of hope in finding common ground highlights the political vacuity of a position that celebrates difference but has scarcely anything to say about the problems of division exacerbated by difference's pursuit. Sure, being exposed to cultural confusion may help to open closed minds and wishing for non-threatening expressions of difference may be a laudable aim. But a good deal more is needed in a divided society if the sources of division are to be dealt with in a politically effective way. Yet looking for more proves disappointing. In sum, a politics that aspires to little else than a containment of difference's excesses promises at best a fragile future, not one that instils confidence. It hardly qualifies as a plausible alternative to a politics of reconciliation which, whatever our differences, attempts to find points of commonality among citizens.

Distrust of the language of commonality is not always easily removed, however. And the emphasis on reconciliation also comes under fire from another, more politically motivated, prioritisation of difference. Put bluntly, this occurs when division may be even seen as an acceptable price to pay for difference's sake. A position that, implicitly or explicitly, admits as much typically suspects that deep down reconciliation cannot escape association with assimilation, and that it involves the imposition of a spurious unity which threatens the integrity, perhaps even the survival, of a valued group identity. On these terms, division may be a regrettable cost, but if its avoidance necessitates the surrender of a group's distinctiveness, then there is no option except to bear it.

There are powerful political motivations at work here, which should not be underestimated: a struggle for the survival of a particular group ethos or way of life, an antipathy to domination, a refusal to facilitate political convenience by exchanging an identity regarded as authentic for one considered inauthentic. Even so, as a replacement of a politics of reconciliation, such a politically inspired prioritisation of difference does not compel. Most obviously, in offering no prospect of our divisions being lessened, let alone overcome, it leaves intact society's rudimentary problems. Perhaps less obviously, but tellingly none the less, its central distinction between inauthentic and authentic identities is open to dispute. This is not to deny that such a distinction can be fruitfully and legitimately drawn, but to suggest that it can be drawn too strictly when put to the service of narrow political interests. This may occur, for instance, when it is inferred that a shared or common citizen identity is necessarily inauthentic, on the grounds that such an identity amounts to little more than a manipulative concoction designed to serve the dominant interests of assimilation. But this inference caricatures any quest for political cohesion or reconciliation. It also implies obliviousness of the susceptibility of a particular group identity to a similar charge: there is no guarantee that what currently counts as an authentic identity is not the product of a group's manipulation by its own elite, or, at the very least, of a very selective reading of its history. Quite simply, it is the fate of all identities to be vulnerable to charges of manipulation and concoction. It just does not wash to think that it is the peculiar fate of those identities that stress what we share as members of the same society despite our traditional differences.

A good deal hangs on seeing this. I am claiming that all identities are in principle contestable, even if most of us most of the time – and some of the time with good reason – act as if they are not. If we discount the crude accounts of assimilation and fundamentalism, this is something that a politics of reconciliation should have no difficulty grasping. It does, however, pose an acute quandary for a politics of difference of the sort presently under discussion. To concede contestability is to demur at talk of difference's alleged intractability and purity. And from here it is but a short step to allow complexity, that is, to admit the multi-faceted nature of many contemporary identities, the fact that they crosscut, and so on. And to allow complexity is to weaken difference's grip, to temper the type of claims made on its behalf; it is to put the search for points of commonality across our differences in an altogether more tolerable light. To say this is not to denigrate the importance of particular group identities, but merely to query their sufficiency and self-enclosed inclinations. There is certainly no intention of diminishing the significance of those powerful motivations of survival, anti-domination and authenticity which a politics of difference brings to the fore and which no plausible approach to reconciliation can afford to ignore.

It is, indeed, an achievement of principled prioritisations of difference to make dealing with motivations like these inescapable, and to expose the shallowness of any attempt to move beyond division that does not take them seriously. But such prioritisations remain inadequate substitutes for a properly conceived politics of reconciliation. In trying to show this, I have also been trying to settle doubts about reconciliation's intentions and implications and, thereby, to open up a space for its reception. What clearly emerges is the need to overcome nervousness about making concessions to the interests of society as a whole for fear that they will signify damaging losses for a particular identity.

If suspicion of reconciliation's intentions is sometimes hard to budge, so too is this kind of nervousness about its requirements. Something like it pervades many layers of society and is manifest not only in the fearful reactions against reconciliation I mentioned earlier, but also in various *practical* prioritisations of difference in Northern Ireland, as witnessed, for example, in 'single identity' projects which attract funding from government agencies. These may be informed by a principled commitment to difference, but they need not be and often, I imagine, are not.

At any rate, the practical prioritisations I am thinking of ostensibly operate on the assumption that it may be important to emphasise difference not for its own sake, but for the sake of reconciliation. Here the rationale seems to be that only communities strong enough in their own sense of themselves can embark upon a path of reconciliation without fearing the consequences. This rationale appears to have gained significant support within community organisations and funding bodies. It underpins growth of the media through which a single identity consciousness is developed and represented, as local communities strive to acquire more self-assured and inventive appropriations of their traditions. Particularly striking examples are on display during the annual West Belfast Festival, where we see increasingly vibrant and self-confident expressions of an Irish republican identity that are out of kilter with the self-understandings and mores of unionist parts of the city. If nationalists and republicans have stolen a march in capitalising on the funding available for creative plans to enhance a single identity consciousness, unionists and loyalists have begun to play catch up. Funding aside, Protestant East Belfast now seems to be treated to annual summer painting sprees undertaken by loyalists anxious to mark out their territory in ways designed to engender self-pride in their Protestant/British identity. Or so we are told.

Now, there is no doubting that many community relations workers regard single identity projects as fitting into the bigger picture of reconciliation between the two traditional communities; and there is no doubt too that the political parties most closely associated with community developments in West and East Belfast – Sinn Féin and the Progressive Unionist Party (PUP) respectively – claim to be keenly interested in reconciliation. But, without querying anyone's sincerity, two main worries remain. First, it is not obvious why, having lived together for three to four hundred years, we still need coaching with our own before engaging properly with the so-called other. It is tempting to retort that when considering how, when, where or if we should dabble in cross-community exercises, there is no better advice than that offered by the Nike advertisement – 'just do it'.

Second, it is not clear that affirmations of our separate identities are making the business of reconciliation easier to conduct; rather, they appear to exaggerate our differences in sometimes unhelpful ways. Decorating East Belfast with red, white and blue paint, loyalist graffiti and symbols, and seeing their equivalents replicated in West Belfast may make (some) people in those areas feel better about themselves, but it does not necessarily make them feel better about each other. Or, more to the point, the better republicans feel about themselves, the worse they are regarded by unionists/loyalists, who are decidedly unnerved by shows of republican self-confidence (and perhaps vice versa). At any rate, not too many Protestants/unionists are keen to participate in the West Belfast Festival, even when invited. And republicans need not even expect to be invited to comparable events in East Belfast.

Playing up difference for the sake of reconciliation may appear to some an attractive idea on paper, but there is a dearth of evidence on the ground to suggest that it contributes much to overcoming division. To clarify, this is not to dispute the entitlements of cultures to celebrate their distinctiveness or differences, nor is it even to suggest that such celebrations have no place in a reconciled society. It is simply to dispute the claim that, in the current context of a deeply divided Northern Ireland, emphasising cultural separateness paves the way to reconciliation.

The strong temptation here is to conclude that, given our differences, we would be better off, and certainly much less prone to self-delusions, by trimming our expectations of reconciliation. Sure, let community relations workers, the voluntary sector, the ecumenical movement, and so on try to build whatever little bridges they can. But do not expect to make much impression in the opposing cultural heartlands of the North, and, in particular, do not expect much political purchase. Thinking along such lines points to a third way of prioritising difference, one that I anticipated in my brief remarks about cynicism in the previous chapter. This is a way of thinking that claims to be based on *realism* about what is politically feasible in Northern Ireland.

No high-wire political acts are going to work said James Molyneaux, former leader of the UUP. Not only do many unionist politicians – especially those opposed to the Agreement – seem to concur, but, curiously enough, so too do anti-Agreement republicans. There is, however, nothing terribly surprising about the fact that overtly partisan political actors, whose interests are not served by a reconciliation of unionism and nationalism, should occasionally present their case in realist terms. More interesting are those, less overtly partisan, academic commentators who also maintain that a candid analysis of Northern politics reveals that hopes of our political differences being reconciled are dashed on the rock of realism.

Writing after the paramilitary ceasefires of 1994, Richard English, for example, maintained that it is simply illogical to press for reconciliation, since it is impossible to square the competing sovereignty claims of unionism and nationalism. Northern Ireland cannot simultaneously be absorbed into a united Ireland while remaining part of the United Kingdom (UK). Moreover, he continued, it is absurd to think of unionism and nationalism as equally legitimate traditions that have a comparable claim to parity of esteem within the North. For this implies wrongly that the 'aspiration to break the Union of Great Britain and Northern Ireland is . . . as legitimate as the aspiration to maintain it'.[14] And, besides, he added, 'the people who have driven the conflict, on both sides, have no belief whatever in the pious suggestions regarding parity of esteem or equal legitimacy: unionists/loyalists believe that their views are preferable and superior to those of nationalists/republicans, and nationalists/republicans believe their views are preferable and superior to those of unionists/loyalists'.[15]

Writing a little later, but still prior to the Agreement, when it was clear that both the British and Irish governments were intending to proceed with negotiations that did not take on board his realist analysis, he offered further advice. Both governments should stop trying to find a solution to the problem of Northern Ireland they expect unionists and nationalists to agree on if it entails engaging the 'extremes', namely those with paramilitary connections. Instead they should prune back their ambitions and concentrate on merely 'managing' the problem. And the best hope he can find for anything approximating reconciliation is the following speculation: 'within a generation [the problem] will be essentially over'. 'The end will not result,' he conjectures, 'from well-meaning initiatives but rather from demographic, economic and wider political changes that are not programmed with a view to peace but which change the nature of the questions people ask.'[16]

Or there is the line Aughey began to develop in the 1996 John Whyte Memorial Lecture,[17] when he invoked the German political theorist Carl Schmitt's distinction between friends and enemies as a more analytically useful tool than anything available in what Aughey elsewhere referred to as 'the banal but corrosive jargon of the peace process'.[18] The idea here is that, by virtue of their opposing constitutional positions, unionists and nationalists necessarily regard each other as enemies and their own as friends. And, politically speaking, that is just the way it is. Thus, there is no point in becoming carried away by impossible dreams of reconciliation.

At a general level, English's and Aughey's pessimistic realist views of the impossibility of reconciliation between unionists and nationalists paint a picture of a present in which a debilitating fatalism looms large. Their implicit – and sometimes explicit – message is: unionists are what they are, nationalists are what they are, and both like it that way. So do not expect changes to come from within these mutually exclusive communities; do not challenge or ask hard questions of their self-understandings; and keep believing that not doing so will deliver a workable society, albeit a deeply unreconciled one. Realism too, it seems, requires a significant act of faith, since why we should think of such a society as workable is anything but evident.

The achievement of the Agreement in 1998 may appear as conclusive proof of the mistaken nature of the realist analysis. The fact that, despite their reservations, it won republican and loyalist commitments is particularly illuminating: the so-called extremes proved not to be the obstacles that the realists imagined, and they appeared to be much more open to what English derisively dismissed as 'pious suggestions regarding parity of esteem or equal legitimacy' than he seemed capable of conceiving. At the time of writing, however, it is premature to make too much of this, since the Agreement's future is still uncertain on account of the conflicting interpretations to which it has been subjected. But, whatever its fate, the fact that it happened at all gives us reason to doubt the realist prognosis.

As I shall argue more fully in Chapters 6 and 7, the Agreement indicates that hope in political reconciliation does not hang on an impossible task of fully satisfying clashing views of sovereignty; it is much more subtle and multi-faceted. And even in a world without the Agreement, there are grounds for being sceptical of key elements of the realist position. For example, since the plantations of Ulster in the seventeenth century, our history has been plagued by some variant of the friend/enemy distinction, so Aughey's resort to Schmitt does not give fresh insight into our political condition. In fact, this sort of distinction has underpinned Irish hostilities for close on four centuries, and has been employed to rationalise every sectarian brutality in the book. And to think merely in terms of it, which Aughey now seems to believe is not necessary,[19] implies a political future that guarantees only stalemate at best and risks considerable unrest if not worse. But unless we are already predisposed to conclude that unionists and nationalists are wired up only to think in oppositional terms, or that they are so determined by their history that they can do no other, it is not obvious why this kind of distinction should be entertained at all. Moreover, as we await the realisation of English's vision of modernity's eventual triumph in the North (through the withering away of traditional allegiances), it is not obvious what he believes will happen to the 'extremes' as their political representatives are told there is no place for them in politics, as presumably they must be if the 'extremes' are to be excluded. And what he supposes the consequences of their exclusion would mean for society at large remains a matter of consternation.

In the end, the reconciliation as impossible thesis advanced by certain politicians and academics is susceptible to the general criticisms I raised against the peace without reconciliation thesis, of which it is probably a variant anyway. Despite its realist claims, it amounts to a flight from political realities in Northern Ireland, and it works with a miserly view of politics which justifies an abrogation of our most compelling political responsibility: creating a decent society for all citizens (not just for friends), and trying to create it now.

The realist view does of course highlight certain difficulties that confront the task of political reconciliation, particularly since views similar to English's and Aughey's are widespread among unionists (including those in the pro–Agreement camp). And the fact that our future remains radically undecided despite the Agreement underlines the enormity of reconciliation's brief. But to accept that differences between unionists and nationalists are permanent fixtures, destined always to thwart reconciliation's ambitions, is simply to give up too easily. Sacrificing hopes of a decent future for all citizens at the altar of difference remains an unpalatable option. And camouflaging this sacrifice through the language of realism adds neither to its intellectual nor practical wisdom.

CONCLUSION

Reconciliation's absence from so much of the life of Northern society now appears less puzzling than it did initially. This is not to say that it appears less disconcerting. But it is not hard to see why the considerable investments in reconciliation in Northern Ireland have yielded such low dividends. Quite simply, inspection reveals complex layers of resistance to reconciliation's appeal; it uncovers an array of reasons why many of the North's citizens may overtly or covertly regard reconciliation as not quite the good thing it is made out to be. And if reconciliation does imply little more than some form of assimilation, then much of the resistance is probably justified and some of the reasons telling.

This is, however, a line I am not prepared to accept. To hold out against reconciliation because we are distrustful of assimilation is largely to miss the point, since what is being resisted is only a caricature anyway. Moreover, the reasons for resistance suffer from a crippling defect: they leave intact the problem reconciliation sets out to address, namely how to overcome the divisions and antagon-isms that handicap much social and political life in Northern Ireland. To give up on reconciliation, or even to scale down its ambitions, is not to be left with very attractive alternatives. And that is partly why it continues to make sense to affirm that recon-ciliation is a good thing. Even so, matters cannot be settled so quickly. The case for reconciliation remains weak if the best that can be said for it is that it wins by default; reconciliation's detractors may lack plausible alternatives but some of their objections may still await further answers; and just what I mean by reconciliation may currently seem tantalisingly vague. So let me now try to strengthen the case for reconciliation by clarifying some of the things I am claiming about it, and by examining another way of thinking of it.

3

A BALANCING ACT?

The reality of division has to greater and lesser degrees always haunted cultural and political relations in Northern Ireland. And a desire to alter it drives concern with reconciliation. This much is obvious. What else I think reconciliation's concern entails may be a little less obvious. I want now to tie together some threads of the discussion so far in order to give a clearer, even if not yet a complete, indication of my view of reconciliation. Doing so also has the advantage of permitting a sharper identification of the main difficulties involved in trying to overcome the problem of division.

Against this backdrop, I then pose a simple question: is reconciliation a balancing act? It may seem that yes is evidently the right answer, one that gives the best clue about how the problem of division may be fruitfully tackled. The big defect of reconciliation's detractors is, of course, their inability to say anything constructive about this problem. When reminded of it, they appear strangely mute, evasively convoluted or depressingly fatalistic. But, without minimising the difficulties involved in dealing with it, there is no need to be floored by the problem of division. The point is to realise that, once surrender or assimilation are ruled out as viable options, balancing opposing claims is what trying to bridge the gulf separating the main sides in a dispute entails. In the context of Northern Ireland, the key is to stress that it is not in the interests of unionists or nationalists, of loyalists or republicans to allow divisions between them to continue unabated. And the trick is to balance the various interests and claims of these rival traditions in a way that each can live with. Thus understood as a means of tackling the problem of division, reconciliation does essentially amount to a balancing act, and refining the act to ensure its success becomes reconciliation's supreme task. Or so the argument might go.

How well this argument succeeds in illuminating essential features of reconciliation's concern and in enabling us to answer its difficulties remains to be seen. Let me give a preliminary account of what I take these features and difficulties to be.

RECONCILIATION AND ITS DIFFICULTIES

For a start, let me say what I do not mean by reconciliation. Obviously, for reasons already canvassed, I do not mean assimilation, fundamentalism, or some state of perfect harmony. It is worth adding that I do not mean a condition of resignation either. This may be an important point to make, since that sense in the English language in which reconciliation connotes resignation can easily be given a political twist. And in the circumstances of a divided society like Northern Ireland, giving an essentially negative connotation this sort of twist is not conducive to building trust between wary, if not hostile, political camps. Take, for example, those pro-Agreement unionists who are reconciled to sharing power with nationalists not because they want to, but because it now appears to them as the least unattractive of the alternatives available. Here reconciliation carries clear overtones of resignation, and may be even accompanied by lament for a political world that has been lost irretrievably. In this case, being reconciled means facing up to a disagreeable yet inescapable reality; it implies making compromises with a heavy heart, granting the political entitlements of one's opponents but reluctantly. On these terms, a reconciled society appears as one in which concessions are made to difference, but only because of pragmatic necessity. This is undoubtedly to envisage a better society than one in which no concessions are made at all.

But to accept this as the summit of our expectations of reconciliation is to be short-changed.

A PRELIMINARY UNDERSTANDING

The sense of reconciliation I have been alluding to throughout Chapters 1 and 2 picks up on the positive connotation also carried by the term. Whereas the negative connotation highlights our being reconciled *to* some state of affairs – such as one in which the claims of difference can be no longer dismissed or ignored – the positive connotation highlights our being reconciled *with* those who are different from us. Whereas one connotation implies a fateful surrender to a world, say, of ineliminable difference, the other suggests an active embrace of it. These two ways of depicting the positive connotation of reconciliation interrelate: it is possible to embrace a world that cannot be divested of difference in so far as we are genuinely engaging with those who are different from us. Together they provide a backdrop against which my various allusions to reconciliation's entailments may be better understood.

Consider, for instance, my claims to the effect that reconciliation matters (1) because the divisions that have attended expressions of our differences in Northern Ireland are destructive and need to be overcome; and (2) because it points to the opening up of a common space we can share and which is indispensable, as without it too many of us are doomed to inhabit only the separate spaces within which divisions become normalised. These claims are empty unless linked to the demand that genuine engagement occurs between members of different traditions. For divisions cannot be overcome in the absence of such engagement and common space cannot be created and sustained. It is unlikely too that this space will be occupied without an embrace of the particular world of difference that exists in Northern Ireland. Quite simply, common space quickly will become vacant without adequate recognition being granted to the different voices required to fill it. The quest for commonality can succeed only if it involves recognising, rather than denying, difference.

Or take another crucial claim I made about reconciliation as a dynamic process through which we are opened up to others and, as a consequence, broadened in our understanding of ourselves and of the world. This claim too assumes a willingness to engage and embrace. Reconciliation precisely does not refer to a final self-enclosed state because engaging with others and embracing a world in which difference is ineliminable makes our horizons and ourselves vulnerable to change. This is to say that reconciliation is always an incomplete, ongoing affair. And it is also to say that a reconciled society is not one from which contradictions, tensions or disagreements have been eradicated. It is, rather, one that has dealt with its destructive divisions through giving sufficient recognition of difference and through shared commitments to basic common goals.

An initial, general depiction of reconciliation is now possible. Reconciliation refers to a set of activities – engaging with others and embracing our world – that are conducted in a certain spirit – most notably one of openness – with an aim to expanding horizons, healing divisions, and articulating common purposes. It is this depiction, I want to argue, that illuminates what it means to quest for a reconciled society.

TWO DIFFICULTIES

The attainment of a reconciled society is extraordinarily difficult for two reasons. First, the spirit of openness essential to the activities of engagement and embrace cannot simply be manufactured. And in a divided society it is sometimes hard to find. As we may appreciate from the earlier analysis, the sorts of indifference, fear, and bitterness that underlie much resistance to reconciliation in Northern Ireland easily choke such a spirit. In fact, possession of a spirit of openness is almost impossible to imagine without the presence of certain character virtues among citizens, in particular those of forgiveness, magnanimity and reasonableness. Accordingly, reconciliation's prospects may be redescribed as follows. A reconciled society is conceivable if we embrace our own circumstances and their ineliminable differences through genuine engagement with those who are different from us. This is to say that it is conceivable if there is a sufficiently widespread spirit of openness and that, in turn, is to say that a reconciled society is conceivable if there is a sufficiently high possession of virtues among citizens. Reconciliation's difficulty is that the fact that divisions prove so durable indicates at root that the requisite virtues are in scarce supply. Thus, in an important sense, lack of virtue appears as a central problem for the achievement of a reconciled society. Just as this problem cannot be plausibly dodged, neither can the demands reconciliation makes of us. In calling for the cultivation of certain virtues it asks for considerably more than a few pious thoughts, a bit of polite conversation and the odd symbolic gesture. In doing so, it appears as anything but a soft option. If taken seriously, it promises to disturb our prejudices and perhaps unsettle our lives.

A second difficulty confronting the possibility of a reconciled society is the one I have flagged up on a number of occasions. It is not obvious how divisions are to be healed and common purposes articulated while difference is simultaneously given its due. Even assuming a resolution of the first problem of virtue is no guarantee of an answer, and, as we have seen, the possibility of coming up with one is regarded sceptically in various quarters. It is one thing to insist, as I have done, on the need to maintain the importance of upholding the claims of both commonality and difference, but quite another to specify just how and what it means to do so.

BALANCING AND INCLUSION

An answer to these difficulties perhaps lies in thinking of reconciliation as a balancing act. In its recognition of the need to take account of the opposing claims of rival traditions, this way of thinking immediately takes us beyond the stalemates and false alternatives encountered in the previous chapter. Two opposing approaches we looked at there seem broadly to agree that a reconciled society is one in which issues of cultural difference among citizens are marginalised for the sake of social and political unity. Although they disagree about whether such a society is desirable, let alone possible, emphases on assimilation and on difference's priority virtually concur in facing us with a stark choice – reconciliation or difference? To think of reconciliation as a balancing act is at once to see that this is the wrong choice. And here there seems to be a nice fit with two of my major contentions: that emphases on difference that downgrade reconciliation, if not make it surplus to requirements, are neither worthy nor practical; and that an advocacy of reconciliation that glosses over difference is seriously deficient too. So thinking in terms of a balancing act makes it a priority to facilitate concerns of difference and of reconciliation, or, more exactly, to show how it is possible to conceive of reconciliation in a way that gives difference its due. And, in doing so, perhaps it reveals how to settle the commonality–difference difficulty. Moreover, since successful balancing has to be practised by the main protagonists in a dispute or a conflict – and cannot simply be done by mediators on their behalf – it may call into play the sort of qualities of character that are required to deal with the other difficulty of virtue's (relative) absence. There is, then, a prima facie case for supposing that to conceive of reconciliation as a balancing act offers an illuminating way out of the difficulties reinforcing division and impeding reconciliation's development.

The potential attractiveness of this case is deepened if it is articulated in reference to possibly its most interesting and powerful source: the concept of parity of esteem.[1] This concept has recently gained prominence in Northern politics, largely through its sponsorship by the British and Irish governments.[2] It indicates both governments' intention to adopt an impartial approach to traditional differences in the North, and their desire to promote among citizens respect of cultural forms other than their own. By highlighting the concept of parity of esteem, it is hoped that traditional hostilities can be overcome and privileged or discriminatory practices brought to an end. Accordingly, it is not difficult to see how the concept fits with an emphasis on reconciliation. On its terms, reconciliation is achievable once we realise our common interest in developing an inclusive society in which unionists and nationalists both have a stake, where their respective cultures are not only permitted expression but are seen as enriching the whole, where the traditional basis of differential social, political and economic treatment is discredited.

Drawing on the concept of parity of esteem in order to explain what it means to view reconciliation as a balancing act has plenty of appeal. It seems capable of incorporating those features which I maintained are constitutive of reconciliation: the activities of engagement and embrace, a spirit of openness, and the goals of healing division, defining common purposes and expanding horizons. And, to the extent that it is, we may think that it is equally capable of providing insights into how to tackle the difficulty of virtue and its lack. Moreover, it offers a resolution of the tension between commonality and difference by effectively construing reconciliation *as* an even-handed treatment of differences. That is why, as I suggested earlier, it may appeal to at least one version of a politics of difference, since there is little fear here of reconciliation being a disguise for assimilation. On the contrary, reconciliation is made benign through its reduction to a balancing of differences. The accompaniment to this conception of reconciliation is a vision of a reconciled society as one in which not only the rights of individuals are guaranteed, regardless of traditional affiliations, but also the competing traditions of unionism and nationalism are seen as partners in running a society which is home to both. In brief, it is a vision of an inclusive society.

Now, this vision may seem decent enough, but there is reason to doubt whether it and its supporting conception of reconciliation are sufficient. Doubts arise because the language of parity of esteem seems to facilitate quite different interpretations of what balancing and inclusion mean in the context of Northern Ireland. Representatives of unionism and nationalism often employ the language to vindicate their own position and vilify that of the other, but rarely to call themselves into question. And they may use it in very different senses: to indicate a substantive ideal or merely a convenient hook on which to hang their demands, to imply morally exacting standards or merely tactically prudent moves. Behind its immediate appeal, in other words, a curious mix of interpretations and

motivations is frequently at play among those subscribing (or paying lip service) to a parity-of-esteem-oriented understanding of
reconciliation. We obtain a better glimpse of these by distinguishing between what I will call accommodation and extreme entitlement models of parity of esteem, which yield quite different takes
on balancing and inclusion. I want to argue that the first model is
mostly exemplary, but the second problematic. There are tensions
between the two, which are in practice often resolved in favour of
the second. As a consequence, and despite the insights of the accommodation model, there are limitations in grounding our approach
to reconciliation in the language of parity of esteem, as there are also
in thinking of reconciliation only in terms of a balancing act, and of
a reconciled society only in terms of inclusion. At best what is on
offer, I contend, is a weak conception of reconciliation, one that
cannot sufficiently illuminate reconciliation's essential features or
answer its difficulties.

ACCOMMODATION

At the moral heart of the concept of parity of esteem there is an
accommodating model of balancing and inclusion, which gives
insight into the meaning of reconciliation. It is comprised of two
central aspirations: to create conditions that make possible a society
in which all citizens have a stake, in which all of their contributions
to make it work are properly valued; and to normalise thinking not
only of how the claims of our own tradition may be most appropriately satisfied, but of how the claims of other traditions may be
too. It recognises that the first aspiration necessitates correcting the
institutional and political imbalance that in Northern Ireland has
historically privileged unionism. It therefore calls on the second in
asking unionists to be open to nationalism's entitlements for the
sake of inclusion and a fair balancing of unionist and nationalist
differences. It also invokes the second aspiration in asking nationalists not to replace what they perceived as traditional unionist
triumphalism with an equivalent of their own. The model's way
of emphasising the entitlements of both traditions, in other words,
makes other-centred concern integral to accommodation. Let's

consider the sort of reasoning it involves.

Other-centred concern is reflected in employment of the language of parity of esteem to expose as unacceptable the denigration of a way of life or a tradition different from one's own. Disrespect of another cultural form appears here as a manifest injustice, to which those concerned with reconciliation cannot turn a blind eye. Individual and group attitudes are here put under the spotlight. As a consequence, various attitudinal tendencies within different communities in Northern Ireland – too frequently left unchallenged – are revealed as simply intolerable: the tendency among unionists, for example, to impugn everything associated with republicanism, if not also nationalism, on the pretext that it serves merely to provide cultural and ideological cover for terrorism; or, equally, the tendency among nationalists to reduce everything associated with unionism to a rationalisation of Orange supremacy and bigotry.

But that is not all. The capacity of institutions to denigrate a way of life is subject to searching scrutiny too. And it is this kind of scrutiny that calls for a correction to a historical imbalance in the public life of Northern Ireland that has traditionally thwarted a fair accommodation of unionism and nationalism. For instance, disrespect of a significant – even if minority – cultural form occurs when a society's major institutions reflect only the identity of the majority community. In a divided society, it is preposterous to imagine that reconciliation is possible without remedying the cultural–political biases inherent in much public institutional life. The recent furore in Northern Ireland over reform of policing is a case in point. Despite opposition from unionists, reforms were introduced in November 2001, even if they have not yet been sufficient to satisfy Sinn Féin, which refuses to nominate members to sit on the new Police Board. Most notably, attempts have been made to make the police service more accountable to the community as a whole – through a more representative Police Board, for example – and to change the culture of policing and make it more acceptable to non-unionists through such moves as replacing the old name of the Royal Ulster Constabulary (RUC) with the new name of the Police Service of Northern Ireland (PSNI). What opponents of reform singularly refused to grasp – not least in their reaction against symbolic changes to the name of the RUC, its uniform and oath of allegiance – was that it is practically implausible to have an institution as important as a police service that reflects only a unionist identity. To block this sort of institutional reform is to jeopardise the possibility of a reconciled society. And it is to do so because, at root, the offence given is grave.

Attempts to block reform of policing have not been allowed to succeed, of course. But it may be that not everyone who approved of blocking measures, and who wished to see Northern Ireland's public institutions retain an undiminished British or unionist character, appreciated just what there is to be offended about here. To some it may seem sufficient that these institutions guarantee in principle, if not always in practice, that all citizens are accorded equal respect through having their individual rights assured. And there is, undoubtedly, a deep-seated unionist suspicion that republicans and nationalists who press for thoroughgoing institutional reform are really pursuing a subversive strategy to undermine the Northern Ireland state altogether. The suspicion is hardly groundless, since it is a declared aim of republicanism to achieve a unified Irish state. But the suspicion may be also used to adverse polemical effect when it is employed to justify derisive dismissals of complaints that purely British symbols alienate a substantial section of citizens. And it is the case that, in the absence of institutional reform, Northern Ireland is destined to remain an unreconciled society, and that, whatever the ultimate intentions of the republican movement, it is unfair to caricature attempts at reform as merely manifestations of a subversive plot. There is something to be offended about here.

It is this that the language of parity of esteem enables us to see. It points to more than individuals' entitlement to live under conditions conducive to self-respect, such as having their status as morally responsible agents confirmed through legal recognition of their rights. The language also refers to citizens' entitlement to live under conditions conducive to self-esteem, such as having their tradition recognised in the public life of society.[3] If it is true, as it is manifestly in Northern Ireland, that many citizens' sense of worth and dignity is tied to their membership of a particular tradition, then public affirmation of that tradition is crucial to these citizens' self-esteem. And it is precisely such self-esteem that is traduced when a tradition is explicitly denigrated or its public recognition withheld. Accordingly, it is possible to say that granting parity of esteem to the North's major traditions matters because the self-esteem of many citizens depends upon it. There are, of course, different ways in which it may be granted. These range from allowing symbols of Irishness to stand alongside symbols of Britishness to devising inclusive symbols, free from old divisive associations, to represent a fresh dispensation of co-operation between traditions in Northern Ireland. I have more to say about unionist criticisms of the constitutional laxity of this type of reasoning in Chapter 7.

For the moment, it is enough to stress that to oppose any institutional change designed to recognise more than a unionist identity is to say that parity of esteem does not matter, which, in turn, is to infer that the self-esteem of many citizens just does not count for much. And it is this inference that is so offensive. For it comes perilously close to making a form of cultural self-annihilation for non-unionists a condition of full participation in the public life of society. This is, as we saw Young note earlier, 'an unreasonable and unjust requirement of citizenship'.[4] In Northern Ireland, at least, it is also an impossible requirement. To demand it simply guarantees the absence of a properly inclusive public realm. Faced with such an absence, it is likely that many citizens will conclude that their need for self-esteem can be satisfied only within the confines of increasingly exclusive communities. And inasmuch as they do, we can be sure that a society constituted by separate social spaces will remain our lot. The painful truth is that these spaces, whatever their value to the self-esteem of their inhabitants, too often exacerbate antagonistic attitudes toward the 'other', and so render meaningless any talk of reconciliation. The point is that without any shared, common space there is no such thing as a reconciled society. It is a considerable virtue of the language of parity of esteem to show much of what is involved if this point is to be taken seriously.

In permitting us to see the importance of cultural recognition to the institutional life of society, the language of parity of esteem also gives insight into another requirement of reconciliation in a democratic society: the inclusive self-rule of citizens. It does so because cultural recognition and self-rule are related in various ways. For example, if the former is necessary to the creation of common space, then, arguably, the latter is necessary to sustain it. The two are mutually reinforcing. Here it is perhaps most illuminating to think of their relation in terms of two interlocking claims. Self-government by citizens is properly inclusive – in a culturally divided society certainly – only in so far as it incorporates a principle of cultural recognition. And cultural recognition is insufficiently valued unless it is displayed through citizen self-rule.

The first of these claims implies that in a divided society simple majority rule is an inadvisable principle for deciding how political power is distributed and exercised, as it may serve mostly to underwrite the ongoing advantage of the largest cultural group. This is an implication with obvious salience in Northern Ireland. As experience of fifty years of unionist government indicated, the implementation of a majoritarian principle risks domination and alienation becoming hallmarks of political life. This is too great a risk to bear in a society with a pressing need for reconciliation. To avert the risk, to avoid problems of domination and alienation, it is crucial to invoke a different principle of political organisation: most obviously a principle of power sharing that issues in an *inclusive* self-rule of citizens. And this is impossible to do without conceding in principle and practice the political status of cultural recognition. Parity of esteem, in other words, warrants political expression.

This is, of course, the thrust of the second claim. A political impulse is always close at hand in demands for cultural recognition. Such demands are made when a society's basic laws and institutions are perceived unjustly to deny those forms of self-government appropriate to cultural recognition. What these forms are may vary. In Northern Ireland one compelling form – though there are others – is where cultural recognition translates into political representation at an executive level: where nationalists, republicans and unionists of various descriptions together are empowered to ensure that society is organised in a way that does justice to its diverse cultural composition. This is the form that appears in the Agreement. To reject this form or, more generally, to imagine that it is unnecessary to confer political status on cultural claims is to misunderstand what it means to give cultural recognition its due. Alternatively, to take seriously cultural recognition and its imperative of inclusive self-rule is to refuse to settle either for continuing direct rule from Westminster or for a form of selective (not fully inclusive) government in Northern Ireland. It is to insist that the goal of a reconciled society remains a priority that cannot be so easily surrendered.

These insights from an accommodating model underscore that rectifying a historical imbalance in cultural and political relations in Northern Ireland is indispensable to the quest for reconciliation. They indicate instances where it is entirely appropriate to think of reconciliation as a balancing act. If parity of esteem is taken solely in terms of this model, it enhances our grasp of reconciliation as a substantive, moral ideal. And it facilitates thinking of an inclusive society as an outcome of an inclusive process in which differences have been balanced through discussions characterised by reasonableness, openness, and a concern to give all participants their due. And, again, this is to think of reconciliation as a form of balancing, which very much depends for its success on the display of certain qualities of character among citizens and on the possibility of a shared sense of common purpose emerging from deliberations over our differences.

EXTREME ENTITLEMENT

Morally motivated accommodation is not, however, the only model of balancing and inclusion that the language of parity of esteem makes possible. As we have seen, the language prompts us to think of the entitlements of traditions. And it allows that it is quite appropriate for traditions to lay out what they believe are their entitlements, and to request that others grant and respect them. In doing so, of course, there is a risk that their request will not be met, at least to their satisfaction. Here there is a danger of entitlement claims assuming an exaggerated form. When this occurs, as it does frequently in Northern Ireland, something like an extreme entitlement model is invoked to justify acting as if esteem is primarily due to 'our' position and only as an afterthought or in a heavily circumscribed fashion to the position of others. Thus, parity of esteem's other-centred aspect gives way almost entirely to self-centred concerns.

At a glance, this model may be regarded as a corruption of the language of parity of esteem, especially since any notion of parity seems to be forfeited altogether. Perhaps it is, but those who operate in terms of it do not typically admit to having abandoned consid-erations of parity. On the contrary, they are more inclined to say that their entitlements are being pressed as strongly as they are pre-cisely because parity is what is being denied to them, because their tradition is being discriminated against in some important way or another. Unionists, who I have suggested are properly asked to accommodate certain nationalist claims, speak like this because they think too much is being demanded of them. They typically talk of excessive attention being devoted to the interests of nationalism and republicanism, of the pendulum having swung too far against them. Some unionists may even deny that there was an institu-tional/political bias in Northern Ireland that needed correcting; others may admit that there was but contend that its extent was exaggerated and that unionism is now incurring losses that are unbearable.

Many unionists regard nationalist pushing for the recognition of Irish symbols in Northern Ireland as disingenuous, and wonder just what sort of expression would be granted to British symbols, say, in a united Ireland, particularly given the republican ambition to purge the island of British influences. And, they might add, whereas nationalists and republicans can wax lyrical about the increased 'greening' of the North, if unionists were to speak in similar terms of making society more 'orange' they would be greeted with howls of outrage and charges of sectarianism.

Certain nationalists, for their part, may think that parity is impossible within the structures of a Northern Ireland which they consider a failed political entity – the Agreement notwithstanding –

and argue that it can be achieved only within an all-Ireland set of arrangements. Here they may think too that the mission of 'greening' the North is a sensible preparatory step for a united Ireland destiny they are convinced inevitably awaits them.

The point is that unionists and nationalists have reasons for resorting to an extreme entitlement model of parity of esteem. It provides a convenient cover – not least in disputes over marching in Northern Ireland – for an obsession with one's own claims that shuts out those of others, typically viewing them as a threat, for an inclination to treat the business of reconciliation if not as irrelevant then merely as an exercise to win the best deal for one's own side, and for a readiness to take umbrage at criticism. On its terms, the language of parity of esteem may be used to underwrite a mix of self-righteousness and self-interest. This occurs when we are told, for example, that it is offensive to a particular cultural identity if the entitlements it demands are not conceded, when what counts is not that claims to entitlement are judged worthy after a process of intercultural debate, but that they are simply demanded. Extreme entitlement claims, in short, may draw on the same moral vocabulary of esteem and offence as accommodating claims, but with very different intent: one that, by making cultural self-interest primary, arguably drains this vocabulary of much of its moral strength. And when these claims are unleashed, reconciliation ceases to function as a substantive moral ideal entailing a genuine reaching out to others and the requirements of balancing and inclusion are easily reduced to tactical ploys useful in the game of maximising one's cultural and political advantage. Considered from the angle of extreme entitlement, serious doubts emerge about the sufficiency of these requirements as signposts for reconciliation.

A stress on inclusiveness, for example, does not necessarily mount an adequate assault on difference's capacity to sustain the divisions that have made acceptable self-government in Northern Ireland so difficult to achieve. For, as I have hinted, inclusiveness here may be perfectly compatible with a politics of cultural self-interest, and may amount to little more than the North's major traditions being given licence to compete for a share of the spoils of devolved government. The problem is that this still leaves us with the prospect of opposing blocs that largely define themselves in opposition to each other, of an ongoing politics of mutual suspicion where a gain for one is characteristically regarded as a loss for the other. Antagonistic cultural and political differences remain untouched in much the same way as they do when difference is granted a practical prioritisation through the sort of single identity community work mentioned in the previous chapter. Inclusiveness, unless defined more stringently than seems possible on the terms of extreme entitlement, does not in itself provide a strong enough antidote to the divisions that have plagued social and political life in Northern Ireland since its inception. And, as a consequence, inclusive self-rule, though crucial, may promise an unstable form of government, one that threatens to collapse under the weight of competing cultural interests.

On the terms of extreme entitlement, the conception of reconciliation as a balancing of differences appears restricted too. This is evident in the notion of commonality it is capable of supporting. To the extent that it is capable of supporting any such notion at all, it offers one that amounts to nothing more than an aggregate of compromises, an outcome of deals of uncertain duration that are struck often reluctantly. Take the prospect of a common political life in Northern Ireland suggested by the Agreement, which is ostensibly endorsed by a range of unionist, loyalist, nationalist and republican parties. In the spirit of extreme entitlement, some republicans appear to support it only because they regard it as an interim measure that hastens the arrival of a united Ireland. And, equally, some unionists appear to endorse it because they believe it is the best available way of shoring up the Union, of stealing a march on anti-Agreement parties, and of serving as a device that may cause severe discomfort to republicans, if not also effect their humiliation. In both cases, commonality's prospects exist virtually at the pleasure of pragmatic calculations and are perpetually susceptible to changes of strategy.

Under these circumstances, commitment to a common political life in the North is unlikely to be deep, precisely because its value is instrumental. So long as it is seen as a tool of other and more pressing loyalties, the allegiance it can claim of citizens is always secondary. When debating what is most appropriate for Northern society, for example, we may doubt whether a majority of unionists or republicans treat the Agreement's attempt to facilitate commonality, through various inclusive arrangements of government, as their primary point of reference. Sure, they may be prepared to work these arrangements to a degree and under certain conditions, but there is a distinct impression that for many on both sides the traditional (and exclusive) sources of their respective traditions still count for more.

There are, of course, various things we may say about a version of commonality that is made possible by a tentative convergence of unionist/loyalist and nationalist/republican interests – that it is the most we can hope for (perhaps), or that it is better than nothing (certainly) – but that its achievement coincides with that of reconciliation is not one of them. To say otherwise is to agree that we may have in common only that which difference's cultural self-interests permit and, even then, only for so long as they permit. And to agree to that is to entertain a strangely depleted view of reconciliation.

TENSIONS AND LIMITATIONS

Rather than complementing each other, parity of esteem's accommodating and extreme entitlement models sit uncomfortably together. They send out conflicting messages about reconciliation's meaning. As a consequence, there are deep *tensions* in those understandings of balancing and inclusion that are grounded in the concept of parity of esteem. And these tensions impair the concept's ability to provide a basis for anything more than a weak conception of reconciliation. They do so partly because the extravagant tendencies of extreme entitlement in practice frequently constrict the expression of accommodating intentions. We may see this with the very language of accommodation. Its moral sense, if not lost altogether, is often overshadowed by the pragmatic sense associated with extreme entitlement demands, such as when a balancing of differences appears not so much as a just accommodation reached through reasonable dialogue, say, but as a convenient accommodation reached through placating competing interests.

Or take the tension and constriction that surround handling of the issue of inclusion. Tension is obvious when inclusiveness is presented as an essential element in a reconciling process, and yet also seems compatible with a cultural and political cold war between competing traditions. The cold war view clearly entertains bleak prospects for reconciliation, whatever the rhetoric of inclusion. It holds among many of those in Northern Ireland who perceive of themselves in typical extreme entitlement terms as bearers of a single cultural identity, the interests of which must be upheld at all costs. What bothers most is the tenacity of its hold here, given that the sectarian connotations historically attached to the enterprise of defending single identity interests are too powerful and pervasive to be ignored, and guarantee ongoing relations of suspicion and hostility. Those working with the accommodating model, by contrast, probably think, as I do, that there is something awry if inclusiveness does not aid in breaking down walls of cultural separation, if parity of esteem does not lead to an increase in mutual understanding between traditions.[5] Reconciliation's prospects are brighter on their terms probably because they are open to perceiving of themselves as citizens bound up in cultural relations that, to borrow James Tully's phrase, 'overlap, interact and are negotiated and re-imagined'.[6] At any rate, it is a perception such as this that is capable of underpinning anticipation of inclusive practices eventually delivering meaningful appreciation of the interdependence of the North's major cultural groups.

The problem here is not only that of a deep ambivalence about what parity of esteem's insistence on inclusion signifies for cultural relations and reconciliation. It is also that of a constriction on the scope allowed to an accommodating interpretation of inclusion. For example, taking Tully's phrase seriously implies cultivating a critically self-reflective attitude. This should not pose any difficulty for a morally energised exponent of accommodation. And yet its advocacy tends to be muffled among those relying on the language of parity of esteem, perhaps because to press its case too assiduously risks upsetting the sensitivities of others who are anxious to uphold the exclusive entitlements of particular cultural interests. But the fact remains that we are not well placed to re-imagine our cultural and political relations with others, or to grasp our interdependence, if we persist in glossing over objectionable, frequently offensive, aspects of our cultural heritages and practices. If reconciliation is to be a serious priority for Northern society, it is simply not enough to request that others respect our right to do what we have always done, or to insist upon our entitlements regardless of any consequence. Rethinking much that we have been content to take for granted, being open to criticisms from within and without our cultural ranks, are not optional extras here. They are, in fact, indispensable. The language of parity of esteem, caught between the tugs of its accommodating and extreme entitlement poles, has difficulty in making them so. It is constricted in saying what often needs to be said.

The language of parity of esteem has *limitations*. Worries that drawing on it may still leave Northern society polarised and traditional expectations and practices uncritically entrenched suggest troubling conclusions. One is that its ability to incorporate the essential features of reconciliation I identified earlier is more uncertain than it initially appeared. It is possible that, inspired by the accommodating appeal of parity of esteem, citizens will pursue the activities of engagement and embrace, will prize a spirit of openness, and will aim to heal division, define common goals and expand horizons. But it is also possible that they will not, or, at least, that they will temper their commitment to these features for the sake of protecting their own cultural loyalties and position. The upshot is that parity of esteem's mixed messages make reconciliation's priority as a goal for Northern society rather less than secure. And an understanding of its meaning is left incomplete by the conception of reconciliation and the vision of a reconciled society associated with these messages. Neither the conception nor the vision is adequate for interconnected reasons. Reconciliation *as* a balancing of differences is an insufficient conception partly because an inclusive society is not necessarily a reconciled one. Or, equally, an inclusive society is an insufficient vision partly because a balancing of differences does not necessarily add up to reconciliation.

A further consequence is that neither of the major difficulties afflicting talk of reconciliation – lack of virtue and the commonality –difference conundrum – is satisfactorily resolved. Potential exploration of the problem of virtue is, as I have suggested, possible on the terms of parity of esteem's accommodating aspect, given that it makes demands of citizens that encourage the incorporation of other-centred concerns in their deliberations. But the space for exploration is cramped by the presence of exaggerated versions of cultural entitlements, which make a mode of calculative reckoning a primary consideration when dealing with other traditions. The tendency is for the question of virtue to be sidelined, as attention shifts to working out how competing entitlement claims may be settled to the satisfaction of the self-interests of traditions.

The quandary of elaborating a conception of reconciliation that gives difference its due also remains. This is principally because, on the terms of parity of esteem, only two notions of commonality seem possible: one reducing it to an aggregate of balanced interests, and the other seeing it as a product of balanced reasons, as an agreement reached after the voices of difference have been given a fair hearing. There is considerable merit in this second view, and I want to return to it in Chapter 5. But even if it were not too easily squeezed out by the first, it still would not be sufficient on its own.

What is lacking is a third notion of commonality, one that is not at the mercy of difference's dictates, that can appeal to something we share in spite of our differences, and that is capable of checking the excessive demands often made in difference's name. In its absence, to think of reconciliation as merely a balancing of differences or of a reconciled society just in terms of inclusiveness is to give difference more than its due. It is to allow the claims of difference to outweigh those of commonality to the point of holding the latter to ransom. And under these circumstances reconciliation cannot function effectively as a priority, since its disturbing, critical edge can be too easily blunted in the name of cultural self-interest. Likewise, the quest for a reconciled society may be halted in its tracks by having to submit to the machinations not infrequently involved in cultural self-interest's advance.

In short, when considered in the light of its accommodating and extreme entitlement models, what is on offer through the auspices of parity of esteem is a weak conception of reconciliation. This conception takes us some distance towards sorting out our problems in the North, but not far enough; it is weak because it cannot deliver a powerful enough attack on the foundations of our antagonisms; it is weak also because it does not demand enough of us.

A PRACTICAL REJOINDER

In spite of its promising contributions to an understanding of reconciliation in general and of what a reconciled society might look like in particular, we need to go beyond the language of parity of esteem if our attempts at understanding are not to be finally frustrated. We need to think of reconciliation as more than a balancing act. This claim is, however, susceptible to a potentially telling criticism.

OVERSTATED CRITICISMS?

There is a point to asking why I am bothering to look for more in the name of reconciliation, as it may be reasonably suggested that I cannot realistically expect more. And this may amount to a simple, yet decisive, objection precisely because it indicates practical limits within which hopes for reconciliation must fall, but which I am trying to exceed. More specifically, the objection, which doubles up as a rejoinder in defence of parity of esteem, might run like this. It does not follow that looking for more than a balancing of differences and an inclusive society is a wise move, even if there are limitations in a parity of esteem approach to reconciliation. Within the context of what is possible in Northern Ireland something like this approach, whatever its mixed signals, may be the best available, at least for now, and it may offer better prospects of success than I have allowed. For instance, given the history of conflict in the North, it is not surprising that cultural–political differences here have absorbed so much attention: those (nationalists and republicans) who believe they have received a raw deal in the past are determined that their cultural interests will be properly represented in the present and the future; and those (unionists and loyalists) who were accustomed to living in a society more or less created in their image are now intent on opposing changes that they think diminish even further valued cultural and political expressions. Accordingly, to aspire to a balancing of differences between the two in the hope of achieving a workable, inclusive society appears as the height of reasonable ambition. Sure, such ambition may seem circumscribed and ambivalent, and to settle for it may be to opt for a thin notion of commonality and a weak conception of reconciliation. But to press for more is naïve, and it is to underestimate the significance of what is on offer.

To explain, the rejoinder may continue, it is quite appropriate that what I have called the extreme entitlement aspect of parity of esteem is currently in the ascendancy, since it is naïve at present to expect many unionists or nationalists to temper pursuit of their particular interests for the sake of some barely perceived common interest. Too much unfinished business involving core cultural–political concerns remains to be decided; business that entails complicated haggling and manoeuvring between the interests of an identity demanding proper public expression for the first time in the North, and those of an identity whose bearers are convinced it has already been forced to concede too much. The only common interest likely to emerge here is one capable of appealing to the self-advantage of both, namely where it appears in the guise of a mutual gain that claims both will be better off in the long run by agreeing to accommodate each other. Given the difficulty of securing even this sort of agreement, it seems fanciful to insist upon more. And it simply is the case that any agreement that is possible is often the result of British, Irish or international mediators and negotiators proposing a compromise solution that falls between the competing claims of local unionists and nationalists. This is another way of thinking of balancing, namely as a positing of a third alternative that requires give and take from all sides, but that may eventually win out because it does not favour one side only and because everyone can find enough in it to live with, even if there are aspects to it that cause everyone discomfort.

To invoke ideals of commonality and reconciliation that look for more than this sort of compromise deal, or that seek to go beyond balancing differences and the achievement of an inclusive society may be theoretically appealing (to some), but it is to overplay one's hand in terms of what is politically attainable: such ideals are doomed to have little practical purchase in the real world that is Northern Ireland today. Moreover, this type of invocation underestimates the possibility that achieving a balancing of differences and an inclusive society may permit thicker bonds of commonality to develop over time. Or, to resort to the terminology I have been employing, it underplays the potential of an extreme entitlement line eventually softening in a more accommodating direction. As the North's citizens become more comfortable with the new arrangements that inclusion, say, would bring, there is a realistic prospect that the current divisiveness of cultural differences would become a thing of the past, and that Northern Ireland would grow into a more deeply reconciled society.

A RESPONSE

I find this sort of rejoinder almost persuasive, and I extend parts of it and give them another run for their money in Chapter 6. As opposed to the pessimistic-realist position discussed in Chapter 2, it offers an optimistic realism, which holds out hope that the North may mature into a reconciled society as we learn to accommodate our differences. Its counsel to prune back overambitious expectations of what is politically feasible is not without merit. And it is quite possibly the case that attaining a balancing of our differences and an inclusive society are as good achievements as we are likely to get in the foreseeable future. Working to enhance their prospects certainly promises to consume much of the reconciling energy most of us possess. In short, I have little difficulty accepting that there are practical boundaries within which aspirations for reconciliation must fall, or that achieving a balancing of differences and an inclusive society (even if only understood minimally) would be significant victories for reconciliation that may open up the prospect of even more in the future.

I still think, however, that there are good reasons for not being prepared to concede everything to this rejoinder, since it casts too narrow a light on Northern Ireland's situation. By concentrating on the constraints imposed on reconciliation's brief by differences between unionists and nationalists, and by mainly handling these in a pragmatic way, the rejoinder screens out too much. As a consequence, it underestimates both reconciliation's potential and the nature of its difficulties. Reconciliation's potential may seem a little healthier, for instance, if we tap into the variety of opinion existing within the camps of unionism and nationalism, and, even more so, if our estimations include reference to the body of thought and sentiment that exists outside these camps in the North. It may be that the rejoinder understates the degree to which certain things are already, or are capable of being, held in common. A danger here is that it acquiesces in permitting our horizons of possibility to be determined by the more obstinate and vociferous advocates of cultural difference.

However that may be, the rejoinder also risks devaluing reconciliation's potential by reducing negotiations between unionists and nationalists to a species of hard-headed enterprise bargaining. No doubt it is naïve to suppose that a lot of political dealing is not conducted in this manner, not least when the aim is to balance differences between unionists and nationalists. But to accept that no more than this can be expected is certainly to diminish politics. It is to accede to the view that politicians should do little else than defend their corner, and it is, at least tacitly, to exonerate a fair amount of bigotry and prejudice. And, frankly, as I suspect advocates of parity of esteem's accommodating aspect understand, this is to take the sting out of reconciliation's challenge, by effectively ignoring the responsibility to pursue the sort of non-instrumental intercultural dialogue that is uniquely capable of throwing up fresh insights and grounds for agreement, even as it calls into question any number of our prejudices. To opt for the lowest common denominator does not necessarily make the best practical sense, in anything other than the very short term.

Another set of problems emerge when focusing on what is achievable in the short term, not least when balancing is taken to imply plumping for an option that falls between those under contention. It is, for example, one thing to persuade two sides formally to accept a compromise deal, but sometimes quite another to count on them sticking to it and making it work. Post-deal, one side or another may falter at the prospect of implementing the disagreeable bits to which it has signed up, or may put a spin on the deal's meaning that is disputed by the other side, and so on. It is typical to see deals in the Middle East unravel for these kinds of reasons, and, as I will note in Chapters 6 and 7, strains suffered by the Agreement can be traced to their door also. That these things happen in situations of acute or long-standing conflict is, of course, unsurprising and highlights just how hard it is to negotiate a durable deal, let alone achieve reconciliation. So the fact of their happening is not in itself a conclusive objection to viewing balancing as a compromise solution in circumstances of serious antagonism. Indeed, there are occasions when trying to persuade opposing sides to find a compromise they can accept is the most that seems possible. But this is no reason to confuse its achievement with reconciliation. At best, the type of balancing of competing interests that yields some compromise agreement or another prepares the ground for reconciliation, most notably by creating conditions of peace.

Matters go awry, however, when it is supposed that an understanding of balancing as a compromise between rival interests serves as a reconciling model. When the block to be removed is defined as that of clashing interests, which may be irrationally, even if intensely, held, there is a tendency to conceive of reconciliation as a technical challenge: one to be met through forms of clever manoeuvring, efficient management or bureaucratic finessing that are designed to bring the recalcitrant natives to their pragmatic senses. This is an unhelpful tendency, as it is not always appropriate, let alone just, to work from the premise that a compromising fix is the best alternative in the face of competing claims. The chances are that on particular issues one side may have a more compelling case than the other and deserves to have it recognised. Yet this is what is undervalued here, because it cannot be recognised when the business of balancing and compromise is conducted in terms of squaring interests and not in terms of evaluating reasons. Behind much of the so-called real world wisdom, which depicts balancing as a compromise between different interests, lurks a disparaging picture of citizens in dispute as being deaf to reason's voice except when it hits a calculative note.

Also lurking behind it are barely engaged and yet very deep-seated cultural obstacles to reconciliation in a divided society. To hope that these obstacles may eventually vanish as we in the North learn to work together may be to underestimate their capacity to subvert the best laid plans of local politicians and governments. Curiously, an exclusive concentration on what seems practically possible now may prove impractical in the long run. Aiming merely to balance different interests, for example, risks leaving intact the sources of our divisions and glossing over the threat they pose to reconciliation. Imagining that we can get along without dislodging the deeper grounds of cultural suspicion, resentment, hostility and resistance to reconciliation is to be blind to why Northern Ireland has been an unreconciled society for all of its history. That is partly why to look for more in the name of reconciliation than the rejoinder offers is not to indulge a flight of fancy, but is to instil another bit of realism about the nature of reconciliation's difficulties into the quest.

CONCLUSION

To return to the question with which this chapter began, I am saying that reconciliation is properly thought of as a balancing act, but that only to think of it in this way may be terribly misleading. Four other things that I am saying explain what I mean. First, when understood in reference to parity of esteem's accommodating model, there are laudable elements in the conception of reconciliation as a balancing of differences and the vision of a reconciled society as inclusive that I wish to appropriate. Second, even when not defined exclusively in relation to an accommodating model, this conception and vision also make some practical sense. But they do not make enough practical sense to be utterly persuasive. In not inviting us to dig deeply in our search for reconciliation, attempts to juggle unionist and nationalist interests in the hope of striking an acceptable compromise leave the foundations of much of our division in the North relatively undisturbed. As a consequence, their achievements risk being short-lived.

Third, although there are instances when it is appropriate to describe reconciliation as a balancing act, we need better ideals of reconciliation than merely those of balancing differences and inclusion: these lack a sufficient notion of commonality and, in their pervasive extreme entitlement and compromise interpretations, do not strictly require practices that interrogate our prejudices and involve us engaging each other in a non-instrumental way. These interpretations in practice cramp the space allowed to the much more promising accommodation interpretation. As a result we are left with too weak a conception of reconciliation, and without the resources that equip us to resolve reconciliation's difficulties.

Fourth, we do not have to settle for what a parity of esteem approach makes available, since there is more to reconciliation than is presently on display. That is why I have been edging towards a defence of a much stronger conception of it, one that refuses to accept that the insights of the accommodation model are justifiably hemmed in by tactical and calculative priorities, and that therefore gives fuller scope to their exploration and expression.

4

FAIR INTERACTIONS

What does reconciliation require? This is a searching question. It is one that I have been wrestling with throughout the first three chapters in my attempt to get a better handle on reconciliation's meaning. But so far I have only hinted at an answer, as my main concern has been to show why certain responses, such as assimilation or a balancing of differences, are inadequate. I have now cleared enough space to allow the question to fix our attention. And by making it central at this stage of the argument, we may see that it acquires a particularly sharp edge: it focuses on what is entailed in treating reconciliation as a priority that calls other of our priorities to account, rather than on how reconciliation's requirements may be adjusted (and diluted) to fit in with other priorities.

Accordingly, to those of us who think that reconciliation is a good thing, not reducible to assimilation and involving more than a balancing act, the question puts us under intense scrutiny. Facing up to it places our motives, practices and beliefs under the spotlight. It makes us answerable for our attitudes towards, and our treatment of, others. It implies that it will not do to squirm out of our responsibilities to heal divisions by invoking any type of self-interest, individual or group. Finding consolation in our communal solidarities, appealing to our rights and entitlements are not, of course, disqualified here, but using these as a cover to dodge our obligations

to those who are different from us and to society at large is. Reconciliation is a hard taskmaster. It lays a claim on us, it makes demands
of us, it ruffles us. It is disingenuous to pretend otherwise.

RECONCILIATION'S REQUIREMENTS

To clarify, in putting the case for reconciliation so unequivocally, I
am not supposing that conflicting cultural and political interests,
loyalties and allegiances will not in part shape the conduct of politics. But I am disputing that they should go unchallenged in dictat-
ing virtually all of political conduct in Northern Ireland. In doing
so, I am supposing three things: first, that by virtue of the fact that
moral self-understandings are important to unionists and nationalists, and to how they justify their respective causes at least to themselves, it is not contrived to say that these are answerable to the
moral challenge of reconciliation; second, that we too readily cease
to hear this challenge once it is qualified through calculations of
unionist or nationalist interests, which encourage treating others
and their causes in purely instrumental ways; and, third, that unless
we think of reconciliation as a priority, which has a call on our allegiance, the chances of overcoming our most serious divisions in
Northern society are remote.

Put another way, the line I am pursuing here is designed to avoid
the problem encountered by the accommodating model of parity
of esteem, namely to prevent the irreducible moral content of
reconciliation from being so heavily circumscribed by tactical and
pragmatic reckoning that its force is disabled. This line is in part
based on a hunch that one of the reasons why reconciliation does
not exercise a hold over more of us is because we rarely allow its
requirements to feature in our reflections. Many of us who bother
with politics at all are too engrossed in the minutiae of squabbles
between unionists and republicans, say, and in the practical
problems these pose to imagine that, beyond some vague aspiration, reconciliation has anything pertinent to contribute to our
immediate quandaries. There is, then, a pressing point to saying that
we need to focus more clearly on what it might mean to treat

reconciliation as a priority for Northern society, and to ask what its requirements are. In the next two chapters especially, I am concerned to do that by concentrating almost exclusively on the normative entailments of reconciliation and by considering the principled objections these have to meet. In Chapters 6 and 7 I continue in a similar vein, but also discuss what sense can be made of reconciliation's requirements in the context of the various political manoeuvrings that have been prompted by the Agreement.

STRONG RECONCILIATION

In considering what reconciliation requires, it is important to bring into play what I have been alluding to as a strong conception of reconciliation. Indeed, the short answer to our question is to say that reconciliation requires nothing less than such a conception. Obviously, this needs teasing out. Building on the discussion to this point, and especially that of the previous chapter, let me start by pulling together the various elements that constitute a strong conception of reconciliation, in order to give a summary statement of its meaning.

On its terms, reconciliation is a priority for a divided society that cannot be justifiably sidelined for calculative reasons. It poses a challenge to our prejudices and many of our practices that cannot be plausibly ignored. The conception invokes the non-instrumental acts and practices of embrace and engagement that are properly conducted in a spirit of openness. These acts and practices entail risk and vulnerability, as we expose ourselves to others in a critically reflective way. They call upon such virtues as reasonableness, magnanimity and forgiveness. In the absence of these sorts of acts, practices and virtues, it is hard to see how reconciliation will not be emptied of much of its content. It is hard to see, in other words, how without them our horizons will be expanded, our destructive divisions healed, and common purposes articulated. These are aims that a strong conception of reconciliation refuses to forfeit.

An expansion of horizons is crucial to underscoring the interconnectedness of traditions in the North, to heightening awareness that one tradition's take on reality is not the only possible valid one. It is an integral part of the business of healing divisions and articulating common purposes. And this is business that requires a thick understanding of commonality, one that gives difference its due without capitulating to the cultural self-interests that exacerbate divisiveness. The vision of a reconciled society bound up with this strong conception of reconciliation is one that anticipates eradicating the cultural and political sources of alienation and division; it is one that shares the spirit of Hegel's idea 'that a reconciled society [can] be understood properly only as an ethically integrated community of free citizens'.[1] This is to envisage a society in which all citizens enjoy a sense of belonging, a sense that is assured through protection of their rights, recognition of their cultural sources of esteem, opportunities of inclusive self-rule, and shared or common commitments.

THREE REQUIREMENTS

Towards the end of the previous chapter, I implied that this strong conception of reconciliation could weather attempts at a quick practical knockout. But can it be defended at other levels and, to continue with the boxing analogy, can it be assured of not ultimately losing on points at the end of a bruising contest? Over the next four chapters, I want to launch what I hope proves a successful defence of a strong conception of reconciliation against stiff philosophical, political and cultural opposition.

The argument that follows incorporates the tasks of defending a strong conception of reconciliation, specifying reconciliation's requirements and tackling the major difficulties that remain to be resolved, namely those of virtue's scarcity, the commonality–difference conundrum, and, I might add, the divisive tendencies inherent in various cultural and political forms in the North. This is not as complicated an exercise as it may seem, since these tasks are complementary. Very broadly, my attempt to handle them goes like this. In the realm of cultural and political relations with which I am dealing, I claim that reconciliation requires at least three things: (1) it requires *fair interactions* between members of opposing groups; (2) it requires that we overcome our antagonistic divisions by occupying *common ground*; and (3) it requires the presence of a society in which all citizens have a sense of *belonging*. I argue that it is only a strong conception of reconciliation that can adequately show what it means to meet these requirements. And, I maintain, it is through the aid of such a conception that we glean how to go about tackling the philosophical, political and cultural obstacles that often make trying to meet them seem too hard. I begin in this chapter with the requirement of fair interactions.

FAIR INTERACTIONS AND CIVIC VIRTUES

FAIR INTERACTIONS

In the first instance, reconciliation requires fair interactions between members of opposing groups, traditions, or political parties. This is a multi-layered requirement. It is also a far-reaching one. It is multi-layered because it envisages interactions operating at a number of levels – individual, community, political – under formal or informal conditions, and serving different purposes – giving victims space to express their pain, increasing mutual understanding, settling a particular dispute, reaching agreement on a raft of controversial issues, and so on. Whatever the level, conditions or purposes, reconciliation calls for interactions to be fair in the sense that all interlocutors are given their due, that is, are allowed to speak in their own voice, are given opportunity to express their views, are permitted to tell their own stories, and are listened to with respect. If the interactions are designed to reach conclusions or agreements on some matter at hand, the expectation is that the deliberations and outcomes will be reasonable, and not simply reflections of manipulation, majority interest, or whatever.

Two important points are involved in recognising that fair interaction is a multi-layered requirement. One is that reconciliation requires interactions of this sort across the board of social, cultural and political life. The best prospects of achieving a reconciled society are obviously when interactions are occurring simultaneously in different spheres, when they are mutually reinforcing and contribute to the development of a reconciling ethos. This is, of course, to project an ideal that falls short in practice. Sometimes community interactions may be well in advance of political interactions between parties. At other times, political parties may have to set the lead in order to arrest deteriorations in community relations, especially during notoriously tense times in the marching season. The other point is that fair interaction is a requirement of all citizens. It may be a responsibility that falls most heavily on political representatives – given that the stakes for the whole of society are so high in their interactions – but in grasping its multi-layered dimensions, we may see that it remains a responsibility of all of us.

Fair interaction also appears as a far-reaching requirement once we start to spell out what is entailed in giving others their due. Straight off we notice that it calls for a willingness to interact, then it calls for a willingness to interact in a certain spirit, and it also calls for a willingness to interact in certain ways. To elaborate, we cannot hope to overcome our divisions unless we are prepared to interact with others. To be unwilling to do so is not just to be sceptical of reconciliation: it is to be opposed to it. And no amount of self-righteous special pleading can disguise this fact. To be willing to interact with those who are different from us is a necessary step on the road to a reconciled society. This does not mean that our interactions guarantee we will reach our end. In fact, various types of interaction block the road to reconciliation: those that are poisoned by mutual condemnations and recriminations, for example, or those that are treated merely as convenient devices for maximising our advantage. Even so, any interaction not involving violence is probably better than none, since even the shabbiest sorts involve some encounter with the humanness of others and may be transformed in the long run.

The pertinent point here, however, is that the challenge reconciliation poses is not simply to interact in any fashion, but to do so fairly. And that means at least interacting in a spirit of openness and in ways designed to build up relations of trust and to give others their due. To imagine these entailments can be legitimately trumped by something else (traditional prejudices, self-righteousness, group loyalties, and so on) is tantamount to saying that reconciliation can be justifiably trumped too. But, as the argument of previous chapters indicates, however appealing this may seem to particular interests at a particular time, it is to surrender to our sectarian divisions and to project a grim future for Northern Ireland and its citizens.

In a society noted for the noise its major traditions make about not surrendering to forces that threaten valued principles and practices, it is perhaps a little ironic that surrender to sectarianism occurs almost effortlessly and is something we in the North are only too familiar with. It is a kind of surrender that is prolonged when particular groups and political parties continue to refuse to interact with others; when many interactions that do occur appear mostly to display a spirit of condemnation; and when many others are conducted in manners that pay scant regard to the principle of giving others their due or to the need to develop relations of trust. Calling for the types of willingness involved in interacting fairly is evidently a tough ask in a divided society with a recent history of violence. Reconciliation is tough business.

THE DIFFICULTY OF VIRTUE

Reconciliation is hard to carry out without virtue. The types of willingness called for by a requirement of fair interactions presuppose certain qualities of character among citizens. And this, of course, is the problem: these simply cannot be counted on in a divided society like Northern Ireland. And yet there seems to be reticence, even among reconciliation's more determined supporters, to draw proper attention to virtue's scarcity and the difficulty it poses here. Perhaps it is perceived as too hard to tackle, or as a difficulty not intrinsically connected to politics and the life of society as such, but as one best left to the Churches to handle or to individuals to settle according to the dictates of their own consciences. Whatever the reason, such reticence is regrettable.

In emphasising reconciliation's need of virtue's presence, I am making two related claims that question the appropriateness of reticence. One is a general claim that the character of citizens matters to the health of public life. The other is a particular claim that the

manifestation of certain qualities amongst citizens is crucial to overcoming divisions in seriously unreconciled societies. We have
already noted obstacles encountered by the second of these claims:
factors such as fear and bitterness frequently block its reception, as
does merely reckoning reconciliation's possibilities in terms of a calculus of balanced interests. And this is why virtue may seem too
hard a problem to resolve. But there is more to it than that. Its difficulties are exacerbated because there is widespread resistance (at least
tacitly) to the first general claim I made, because reticence is nourished by a pervasive tendency to de-politicise virtue. Let me
explain.

To speak of citizens' characters mattering to political life sounds
odd to those who think of politics only as a power play between
competing interests. It also strikes a discordant note among those
in tune with a refrain that restricts virtue's domain to a sphere of
private morality (except when scandals concerning sexual infidelity
or financial corruption are brought to public attention). The *privatisation of virtue*, in short, appears to put the issue of citizens' characters out of the proper reach of politics. Or, at best, it says that the
issue is relevant indirectly. For example, it may be considered a
bonus to have citizens with honest, industrious, thrifty, sober and
law-abiding characters – to cite the Puritan virtues traditionally
extolled by unionists – but these are traits that are only incidentally
linked to citizenship. They are primarily acquired through the manner in which individuals attend to their private responsibilities, dis-
charge their domestic duties, or conduct their business affairs. They
do not presuppose any necessary regard for politics or the larger
concerns of society. They lack a specifically public focus.

An upshot of virtue's privatisation is low expectations of what
should be asked of citizens and their political representatives in
divided societies. The presence of Puritan virtues has not halted the
spread of sectarianism in Northern Ireland, not least among those
boasting high possession of them. Nor has it curbed the development of a politics of cultural self-interest, a politics that makes minimal demands of us as citizens and requires our representatives above
all else to defend our corner, to minimise concessions to our

opponents, and to outwit them whenever possible. Political experience in the North suggests that moves to privatise virtue leave too much to be desired: supposing that the character of citizens is a matter of indifference to politics, or one of indirect relevance only, reveals an implausibly slender grasp of what is required to create and sustain a decent society. A civic republican tradition of politics has always recognised this. From Aristotle's account of the practical virtues, or Machiavelli's notion of *vertu*, through to Michael Sandel's recent defence of a 'formative politics' that 'cultivates in citizens the qualities of character self-government requires',[2] a recurring republican theme is that a good society is conceivable only if there are good citizens. A society that devalues civic virtues, that imagines it does not need citizens who have a concern for the good of the whole and who develop moral bonds with other citizens, is a society threatening to atrophy.

Interestingly, there is renewed concern in certain liberal quarters that the privatisation of virtue may have gone too far. Will Kymlicka and Wayne Norman, for example, contend that 'the health and stability of a modern democracy depend, not only on the justice of its institutions, but also on the qualities and attitudes of its citizens'.[3] And William Galston draws a list of general, social, economic and political virtues he thinks are hallmarks of responsible citizenship, and that are necessary if democracies are to flourish. Without citizens who possess these qualities, he writes, 'the ability of liberal societies to function successfully progressively diminishes'.[4]

Direct talk of virtue, then, is anything but misplaced in politics in general. Affirming the appropriateness of such talk instantly undermines one type of objection to the particular claim that reconciliation requires certain qualities of character of citizens, and one of the grounds for reticence. But, as I have indicated, the stress on civic virtues meets other difficulties in divided societies. Its appeal is complicated in Northern Ireland, where the very existence of the state is in dispute, where terrible deeds have been committed, and where many people define themselves in terms not of a common citizenship but of exclusive identities. It is, however, no answer at all to give up on (civic) virtue under such circumstances. And to continue with reticence is hard to defend. Deprived of a plausible appeal to virtue's lack of political relevance, reticence amounts to a failure to take seriously a central requirement of reconciliation, and is complicit in reducing reconciliation's pitch to forms of private coaxing. That is partly why it is so easy for politicians to bristle with irritation at occasional talk of virtue having some bearing on their affairs – such as when it is hinted they have something to learn from victims of appalling deeds who have forgiven their victimisers – and to dismiss it as just so much sanctimonious blather. But faced with divisions that breed fear, bitterness, manipulation and calculative reckoning, an emphasis on virtue's civic dimension actually becomes more pressing, and is at the heart of the challenge reconciliation poses to us all in the North.

The civic dimension of virtue is so crucial here because its focus is the good of society as a whole. In culturally diverse and divided societies, of course, this focus also has to include reference to the competing goods of rival traditions. But it keeps to the forefront those attitudes and qualities that necessitate citizens to think of more than the good or interests of their particular tradition, those that make an accommodation of our traditional differences an imperative for the sake of the good of all of us. And since interacting with others is indispensable to realising a common good, this means highlighting attitudes and qualities that enable interactions to be conducted in an appropriate spirit and in appropriate ways.

Working out what an emphasis on civic virtues means may vary across societies. In a society such as Northern Ireland, initial attention needs to be paid to qualities of character that are peculiarly suited to healing our divisions, that engender a willingness to interact fairly – those of forgiveness, magnanimity and reasonableness. Their salience is this: in a society scarred not only by the dreadful torment and loss some citizens have suffered at the hands of others, but also by sectarian practices and attitudes that warp our relations with each other, such virtues are necessary if we are to be snapped out of ways of thinking and acting that restrict our capacity to envisage a society that is good for all of us. They project us beyond bigotry, and also beyond the forms of pettiness, mean-spiritedness, self-righteousness and intransigence that wither our imaginations and lock us into visions of society that may offer plenty to our friends but considerably less to our so-called enemies.

For example, forgiveness, as I argued in Chapter 2, serves as an antidote to bitterness and to the tendency to absolve ourselves of any responsibility for our divisions by placing all of the blame on others. Forgiveness releases us from the power of a convenient but distorting kind of stereotyping that reduces a cause (whether loyalist, republican, or whatever) to the atrocities committed in its name. In doing so, it also undermines a self-righteousness that feeds on such stereotyping and that rationalises sectarian attitudes. Forgiveness allows us to see others (and their causes) in truer perspective, and as part of who we collectively are as a society; it enables these others to figure in our conceptions of a common good; it takes seriously the implication that, as Arendt puts it, 'every man is, or should be, more than whatever he did or achieved'.[5] Magnanimity, in a sense, extends the possibilities opened up by forgiveness in its display of a generosity of spirit to others that contributes to replacing relations of suspicion with those of trust. It eschews a niggling, quibbling attitude that insists on the sort of hyper-procedural exactitude that ends up not seeing the wood for the trees. Magnanimity, rather, allows certain latitude to those, say, who have resolved to end conflict in the North; it encourages focusing on the bigger picture of healing divisions and moving towards the creation of a society we all can share. And reasonableness proves a necessary complement to forgiveness and magnanimity because it does not instantly alienate others by expressing non-negotiable preferences, making demands or issuing threats. On the contrary, it indicates a preparedness to persuade and to be persuaded by reasons.

To repeat, meeting reconciliation's challenge entails saying that these are not merely admirable private qualities some individuals possess, but also civic qualities expected of all citizens and their representatives. The obvious problem that, with the possible exception of a diluted version of reasonableness, they are not recognised as anything of the sort, is less distracting than it seems once we refuse to accept the privatisation of virtue. Sure, it is easy to feign deafness to the language of civic virtues when political conduct has been shaped for so long by habits of cultural self-interest. And of course there is no guarantee that exhortation to interact fairly with those we are accustomed to thinking of as enemies will not continue to fall on deaf ears. But it is important that an insistence on the political salience of virtues deprives such deafness of its customary justification.

I am contending, then, that reconciliation's requirement of fair interaction calls for the *cultivation of civic virtues* among citizens and their political representatives, and that the grounds for resisting this call are flimsy. We should expect these virtues to foster a willingness to interact openly with others in non-instrumental ways. But it is not just a matter of being willing. It is also a matter of doing. Responding to the call of fair interactions implies not so much whipping ourselves up with forgiving, magnanimous and reasonable thoughts, as it does performing forgiving, magnanimous and reasonable deeds. Failures of performance, in other words, cannot be excused by pleading good intentions. Of course virtues have to be internalised and affect our motivations, but they must do more than that. Deep introspection is not the key to their emergence. They cannot be conjured into existence by merely learning a set of rules. And they do not appear pre-packaged in a simple, ready-to-use way. The crucial point about virtues, or qualities of character, is that they are developed through experience, through engaging in certain forms of activity.

The challenge to display these qualities, then, is simultaneously the challenge to act in a certain way, to participate in certain forms of endeavour. Civic virtues are manifested through acts and practices. It is by involving ourselves in these that such virtues become more deeply ingrained in our lives. So rather than being hamstrung by their scarcity in political life in Northern Ireland, the point is not only to advocate the wisdom of citizens interrogating their attitudes and motivations, but also to emphasise the activities that are conducive to the development of virtues. Here too is the point for those who are hesitant about interacting with traditional enemies in a situation like Northern Ireland, not because of bad faith, malice or overt sectarianism, but because of a deep-seated wariness: it is only by interacting in the first place that we put ourselves in a situation in which it is possible for civic virtues to be cultivated in our lives as citizens; it is only by interacting that we may learn how to interact fairly. In the absence of involvement in fair interactions, in other words, claims to possession of the virtues needed in a divided society are likely to be shallow. One way of grasping what this means is to explore the acts and practices I am calling embrace and engagement. These exemplify what I understand fair interactions to entail and, in doing so, serve as potential vehicles of the kind of civic virtues I think are essential if our antagonistic divisions in the North are to be overcome.

EMBRACE AND ENGAGEMENT

The terms *embrace* and *engagement* underscore the importance of non-instrumental acts and practices to the business of fair interaction. In general, they are intended to intimate that there are no short cuts available to achieve the goals of reconciliation. On the contrary, aspirations to heal divisions, articulate common purposes and expand horizons are integrally linked to acts and practices that eschew the use of manipulative techniques, clever subterfuges or calculative ploys. Such instrumental devices may be occasionally masqueraded as having reconciling intent, but they are typically deployed to outflank or dupe one's opponents (or, often just as importantly, one's supporters) in an attempt to advance one set of interests at the expense of another. The terms embrace and engagement are employed here to gesture at something completely different, something suggested by a requirement of fair interactions: that reconciliation is a morally taxing ideal, which is tied to certain ways of treating people; that it becomes weakened or seriously distorted if detached from practices that refuse to treat others as mere means to the pursuit of a particular set of ends. They are continuous with what I referred to in the last chapter as the accommodating aspect of parity of esteem. More specifically, the terms also carry at least the following implications.

EMBRACE

Embrace primarily implies a mode of response to the fact that we inhabit a world of apparently ineliminable differences (of culture, religion, values, and so on), one that signifies welcoming acceptance of, and participation in, this world. It is appropriately depicted as an embodiment of the spirit of openness that fair interactions require. Accordingly, there are various expectations we should have of those who exhibit such a spirit: that they fully acknowledge the irreducibility of cultural plurality and see it as a source of enrichment rather than as a threat; that they recognise the entitlements of cultures and religions, say, to self-expression and perhaps, under certain circumstances, to self-determination; that they resist imperialist or colonial ambitions to flatten 'alien' forms of life for the sake of hegemonic control; that they demur from a priori judgements about the worth of ways of life beyond their immediate ken; that their presentations of the benefits of their own ways of seeing and doing things are characterised by an appropriate measure of circumspection. In the context of Northern Ireland, embrace as a mode of response entails accepting that the institutions of a society composed of unionists, loyalists, nationalists, republicans, and others, should reflect more than one cultural identity; that differences of cultural and political outlook cannot be legitimately suppressed or marginalised; that alternative traditions are better treated as allies than as enemies.

Two essential features of what I am calling embrace are those of *indebtedness* and *inclusion*. Embrace, in other words, seems an entirely appropriate response to the reality of cultural plurality in general, and to its presence in Northern Ireland in particular, once we acknowledge (1) that we are interrelated with those who are different from us and that we cannot get by adequately on our own, and (2) that there is no justifiable reason why any category of humans should be excluded a priori from embrace's reach. Not to acknowledge these features is to fail to display openness in our interactions, yet to acknowledge them fully is demanding.

Acknowledging *indebtedness*, for instance, evidently means

disowning crude sectarian denials that Northern Ireland can be properly home to our major traditions, either because Protestants are viewed merely as vestiges of a colonial presence that must be finally banished for the sake of Irish freedom, or because Catholics must be allegedly kept in their place, not least since they are currently threatening to upset the power balance that partition was intended to secure for the Protestant majority. But more is involved than distancing ourselves from these examples of offensive nonsense. Acknowledging indebtedness in a society like Northern Ireland may also entail saying with Honneth that 'only to the degree that I actively care about the development of the others' characteristics (which seem foreign to me) can our shared goals be realized'.[6] Or, even more strongly, it may be to say with Tully that the loss or assimilation of one of our traditions would be experienced 'as an impoverishment of one's own identity'.[7] Now clearly, not many people in Northern Ireland have internalised the sentiments of indebtedness to the extents suggested by Honneth's and Tully's remarks, and they are conspicuously lacking in our political discourse. But these are the sorts of sentiments that such virtues as forgiveness and magnanimity open us up to, and that serious concern for reconciliation aims precisely at cultivating, not least through encouraging an act of embrace.

Facing up to *inclusion* is difficult enough too. I have already noted that, in the context of Northern Ireland, it suggests institutional arrangements that no longer express the exclusive privilege of a unionist identity, and that it sits more easily with a notion of power sharing than with a notion of majority rule. These suggestions may be counted among inclusion's possible external outcomes. Such outcomes do not just suddenly appear, of course, but are products of some process or another: of conflict resolution, political discussions, government initiatives, and so forth. And it is not unreasonable to suppose that the best prospects of achieving inclusive external outcomes stem from processes that are inclusive too. Put another way, inclusion also refers to internal conditions that should characterise a process aimed at reaching agreement on matters of political and cultural dispute, and at making it work.

Inclusion's internal conditions include those formal requirements of political equality that are typically considered essential for an agreement or law to have normative legitimacy in a democracy. One obvious requirement, for example, is that those affected by an agreement, say, are represented in the negotiations that produce it. But more than formal requirements are involved here. The stipulation that all representatives or participants are given their due is at the heart of the notion of an inclusive process, and with it the belief that where this occurs all claims will receive a fair hearing and ensure a just (inclusive) outcome. Giving everyone concerned their due suggests more than attending to a set of procedural rules. And it does so for a range of reasons: because procedures may be regulated in ways representatives of minorities find intimidating or alienating, or because they may enforce norms of deliberation that are culturally biased, or because they simply cannot ensure that what counts as a compelling reason for one group or tradition counts as a reason for others, and so on.

It is possible, for example, to abide by inclusion's procedural requirements and yet treat other interlocutors with contempt, hostility or suspicion. And where this possibility is realised, it is more likely than not that some interlocutors will feel intimidated or alienated, and that questions of cultural bias and conflicting reasons will not be dealt with satisfactorily. Accordingly, there is a point to saying that another of inclusion's internal conditions involves giving others their due by recognising their basic humanness either prior to or as part of negotiations. More than cosmetic niceties are involved in gesturing at relations of trust which pave a path for fruitful discussions between interlocutors, in extending embrace's reach in a way that diminishes intimidation's likelihood and that enhances prospects of issues of cultural bias and conflicting reasons being addressed without rancour. This is what Young is driving at when she maintains that 'greeting' is an indispensable component of inclusion. As she puts it, through forms of public greeting (handshakes, hugs, compliments, and so forth), 'a speaker announces her presence as ready to listen and take responsibility for her relationship to her interlocutors'. Indeed, she continues, 'if we were to imagine a communicative interaction in which such modes of greeting were absent, it would feel like the science fiction speech of an alien'. And these modes are nowhere more important than in conflict situations. For 'the political functions of moments of greeting are to assert discursive equality and establish or re-establish the trust necessary for discussion to proceed in good faith'. And especially when groups confront one another over issues about which they will disagree, 'rituals of greeting and politeness are important for getting and keeping the discussion going through difficult times'.[8]

Giving others their due also implies certain substantive relations of equality between interlocutors and points to another of inclusion's internal conditions that go beyond procedural rules. We may see this in the requirement that all interlocutors should be allowed to speak and to be heard in their own terms. Tully, writing in a Canadian context, captures this requirement nicely when he argues that a just form of constitutional discussion is one in which all interlocutors are permitted to appear in ways true to their particular cultural identities.[9] This is a form in which culturally distinct ways of speaking and acting are mutually recognised and comprise an intercultural dialogue, the language of discussion is itself just and not loaded in favour of the dominant group, and all participants learn to listen to the voices of others. A discussion constituted along these lines may be capable of overcoming those problems of intimidation, cultural bias, and conflicting reasons that adherence to procedural rules alone is powerless to address. It may give substance to the hope that the outcome will amount to a just settlement, since everyone involved has been guaranteed a substantively fair hearing.

Now, it is clear that the best hope of such a settlement that Northern Ireland has arguably ever had – the Agreement – was arrived at without going much beyond the procedural requirements of inclusion. This suggests either that the sort of additional conditions raised by Young and Tully are not necessary at all, or that the Agreement suffers from the lack of them. I will argue later that the latter is the more plausible suggestion.

ENGAGEMENT

Leaving that aside for the moment, I am claiming that the act of embrace – with its emphases on indebtedness and inclusion – illustrates the spirit of openness called for by fair interactions. It also spills over, as it were, into what I am calling engagement, namely practices involving honest, committed encounters with others, not least those with whom we disagree most. Greeting, for example, is simultaneously an act of embrace and a practice of engagement. And references to the internal conditions of inclusion such as those raised by Tully already indicate much of what should go on in perhaps the pivotal practice of engagement, that is, dialogue.

Besides greeting and dialogue, practices associated with engagement also include storytelling, rhetoric, drama, dance, music and others. These practices serve different purposes at different times and, to repeat an earlier point about fair interaction being a multilayered requirement, reconciliation has need of all of them. What is crucial about these practices is that through them others are opened up to us and we to them, others are permitted to be heard in their terms and we in ours. Speaking and listening are valued as two sides of the one coin, as indispensable to interacting in ways that are fair. This is especially the case with the practice of dialogue, which is uniquely suited to breaking down enmities and reaching agreement on controversial issues. Dialogue is a primary vehicle of civic virtues; it is a practice at the heart of politics that cannot be substituted without enormous loss to the quality of political life. We have already noted that dialogue entails forms of procedural and substantive equality among interlocutors. By extension we may now see too that it involves vulnerability and reciprocity and, in doing so, underline further what it means to interact fairly.

By engaging in dialogue we are made *vulnerable* by permitting others to scrutinise our views and reasons, as well as by listening to theirs and allowing them to challenge ours. This is to say that dialogue is a risky exercise, since there is no guarantee that as a result of it we will emerge exactly the same persons as we entered, that is, as persons carrying precisely the same baggage, holding precisely the same opinions with precisely the same conviction, and so on. And this is the case because dialogue is a peculiar practice: it is unpredictable and uncontrollable and offers no refuge from vulnerability without ceasing to be dialogue. Immunity from vulnerability may be possible through other communicative practices in which speech is regarded as a tool we use to convey information or to impose our will on others. But these are practices that should never be confused with dialogue. That is why, in an important sense, the conduct of dialogue is properly said to lie beyond the wills of its participants. As Hans Georg Gadamer suggests, it is perhaps more accurate to say that we 'fall into' or 'become involved in' dialogue rather than that we oversee it.[10]

The process of dialogue, with its to-and-fro movement, with one word following another as the conversation takes its own twists and turns and reaches its own conclusions, may well be conducted in some manner, but those participating in it seem far less the leaders than the led. Accordingly, the outcome of dialogue is uncertain, and the understanding we may achieve through it is like a process happening to us. And since this is a shared experience over which nobody has mastery, dialogue exemplifies a kind of fair interaction that hinges on an equality of vulnerability among participants. This is a particularly apt point to highlight in a situation like Northern Ireland's, where fear of losing out to the 'other' acts as a serious impediment to engagement. One striking reason why dialogue is so important here is that the idea of equal vulnerability it conveys addresses, and may help to alleviate, precisely that fear.

This understanding of vulnerability, together with what we have already observed about inclusion's implications, indicates that dialogue centrally entails *reciprocity*. It does so in the obvious sense that it cannot occur without a relation of reciprocal recognition between interlocutors in which the distinctness and personhood of each is acknowledged. Beyond that, in circumstances of conflict or contestation, reciprocity refers to interlocutors' preparedness to come to terms with each other's readings of matters of dispute between them, and with the reasons and feelings these readings reveal. Reciprocity here calls into play mutual empathy. It asks those engaged in dialogue to take an imaginative leap whereby they not only endeavour to grapple with readings different from their own, but even perhaps try to see themselves as others see them and try to see others as they see themselves. Once we concede equal vulnerability this is much easier to envisage.

Listening to others in the process of dialogue implies taking on board their accounts of themselves and their positions. It encourages removing the mote from our own eye, so that we might obtain a more illuminating glimpse of the totality of the contested situation in which we find ourselves. And even if translucency of vision is an elusive goal for finite beings, even if we cannot escape seeing through a glass darkly, there are degrees to which we suffer from impaired sight. It is possible to see better than we currently do, just as it is possible to understand better than we presently do, and to appreciate the position of others better than we typically do. It is by attempting to empathise with others in the course of dialogue that we may enhance our prospects of seeing, understanding and appreciating better.

Of course, empathy is limited in the sense that our imaginative leaps into another's view of our common yet contested situation can only yield partial returns: we cannot finally perceive things exactly as others perceive them, any more than we can know others as they know themselves, or stand in their shoes as they stand in them, without ceasing to be the persons we are. So the point of saying reciprocity is a necessary feature of dialogue that involves empathy is not to smuggle in some daft demand for interchangeable identities, where I can as easily be you as I can be myself, and vice versa. It is, rather, to say that through empathising as far as possible with others, and through subjecting ourselves to the give and take that reciprocity implies in dialogue, we allow our perceptions and prejudices to be disturbed. What matters, ultimately, is that by attentively heeding the voices of others, we broaden our horizons in a manner that may enable us together to move beyond our difficulties. For what we are exposed to here is the partiality of our own grasp of things, and it is through our shared exposure that it becomes possible for us to contemplate changes .that may previously have seemed impossible.

In a dialogical exchange characterised by equal vulnerability and reciprocity, it no longer appears far-fetched for us reasonably to moderate our requests of others, to make concessions to their requests, and to adjust our position without an overriding sense of loss. And inasmuch as it does not, we arrive at a deepened understanding of reconciliation's requirement of fair interactions. By not contriving to advance our own view at whatever cost, but by adapting to the views of others, by being open to their insights, by admitting our own blind spots, by modifying and expanding our perspective in the light of our dialogical encounters, we relinquish any desire to dominate, manipulate or coerce others, or to gain a victory at their expense.

THE PROBLEM OF LANGUAGE

Fair interactions are important in themselves regardless of any other consequence. But they also provide an indispensable backdrop against which the goals of reconciliation may be understood. They are, in fact, integral to the business of trying to achieve these goals. Thought of in this way, we can say that there is a fit between the means and ends of reconciliation. By recognising the humanness of others and incorporating the reality of different perspectives, fair interactions between members of our major traditions already contribute to the goals of broadening horizons, healing divisions and finding common ground. They amount to partial realisations of these goals.

That at least is their promise. Of course, this is a promise that may never be fulfilled, either because fair interactions represent an unattainable ideal, or because we do not rate reconciliation highly enough to pursue them. Let me leave aside until the next chapter discussion of why it may be thought that we are dealing here with an ideal that is in principle unattainable, and why I disagree. Instead I want to take up the point that fair interactions gesture at possibilities that are unlikely because they presuppose a commitment to reconciliation that does not exist.

I have already suggested why various of the reasons that account for a lack of commitment to reconciliation – from indifference, fear and bitterness through to preoccupation with narrowly defined unionist or nationalist interests – are less than compelling. Although real enough, these sorts of reasons are not easily justified, and they do not pose obstacles to reconciliation that are in principle impossible to overcome. There is, however, another type of reason why commitment to reconciliation may be inhibited, one that comes more sharply into focus once emphasis falls on the requirement of fair interactions. And this presents a problem of considerable importance, since it indicates a deep-seated cultural level of resistance to reconciliation. Stated generally, the problem is this: inasmuch as reconciliation requires fair interactions, it seems destined to want for adequate commitment because it relies on a view of language that simply does not resonate across the North's cultural divide.

DIALOGUE AND MISUNDERSTANDING?

To elaborate, the depiction I have given of fair interactions puts immense stress on dialogue. At a stretch, it may be possible to manifest civic virtues and to embrace and engage others in non-dialogical ways, but not adequately. Dialogue-free understandings of civic virtues, embrace and engagement are seriously incomplete. And, in the absence of dialogue, neither politics nor reconciliation can appear in other than very distorted forms. Dialogue, in short, is central to the life of a thriving democratic polity and to the tasks of sorting out misunderstandings and reducing hostilities between people. None the less, appealing to dialogue in order to enhance reconciliation's prospects is more problematic than I have so far allowed. For it to play the central role I think it must, interlocutors have to work at hearing and understanding one another. And yet this happens only rarely in Northern Ireland. Part of the difficulty, which I have more to say about in subsequent chapters, is that unionists and republicans, say, invoke different moral and political vocabularies and so succeed mostly in speaking past one another. Padraig O'Malley suggests that the gulf in understanding here is sometimes so great that there is a need for both sides to learn 'what Alasdair MacIntyre calls a "second first language" – a common idiom that will allow them to articulate shared values and overlapping aspirations without having to submit them to the litmus test of mutually exclusive political legitimacies – if they are ever to explore common ground'.[11]

O'Malley is certainly on to something important. Beyond the examples he draws on from reactions to the republican hunger strikes of 1981, we can see evidence of the gulf in understanding in the ways in which potential political progress has sometimes been stunted in recent years through one side's inattention to the significance of changes in the language of the other. For example, republicans saw Sinn Féin president Gerry Adams's denunciation of the Omagh bombing,[12] carried out by the Real IRA in 1998, as signalling a decisive statement of their movement's commitment to pursuing its goals through exclusively peaceful means. But its significance was apparently lost on unionists, most of whom barely registered that Adams had said anything out of the ordinary. It is, however, too quick and, as I argue in the next chapter, too unconvincing to conclude that there is an unbridgeable misunderstanding at work here. The uncomfortable fact is that it suits certain interests to misunderstand those they think of as their enemy. Not hearing what others are actually saying is convenient when we do not want old prejudices disturbed. In other words, part of the difficulty posed by different languages in Northern Ireland could be sorted out if what I have called civic virtues were taken seriously. In this sense the problem does not lie with language itself.

In another sense, however, it does. And to get at the problem in question we cannot settle for O'Malley's solution of learning a 'second first language', since this presupposes what is in fact often missing, namely a willingness to learn for the sake of making effective dialogue possible. The deeper problem is that lurking behind much of our talking at cross-purposes and failure to connect with one another lies a suspicion of dialogue per se, which hinders receptiveness to O'Malley's recommendation. This suspicion cannot be wholly explained by the relative scarcity of appropriate civic virtues in a divided society. It is also linked to predominantly instrumental views of language in which dialogue has already been allotted a subordinate role. In the context of Northern Ireland two such views stand out.

THE LANGUAGE OF VIOLENCE

One view typically subordinates dialogue to a type of violence that is presumed to speak with a peculiarly powerful political voice. Here, of course, I am taking language in its broadest sense as a medium of meaning, which allows us to refer to the language of art, or of music, or, as in this case, of violence. What has been traditionally known in Ireland as *physical force republicanism* exemplifies the view I have in mind. Its characteristic stance is that political dialogue is of secondary importance in achieving republicanism's goal of convincing the British to terminate their rule in Ireland. Violence, we are told, is the only political language that British governments understand; it is bombs and bullets, rather than any subtler dialogical art of persuasion, that are taken to concentrate British minds on matters Irish.

This view of language is now on the wane among republicans. The Official IRA unceremoniously ditched it back in the 1970s. Its principal advocates throughout the period of the conflict, the Provisional IRA, have more recently abandoned it. And it is presently confined to dissidents associated with the Continuity IRA and the Real IRA. There is little that is intrinsically interesting about it, since violence represents a very crude instrument of persuasion that has failed to force a British withdrawal from Northern Ireland, even if many believe that it helped win political advantages essential to the present negotiating position of Sinn Féin. At its core, this view is the antithesis of the view of language integral to reconciliation: its sidelining of a mode of politics to which dialogue is indispensable reflects a closed and an uncompromising spirit, which cannot begin to hear the voices of others or to recognise their entitlements. Accordingly, it is a matter of some consequence that, as things currently stand, such a radically anti-dialogical perspective on language no longer constitutes the formidable obstacle to fair interactions that it once did.

The relative decline of the notion that violence serves as a uniquely effective political language in the North contains salutary and cautionary lessons. It is *salutary* to see that even in circumstances of deep division and historical antagonism reconciliation's hope is never entirely snuffed out, since human agents are not doomed to play out pre-determined or culturally inflexible roles but are capable of effecting substantial change, not least within their own culture. And the republican shift from a language of violence to a language of reconciliation is a particularly striking instance of such change. Without denying the strategic rationale of the shift, it is too cynical only to see here one instrument (violence), which has out-lived its usefulness, being swapped for another (political dialogue), which promises a more efficient realisation of republicanism's goal. Or at least it is on the terms of a reading of republicanism that I discuss in Chapter 7, even if other readings admittedly reinforce cynicism. The point is that only to see a cynical change of instru-ment here is to overlook what is potentially most interesting and significant, namely that in the move from one language to another, republicans' interpretations of political reality and of their goal are subtly transformed. What was clouded, if not impossible to see pre-viously, now comes into clearer light.

Take, for example, republicanism's attitude to unionism. Mar-ginalising unionists is integral to the physical force view of the language of violence: unionists appear as little more than lackeys of Ireland's colonial oppressors and do not warrant being taken ser-iously on their own terms; they are treated more as irritants rather than as central players in the big game of achieving total Irish inde-pendence from Britain. Thus, on these terms, the goal of Irish unity is properly pursued not by convincing unionists of its merits, but by forcing the hand of the British government. More than tactical con-siderations are involved in the move away from this view towards political dialogue. A different interpretation of political realities in the North is also invoked, one which crucially includes recognising unionists as authentic bearers of a British identity rather than as vic-tims of a false consciousness, and engaging them as pivotal, rather than as bit, players. Moreover, while the goal of Irish unity remains, other arrangements – most notably those on offer in the Agreement – are acceptable in the meantime, and the sort of unity that is envisaged is no longer one implying a cultural homogeneity alien to unionists, but one reflecting a cultural plurality that would accommodate unionists' Britishness.[13]

There is much to be encouraged by here. Even so, it is prudent to add a *cautionary* note to Provisional republicanism's transition from violence to political dialogue. This sort of transition is rarely neat and, even if it signals the breakdown of a major barrier to fair interactions, we cannot suppose it implies the easy removal of other barriers. Its significance is at once blunted, for instance, unless it is recognised by others, particularly unionists. Yet unionist recognition has not been forthcoming, and cynicism rather than enthusiasm typifies its response to Sinn Féin's discovery of the language of reconciliation. When Gerry Adams, for example, speaks of reconciliation depending on 'the willingness of Irish people to leave aside their fears and prejudices, to forgive and be forgiven, and to embrace each other as neighbours in building a new society which reflects the diversity of our nation',[14] he may as well have been whistling in the dark as far as most unionists are concerned. As we shall see shortly, there are problems specific to unionism that partly account for its response. But difficulties internal to republicanism's move from one language to another must also be reckoned with.

The transition from violence to dialogue is frequently complicated by the need to convince reluctant or sceptical supporters of its appropriateness. And, indeed, it is sometimes the case that the significance I have attributed to it – of representing a shift to more inclusively inclined interpretations of Northern political realities and of republicanism's goal – is played down by Sinn Féin, especially when its own constituents are being addressed. Or, at least, the language of reconciliation has to vie with calculations of Sinn Féin's strategic interests, with its determination to prevent splits in its ranks by prioritising the unity of the republican movement, and by emphasising the continuity of republican policy. Accordingly, the break with violence on occasions seems less than decisive.

Doubts about the break are harboured through continuing references to the Provisional IRA as an undefeated army, which has not gone away but has played a legitimate and constructive role in creating conditions for peace, and to its volunteers as brave, honourable soldiers. And these doubts are reinforced by the reluctance the Provisional IRA showed in relinquishing weapons, and the suspicion that it finally conducted an act of arms decommissioning in October 2001 only because of intense pressure from the US in the wake of Al Qaeda attacks on the World Trade Center in New York and the Pentagon in Washington DC on 11 September 2001. No doubt Sinn Féin perceives these references and this reluctance as justifiable, and indeed unavoidable, if republican morale and cohesion are to be upheld. The problem is that they recall memories of the old language in which unionists were effectively defined out of existence. Mixed signals are therefore sent out to unionists, which is of course why it is so easy for them to dismiss Sinn Féin's use of a language of reconciliation as a disingenuous flirtation.

There is room to doubt how well Sinn Féin grasps the depth of unionist feeling here. Absorbed for so many years by their own sense of grievance and by their justifications of the Provisional IRA's armed struggle, some republicans appear strangely oblivious to the fact that unionists were terrorised by the Provisonal IRA's activities, and to the threat unionists perceive in its continuing existence in a post-Agreement North. It is also questionable how much responsibility republicanism admits to bearing for sowing seeds of bitterness and deepening sectarian divisions as a consequence of its armed struggle. Republicans face serious difficulties on these and related issues, which I return to in Chapter 7.

This cautionary note about the difficulties of moving from violence to dialogue is not meant to nullify the salutary note I raised earlier. It suggests, rather, that existing possibilities for reconciliation may be squandered due to lack of adequate cultivation. But this is something we can prevent by adopting the attitudes and practices associated with fair interactions. It is the relative absence of dialogue between unionists and republicans that severely diminishes the prospect of bridging the gulf that separates them. The upshot is that reconciliation, far from being dismissible as an abstract wish, is the one option that makes compelling practical sense in Northern Ireland today. The onus is on those who think otherwise to show why it is unreasonable to maintain that its requirement of fair interactions lays a claim on us that cannot be justifiably avoided.

This is not only a responsibility of republicans when, for whatever reason, they slip back into their old language with its connotations of violence, or, as it seems to unionists, when they refuse properly to cut themselves adrift from it. It is also a *responsibility of unionists*, since fair interactions ask for considerably more than they have ever been prepared to give. One counter is that too much is being asked of them. The typical reasons produced in support of such a counter are unimpressive. Anti-Agreement unionists cannot get off the hook here by citing scepticism of republicans' motives and sincerity as grounds for non-engagement. Without being put to the test through dialogue this sort of scepticism easily becomes a convenient cloak for hiding any number of self-serving prejudices. And self-righteous posturing about being unwilling to trade as a matter of principle with those who are too closely associated with the language of violence has an utterly hollow ring. Northern Ireland only exists because unionists were more than prepared to employ such language on a grand scale; the Northern Ireland state under unionist control used its coercive powers in a highly partial manner; and much loyalist violence has been prosecuted with a singularly sectarian intent. Moreover, it is an unedifying spectacle to witness mainstream unionists, who have been untroubled in forming pacts with loyalists from paramilitary backgrounds, seeking exemption from the requirement of fair interactions because their consciences are burdened by the thought of dealing with republican men and women of violence. The language of violence has tarnished unionism and nationalism alike, and neither is due special dispensations from reconciliation's demands.

LANGUAGE AS A TOOL

Perhaps, though, unionism represents a peculiar case in another sense: the requirement of fair interactions may ask too much of unionists because it relies on an assumption of dialogue's centrality, which sits uncomfortably with much of their experience. Unease with a heavy emphasis on dialogue, in other words, does not always betray violent proclivities. Many members of a Northern Protestant culture, shaped in large measure by Presbyterianism, are attached to another view of language in which dialogue plays a minor role. In this view, what counts most is the instrumental function of words, namely that they serve as useful tools for achieving a given set of purposes. It is a view that fits with the familiar cultural image of hard-headed, taciturn Northern Protestants who, as John Dunlop remarks, are 'more interested in engineering than in art'.[15] And it is out of respect for this cultural image and the view of language it entails that unionists are entitled to relief from the more stringent dialogical demands of fair interactions. Or so it may be implied. An immediate qualification is needed here to avoid saying something preposterous. The claim is not that dialogue is foreign to unionists – since pressed to its limit this would be so absurd as to call into question their membership of the human species – but that it is a mistake to make too much of it, especially since it is not as essential to resolving Northern Ireland's problems as my account of fair interactions supposes.

Unionist practice expresses this claim in two ways. First, it implies that it is possible to settle important issues without the aid of dialogue. Thus Orangemen expect disputes over controversial marches to be resolved in the absence of any meeting with local residents or any factoring in of their objections. Or, perhaps most tellingly, the UUP was involved in multi-party talks negotiating the Agreement without engaging Sinn Féin, presumably believing that a deal for the future of Northern Ireland could be successfully struck and implemented independently of direct acquaintance with or distraction by republican concerns. Second, those encounters between pro-Agreement unionism and republicanism that have subsequently occurred, and which may be thought to give promise of an overdue engagement, have had little to do with dialogue as such. For unionists these have been primarily confrontational opportunities, when Sinn Féin can be told of what is demanded of republicans, and of how these demands act as pre-conditions of further political progress. Reflecting the general lack of curiosity among their constituents about what makes republicans and nationalists tick, unionist politicians typically treat listening to Sinn Féin as a superfluous condition. And, strikingly, complementing this downplaying of dialogue's significance, there is a conspicuous lack of reference among unionists to the broad language of reconciliation so freely employed not only by Gerry Adams but also by a range of other non-unionist politicians. Instead, UUP leader David Trimble speaks openly of unionist politics following the Agreement as 'a continuation of the so-called war by other means'.[16] Aughey's scorn of the 'banal but corrosive jargon of the peace process'[17] evidently has cultural and political reverberations among unionists.

There is little doubt that these anti-dialogical practices create enormous barriers to the realisation of fair interactions. But does the view of language that underpins them succeed in showing that dialogue is not as necessary to sorting out our Northern difficulties as I have made out, and that unionists have solid grounds for pleading exemption from dialogical demands? The answer can be yes only if we are prepared to entertain extraordinary beliefs about language, politics and the privileged status of unionism. These beliefs are transmitted through two major facets of an instrumental view of language: a substitution of confrontation for dialogue, and an aspiration for an unambiguous use of words. Let's consider each in turn.

In the current context of Northern Ireland, unionists' substitution of dialogue with various *confrontational techniques* appears in attempts to make republicans bend to their will. The substitution also appears in so-called prophetic exposures of perceived error and evil. Unionists of all persuasions practise both forms of substitution even if those opposed to the Agreement do so more unrelentingly than others. The forms imply different criteria of judgement, with one inviting evaluation in terms of its consequences and the other not. But both share a common defect, namely reliance on devices that are politically inept at healing divisions in an unreconciled society.

Take confrontation's expression as an imposition of a *unionist will*, which is evident in efforts to force republicans into line by issuing demands, ultimatums, threats and sanctions. This form of confrontation seems misguided, particularly given the ethos of resistance that characterises the republican movement. It is far-fetched to believe that a transformation within republicanism can be engineered in such a fashion. Pro-Agreement unionists may beg to differ, especially since the Provisional IRA finally decommissioned weapons as unionists insisted it must. Thus confrontation appears to have paid off; it has had its desired consequence. This is very debatable. Confrontation's dividends are more uncertain than they seem to pro-Agreement unionist eyes, not least because in Northern society confrontation reduces politics to a counterproductive game of inconclusive strategic jostling. The result unionists present as a vindication of their approach may be plausibly construed as nothing of the sort.

For example, an explanation of a pro-Agreement unionist case for the beneficial effects of confrontation could run like this. What matters most for unionists is the political imperative of defending the Union. Through the role it grants to the principle of consent, the Agreement seems to facilitate this imperative by underwriting Northern Ireland's constitutional status within the United Kingdom. The prolonged republican refusal to decommission weapons, however, threatened such a unionist interpretation of the Agreement's significance, since it implied non-compliance with its constitutional provisions, even if the Agreement omits reference to any specific Provisional IRA undertaking to decommission. Accordingly, Sinn Féin had to be faced down over its reluctance to deliver a surrender or destruction of Provisional IRA arms. For the sake of the Union, a unionist will had to prevail here. Confrontational pressure therefore had to be exerted on republicans, including vetoing official meetings between republican ministers of the Northern Executive and their Southern counterparts. Unionists conjured with a number of possible outcomes of their confrontational approach: a decommissioning of Provisional IRA weapons, which could be taken to justify their support and interpretation of the Agreement, if not also effect the humiliation of republicanism; or, in the absence of decommissioning, the exclusion of republicans from government offices; or, failing either of these, a renegotiation of the Agreement.

In a sense, the strategies that accompanied these potential outcomes inferred that although republicans were the butt of unionists' harsh language, its primary audience was the British and Irish governments. Unionists had to be aware that republicans were hardly likely to decommission arms in direct response to their invective. But by declaring that they would not indefinitely tolerate the Provisional IRA's refusal to decommission its weapons, the unionists' intention was to put republicans under maximum pressure. Thus they signalled to London and Dublin that they must squeeze Sinn Féin on this issue in order to avert a political crisis. And perhaps such pressure would prove so irresistible that it would result in the desired movement on arms. Alternatively, assuming that republicans continued to resist, the unionist hope was that both governments and other political parties would accept that it was republican intransigence that was the obstacle to political progress in Northern Ireland, and that there was little option but to exclude Sinn Féin from the political Executive. Should these hopes be dashed, then the tenor of unionists' language was designed to leave nobody in doubt that the present arrangements had not worked and that something like a review or renegotiation of the Agreement was required. When Provisional IRA decommissioning eventually occurred, well over three years after the signing of the Agreement, pro-Agreement unionists could boast that confrontation had borne fruit.

This is not the only available explanation for Provisional IRA decommissioning, however. It is possible to offer a very different one that says that unionism's confrontationalist stance can claim little, if any, credit for republicanism's movement on arms, that it has been more of a hindrance than a help, that movement occurred only because it fitted with republicans' strategic interests, and that it does not carry the political significance pro-Agreement unionists want to believe. For instance, the Provisional IRA's decision to begin decommissioning weapons was undoubtedly taken in the light of unprecedented American pressure following the US's recent move to engage in an international war against terrorism. And this had nothing to do with republicans folding their hand because they had been outwitted by David Trimble's skills as a political poker player.

Prior to the attacks in New York and Washington DC on 11 September, there was no sign that Trimble's threat to withdraw unionist ministers from the Executive, in the absence of decommissioning, was making much impression on the Provisional IRA. It is more that not incurring American wrath made more strategic sense to republicans than did refusing to put some of its weapons beyond use. Besides, the Provisional IRA had already made a number of gestures on arms that indicated movement here had long been possible. If anything, the stumbling block to delivery was unionism's confrontationalism. For its own reasons of honour, the Provisional IRA could not be seen to be surrendering to unionist demands. Furthermore, republicans argued that decommissioning was only one part of a bigger picture of change depicted in the Agreement, and that it could not be dissociated from issues such as demilitarisation and reform of Northern society. And, it might be added, it was only able to happen because it was accompanied by assurances of more British moves on demilitarisation and of pro-Agreement unionist willingness to stop blocking the functioning of North–South institutions.

Once more, in other words, republicans estimated that there were strategic advantages in decommissioning weapons when they did. And this is manifestly because decommissioning did not carry the political connotations for them that it did for unionists. Rather than indicating their acquiescence to the Union, it could be rationalised as merely another step on the road to Irish unity, one that makes sense because unity is now being pursued via a non-military route.

I have skimmed over aspects of unionist and republican reasoning on decommissioning and related matters that I return to in

Chapter 7. The point here is not so much to investigate the details of the respective explanations of their reasoning I have just sketched, or even to question whether decommissioning is a good thing – I think it unquestionably is – as to cast doubt on unionism's substitution of confrontation for dialogue. This is not to deny that there may be occasions when the language of confrontation has its place: for example, as a response of citizens to those who have committed atrocities, or to cases of corruption or overt sectarianism, which offend against our most basic commitments to building a decent society. Put another way, righteous indignation deserves a political hearing, since it highlights the offensiveness of tolerating instances of manifest injustice and strongly cautions against turning a blind eye to deadly or demeaning modes of behaviour. But, given the history of Northern Ireland, it is incongruous to think that unionists have a monopoly of it. Indignant confrontational language may be as appropriately directed against various unionist, loyalist and British government practices as against certain republican or nationalist ones.

Most importantly here, the language of confrontation is best considered as an occasional supplement to dialogue, and not as a substitute. As I have tried to suggest, confrontation, even on its own terms, has uncertain consequences in Northern Ireland. What looks like success for unionism from one angle may appear as something else altogether from another. Or it may be that confrontation just engenders political stalemate. A partial decommissioning of weapons may have ended stalemate in the short-term because it suited the strategic interests of pro-Agreement unionism and republicanism – but doubts about the longer term were never properly put to rest. Anti-Agreement unionists remained resolutely unimpressed by acts of decommissioning, and it was entirely predictable that they would be satisfied with nothing short of the disbandment of the Provisional IRA. Now with pro-Agreement unionists also insisting on disbandment as a new condition for sharing government with Sinn Féin – following allegations about ongoing activities by the Provisional IRA – stalemate has returned with a vengeance. As matters currently stand, relations between republicanism and all strands of of unionism are so poor that direct rule from Westminster has been reimposed in an attempt to prevent a complete collapse of the Agreement. The politics of Northern Ireland have taken another uncertain turn.

There is, however, a deeper problem than uncertain consequences or potential stalemate. It is that once political language is locked into a confrontational mode, strategic considerations become all-consuming. Politics is reduced to calculative moves, to outfoxing one's opponents, to seeking victory. And unless one side is simply vanquished or surrenders, crisis then becomes endemic in the political process of a divided society. And this is what is so mis-guided about dialogue's replacement by confrontation: victory for one side, even if possible, would not be worth winning. It would risk deepening divisions and make a return to serious violence a realistic prospect. Whatever the substantive merits of its case, which I discuss in later chapters, unionism is culpable for exacerbating these risks due to its conviction that confrontation, not dialogue, is the language best suited to dealing with Sinn Féin. And such a highly specious view makes unionists vulnerable to accusations of either desperation or ruthlessness, where resistance to the inclusive requirement of treating all parties as equal political partners is so strong that the impulse to impose a unionist will on republicans at least cannot or will not yet be relinquished.

Whether prompted by desperation or ruthlessness or, as unionists prefer to believe, by constitutional rigour, it is to court extraordinary beliefs about politics to think that the confrontational language adopted by unionism points to a non-dialogical route through our difficulties in Northern Ireland; or even that it is the surest way of securing the Union, since it threatens to alienate precisely those citizens whose allegiance is required if subversion is not to pose an ongoing difficulty. The simple fact is that without dialogue between unionists and republicans, the North's deeper problems – of which paramilitary weapons and organisations are only symptoms anyway – remain untouched. There is no short-circuiting available here. The language of confrontation, even should it succeed unambiguously, is inherently limited in what it can hope to achieve in a divided society. It is utterly ineffectual in helping us to overcome sectarian divisions and to chip away at the layers of mistrust that jaundice relations between large sections of our major traditions.

Of course, in another reading of what unionists are up to in substituting confrontation for dialogue, this apparent limitation counts for very little. On this reading, what we see are unionists playing out their self-appointed role as *prophetic witnesses*, a role that demands the use of strong language against republicans as a matter of duty, irrespective of its consequences. Here the hope of republican transformation may not be entirely forfeited, but unionist faithfulness in not hesitating to denounce what seems to them manifestly wrong is the crucial consideration. This reading makes sense if we allow that unionists' confrontational language represents an extension into politics of a cultural-religious style derived from the central role the evangelical sermon plays in their worship. Religiously speaking, it is a style that assumes a recognised authoritative source (the 'Word of God'), and a trustworthy representative of the source (a faithful preacher/minister). It assumes further that the message conveyed through this representative is aimed at the hearts of the congregation – through authoritative words that have the power to pierce our consciences and convict us of sin – and that the responsibility is ours whether to heed or ignore them. Dialogue is beside the point here: the language model is monological not dialogical. The words of the sermon are delivered as judgements of sin and are directed to the conscience not the intellect. Accordingly, they are to be accepted or rejected, but not debated, or set in a context of alternative views, or weighed up against other considerations, or queried in any manner. As instruments of a divine will, these are authoritative words that have the intrinsic power to trump our doubts, hesitations and equivocations.

Ian Paisley, needless to say, explicitly transfers this model to politics, and his political denunciations of republicanism are mixed with religious connotations and are intended to carry the same moral force as his other denunciations of sin. But even when the explicit religious overtones are absent, as with unionists of a more secular disposition, traces of the model remain. Republicans are depicted in the worst possible light, as the political equivalent of the most dangerous of sinners. Thus they may be variously referred to as enemies of Ulster, or as subversive terrorists, or as blights on the democratic landscape, and so on. And in condemning the activities and motives of republicans through confrontational language, even secular unionists sometimes seem to perceive themselves as faithful witnesses to a truth they are duty-bound to represent. Moreover, because they are so unreflectively assured of the appropriateness of their casting in the role of prophetic witnesses and denunciators, many unionists are undeterred by republican indifference or hostility. Rather than indict the futility of their approach, it merely reveals that republicans remain unreconstructed terrorists at heart. It is as though republicans' refusal to receive the political message conveyed by unionists confirms their status as unrepentant sinners whose hearts are hardened against truth. Thus the major task remains that of faithfully exposing republican error whatever the consequence. To enter into dialogue is to misunderstand what the task requires, since it is to allow the unthinkable, namely that republicans' views may be as valid as unionists', that error may be as valid as truth, that bad may have something to teach good.

Now evidently, the language model of the sermon serves only polarising and polemical political purposes. Whatever its religious salience – a matter of dispute I leave aside here – its political implications are dreadful. Political relations between opposing parties cannot even begin to be established if one party insists on operating in a monological voice. Thus there continues to be an abysmal relationship between anti-Agreement unionist parties and Sinn Féin. Prior to the Provisional IRA's act of decommissioning weapons, relations between the UUP and Sinn Féin were only marginally better, and how they develop in the future remains an open question. The point is that there is a strong tendency within unionism as such to subject republicans to a monological form of address. This was illustrated by remarks made by David Trimble during his Nobel Peace Prize lecture. Here he appropriated the advice of George Kennan to the US State Department on how to deal with 'the State terrorists of his time' in order to back up a confrontational/sermonising stance to republicanism. 'Do not act chummy with them,' advised Kennan, 'do not assume a community of aims with them which does not really exist; do not make fatuous gestures of goodwill.'[18] These are disconcerting sentiments to express at a time when the UUP and Sinn Féin were signatories to the same Agreement, members of the same Assembly and political Executive, citizens of the same society, and supposedly partners in trying to make the North work. There are political quandaries here that I leave aside until the final two chapters.

At the moment, the only question to decide is whether the influence of a cultural–religious style of sermonising in unionist politics should be respected to the point of immunising unionists from the requirements of fair interactions. To give such respect is to concede at least the following: that unionism properly enjoys a unique status among political positions in Northern Ireland, and that unionists are entitled to claim privileged access to an authoritative source, which they alone are peculiarly equipped to represent. It is also to allow that unionist hubris excuses them from larger concerns of equality in Northern society and from the risk and vulnerability that dialogue entails. And, not least, it is to capitulate to forms of religious and/or political fundamentalism that have no defence other than dogmatism, and that are inimical to any plausible idea of a reconciled society. These considerations give pause to any temptation to grant unlimited respect to unionism on cultural-religious grounds. It is, frankly, too extraordinary a request to accept that any exemptions from dialogical requirements are due to unionists because they arrogate to themselves a special prophetic role.

One other possible ground for exemption is worth considering. The notion that issues of political importance in a divided society can be settled with minimal deference to dialogue ties in with those features of a language of confrontation I have identified. But it does not have to rely on these alone. There is another dimension of an instrumental view of language – bound up with various cultural concerns and habits of unionists – to which appeal may be also made. Dunlop gives a hint of it when commenting on attitudes to language common within Presbyterian or unionist culture. This is a culture seeking consolations of certainty to alleviate its fears of siege; it is one whose members 'have a tendency to tame whatever they touch', since they 'do not like too much untidiness' and 'do not live easily with studied ambiguity'.[19] The attitudes to language that reflect these cultural interests in certainty, taming and an absence of ambiguity are disclosed in a strong inclination to think of *words functioning primarily as precise tools of truth and control*. Interestingly, this inclination is in line with the culture's respect for science, where 'the desire for precision is a precondition for accurate scientific enquiry'.[20] It issues in a fixation on the literal sense of words, with only sparse attention granted to their symbolic or expressive connotations. So much so, indeed, that the meaning of a document, say, is taken to consist merely in 'the sum total of words used'.[21]

Here we have the bare bones of a radically monological approach to language. If a fundamentalist understanding of the sermon provides one model for such an approach, then, playing on the language–science link suggested by Dunlop, it may be that a specific conception of the use of words in scientific enquiry provides another. At any rate, infatuation with precision in language finds its ideal type – which has been in vogue in the West since the modern scientific revolutions of the seventeenth century – in the disengaged philosophical or scientific enquirer who aspires to an interpretation-free definition of words, so that they can be applied exactly as names for objects, as tools that are of use in giving a clear explanation of how things work, of how we may claim certain knowledge, and so forth. This is to envisage the enquirer standing apart from language, as it were, sifting through the words at his or her disposal and choosing to employ only those with transparent meanings, that is, meanings purged of ambiguity because they precisely designate particular objects. This activity does not require company. An ambition even may be to build up a lexicon of tightly defined terms – where each word is added separately as it passes a test of transparency – in order to equip enquirers with a set of linguistic instruments perfectly within their control.[22]

Such an approach to language contrasts sharply with that associated with dialogue, particularly one with an intercultural focus. Dialogue presupposes engagement. Interpretations are its stuff, as are nuances, shades of meaning and ambiguities. In dialogue the expressive meaning of words, which calls on a range of emotional states and experiences, counts as much as its designative meaning. Through dialogue we may aim to become clearer about things – our confusions, misunderstandings, and so on; we may try to figure out how we can together work through our difficulties, as we strive for better interpretations of our problems, circumstances, and respective positions. But our various attempts to become clearer, work through issues and interpret better are always provisional. They are never absolute. That is why the goal of total transparency or an interpretation-free condition is misplaced.

It is also why a dialogical approach to language seems a problem to certain advocates of precision. On dialogical terms, as I have already mentioned, language does not function as a tool over which we have complete mastery; and risk, vulnerability and uncertainty cannot be expunged without dialogue ceasing to be dialogue. The trick, then, is to relegate dialogue to a lower order of significance on the grounds that it is not essential to scientific or philosophical enquiries. Indeed, it may be even taken to distract from them, which is why we are told it is prudent to be wary of most of language's uses: if not harnessed correctly, language has ensnaring tendencies. It is just such a thought that is echoed in many Northern Protestants' suspicion of those 'bearing a wealth of vocabulary',[23] of 'those who rely overmuch on their words',[24] and that is captured in Thomas Hobbes's remark that words are 'the money of fools'.[25] Language, like nature in this view, must be tamed; its seductive powers must be resisted if it is not to turn our heads, take us over, and doom us to stumble around in a world of myths and illusions. Important issues of truth and knowledge can be only decided when words are precisely defined and so operate as instruments of control. A peculiar form of austerity and rigour, alien to the conduct of dialogue, is called for.

Although this ideal type of disengaged enquiry has exercised a powerful influence in Western civilisation, it barely withstands scrutiny. This is not, however, the occasion to probe its manifold problems. It is sufficient to say here that there is ample room to doubt its central aspirations, which we can do without denying the spectacular successes of modern science. For instance, we may doubt whether standing outside language (and culture) is a feat that lies within the scope of human accomplishment – austerity, rigour and discipline notwithstanding; or whether total transparency is possible and therefore whether a necessary condition of language serving as a precise instrument of control can be satisfied; or whether it makes elementary sense to conceive of a lexicon being built up item by item as each word is added separately and in isolation from its larger context of meaning.[26] If it is reasonable to doubt these aspirations, then it is equally reasonable to doubt whether there is a model of language capable of justifying unionist reservations about dialogue.

Now, even if we do not doubt these aspirations, even if we think that a monological model works for science, it is still reasonable to doubt that unionist reservations are somehow vindicated. There are difficulties in translating the model into the realm of cultural and political relations. Most obviously, unionists are in crucial respects different from the ideal type of scientific or philosophical enquirers. Unionists are engaged not disengaged, interested not disinterested, partial not impartial, situated not detached. So to appeal to a model of language that presupposes features unionists cannot possibly possess is not convincing. Put bluntly, unionists may hope to approximate to the ideal type only by not being unionists (or committed cultural–political actors of any kind). Whatever important issues may be settled monologically, they do not include sorting out problems between culturally encumbered traditions in a divided society.

Politics cannot work satisfactorily in terms of monological models, either religious or scientific. They provide no secure refuge from dialogue for unionists. Sure, many unionists may be uneasy with dialogue because of its uncertainties and because of their contempt for other interlocutors. And they may prefer to use words more sparingly than would be sensible in a dialogical situation, even though dialogue is as much about listening as it is about talking (and overlooking the fact that many of unionism's political representatives show little reticence in putting their case). But the requirements of fair interactions cannot be justifiably bypassed out of deference to a so-called scientific view of language that is either wrong-headed in principle or inapplicable to politics (I think it is both), and that makes coming to grips with our problems in Northern Ireland more difficult than it need be.

CONCLUSION

To wrap up, fair interactions are an indispensable requirement of reconciliation. They entail non-instrumental practices, which are conceivable only if civic virtues are cultivated among citizens. A relative lack of these virtues poses a major obstacle to their enjoyment, as do views of language that diminish the significance of dialogue. There is no guarantee that these obstacles will be swiftly removed in Northern Ireland, not least because they reflect entrenched cultural beliefs and dispositions. The quest for reconciliation therefore continues to be thwarted. And that is why I do not believe it can be achieved through short cuts that gloss over the depth of opposition to its demands. The emphasis on fair interactions illustrates perhaps more effectively than any other just how exacting these demands are. But what we can do is show that the obstacles of lack of virtue and non-dialogical understandings of language do not have to be considered insuperable blocks to reconciliation. I have tried to do that in this chapter by arguing that only poor reasons can be elicited in their support. There are, in short, compelling reasons to interact fairly, and the onus falls on those who think otherwise to show why these should not count decisively in reconciliation's favour.

5

POSSIBILITIES OF
COMMON GROUND

Another requirement of reconciliation is that we overcome our antagonistic divisions. Striving for fair interactions is part of what trying to meet it involves. But, in themselves, fair interactions do not guarantee its satisfaction, for it implies more than having citizens who act virtuously, who embrace plurality, and who engage each other. Contrary to a caricature, reconciliation's message is not that if only we were nicer to one another the sources of our conflict would disappear. For it is possible that, despite our best efforts, we will not agree on how to settle the basic issues that divide us. Of course, if there are fair interactions between citizens, then there is every chance that the sting will be taken out of our disagreements, and that divisions will be drained of much of their antagonism. And the prospects for agreement are enhanced enormously if we share an appreciation of each other's point of view and of the incompleteness of our own. Fair interactions already open us up and broaden us out in a manner that involves us overcoming some of our antagonistic divisions, and that makes it much easier to sort out those that remain. But, if these kinds of interactions were to be experienced and yet failed to deliver any substantial agreement between citizens from different traditions, it is hard not to think that they would prove difficult to sustain in a divided society. Quite simply, fair interactions do not clinch reconciliation.

THE COMMONALITY–DIFFERENCE CONUNDRUM

What is implied in addition is that it is possible for us to deal with the content of our differences in a manner that ends the divisions between us. And this means discovering common ground we all can occupy. It suggests we can reason our way through our differences to reach agreement on how we may live together without anyone suffering a justifiable sense of irreparable loss. Or, if that is too ambitious, it suggests there are losses we are prepared to bear for the sake of the bigger gains on offer. Here we confront again the difficulty of the commonality–difference conundrum. Even under conditions of fair interaction, how can we conceive of commonality without sidelining difference, or, equally, how can we give difference its due without giving up on commonality? So far these questions have not received satisfactory answers. To reiterate, the answer of assimilation mishandles the claims of difference, just as the answer of prioritising difference mishandles the claims of commonality. The slightly more hopeful answer of balancing the interests of rival sets of difference, such as those of unionism and nationalism, does not succeed either, as it curtails concerns of commonality for the sake of placating the interests of difference.

I want to argue now that more plausible answers to the questions thrown up by the commonality–difference conundrum lie in two understandings of commonality: one that sees commonality as a *possible product of reasonable engagements with our differences*, and another that sees commonality as *a possibility that exists despite our differences*. These are interrelated. In the context of an intercultural dialogue, say, it is likely that they frequently overlap. Hopes of commonality emerging through discussion of differences are doubtless sustained by the conviction that we already share much that our differences are occluding. And, equally, the expressions given to what we share are shaped by our appreciation of what separates us, and probably can appear in non-distorting forms only to the extent that we explore our points of separation and evaluate whether they admit of any bridging and whether they should be permitted to block attempts to occupy common ground. Even so, the two understandings of commonality's possibility have different emphases and confront different challenges.

The first undertanding anticipates the unexpected; it opens up the prospect that through deliberating together about our differences new articulations of our respective positions may arise that bridge the gap between us. It has to withstand potentially crippling objections, namely that it chases the impossible and must fail because its pursuit necessarily violates plurality; or that it unwisely refuses to concede the incompatibility of the North's major traditions and falters in face of the non-negotiability of their respective identity claims. I try to show that objections such as these are wide of the mark.

The second understanding, besides reinforcing the first's anticipations of commonality, acts as a kind of moral guarantor. By stressing the importance of certain things we share, it sets limits on difference's legitimate pursuit. And, I maintain, it is hard to avoid admitting that some form of commonality is possible despite our differences: the difficult question to decide is what form(s). Responses to this question matter a great deal, since they affect the political scope allowed to ideals of reconciliation. It is largely agreed in influential schools of contemporary political thought that only 'thin' forms of commonality are possible, and that differences among citizens can be protected only if reconciliation's political scope is accordingly quite narrow. I give reasons for dissenting from this consensus. I suggest that we need 'thicker' forms of commonality that widen the political scope of reconciling ideals.

COMMONALITY THROUGH DIFFERENCE

A clear upshot of the discussion on fair interactions is that, given the right conditions, it is entirely possible that through dialogue about our differences a shared notion of commonality may emerge. This is a possibility I also hinted at in an earlier discussion of the accommodating aspect of parity of esteem. In an important sense, the Agreement already provides evidence of it and gives an indication of what it might mean. Multi-party negotiations, despite their inadequacies, ostensibly resolved the long-standing constitutional disagreement between unionism and nationalism in a way that previously seemed inconceivable. And, in doing so, they laid a basis for a common political life in which all citizens may participate. In another sense, however, the achievements of the Agreement do not count as sufficient evidence of commonality's possibility. To foreshadow the agenda of Chapter 6, the Agreement may yet be undone, especially since it is under immense strain on the unionist side; its achievements arguably rely on a fragile convergence of interests rather than on deeper convictions of reasonableness; and even its most optimistic supporters cannot fail to notice that the Agreement scarcely arrests those cultural antipathies in the North that put enjoyment of a common life on the long finger. Given that I am advocating a reason-grounded understanding of commonality, which aims in part to shore up the rationale of the Agreement, these are very awkward considerations. They suggest that my endeavour to promote commonality's possibility is susceptible to the twin charges of seeking the impossible and of ignoring obdurate cultural–political realities in Northern Ireland.

Both of these charges have been touched on already in Chapter 2, where I discussed various ways in which difference was prioritised at the expense of reconciliation. There I was mainly trying to show that none of these ways was helpful, since they left undisturbed the root problem prompting concern with reconciliation – how to overcome the antagonistic divisions that accompany many expressions of our differences – and that, in cases, they harboured very misleading notions of reconciliation's project. But I also indicated that these shortcomings might not exhaust their critical energy: they may still have the power to undermine the particular conception of reconciliation that I am advancing. I now want to test their subversive power by considering the doubts they raise about the possibility of commonality emerging from reasonable engagements with our differences. Thus I reintroduce, and discuss in more detail, the question of how experience of plurality can admit of commonality without plurality itself being denied. And I also provide another response to the claim that traditional differences in the North, which issue in conflicting identity claims, do not admit of reasonable resolution.

PLURALITY VERSUS COMMONALITY?

A fundamental doubt is that the very notion of commonality appears to fly in the face of the irreducible plurality of humans' experience of the world. It is as though the act of embracing difference is instantly compromised by practices of engagement, as soon as the latter are taken to involve searching for points of unity or a common good. This is to say that plurality is constitutive of our world in such a way that it denies commonality's legitimate possibility. Here commonality seems only illegitimately possible. This is most obviously the case when it is introduced as a violent cure to curb unruly expressions of plurality, such as when colonisers seek to bring the colonised to heel by destroying their local cultures and imposing upon them some brand of imperial unity. Less obviously, and potentially more damaging to the position I am advancing, it is also said to be the case where emphasis falls on commonality being arrived at through practices of democratic deliberation. 'To arrive at the common good it may be necessary to work through differences,' contends Young, 'but difference itself is something to be transcended, because it is partial and divisive.'[1] And this she thinks is unjust, because it favours the powerful and discriminates against the weak.

Doubt about commonality continues to plague, then, because commonality appears as a bogus quest, one that should be dispensed with if we are to remain faithful to the plurality displayed through human experience. As I have just depicted it, two principal assumptions underlie this expression of doubt, and neither is convincing. One is that a *sociological* generalisation can be invested with more philosophical weight than it can bear. The generalisation is that talk of a common good always betrays a strategy of the powerful to dominate the weak and therefore functions as a device to control difference. But the best that can be said about it is that it is contingently true, that is, there are many instances when this has been and is the case. What cannot be said is that it is necessarily true, that is, it cannot be taken to cover all possible instances. To put the point another way, under conditions of unfair interaction – where no attempt is made to offset the influence of unequal power relations – the generalisation has prima facie plausibility. And there is some substance to Young's contention that it holds even under certain conditions of democratic deliberation, as I indicate more fully later. There is, however, no reason to accept that it holds under the conditions of fair interaction I described previously, since these preclude the legitimacy of invoking the language of commonality to privilege dominant interests or to suppress difference.

More than a sociological generalisation is needed to vindicate doubt about commonality here. A second assumption, which makes a deeper and more *radical philosophical* attack, ostensibly supplies what is lacking. This is the assumption that plurality is so ingrained in humans' experience of things that any attempt to find points of commonality necessarily violates it. Now such an assumption may have multiple meanings. Among its more prominent are those that issue in something like the following pattern of reasoning: (1) endeavours to make sense of human experience produce a multiplicity of perspectives of the world; (2) these cannot be reconciled because there is no world independent of our various perspectives of it to which appeal can be made; (3) as a consequence, we are confronted with incommensurable discourses, which invoke non-comparable standards, and which we need to accept as such.[2] On these terms, the very idea of fair interactions is fanciful in principle. It is simply unrealisable and failure to recognise this cannot but entail a violation of plurality (such as the marginalisation of some inconvenient perspective or another). Thus, since the conditions of fair interactions cannot be fulfilled, the search for commonality is bogus. And they cannot be fulfilled because they wrongly imagine that experience of our world(s) can be other than it is for us.[3]

If true, such a radical pluralist pattern of reasoning is a devastating blow to the project of reconciliation. And this much can be conceded to it: that we do not enjoy unmediated access to the world as it is in itself, but only access mediated through our various descriptions; that our culture's perspective or description of things is only one amongst others; and that there is something spurious about the quest for commonality if what we really mean by it is getting others to agree to our way of doing and seeing things. But these concessions do not have to translate into a radical anti-commonality thesis. They do not have to be reduced to saying that one description is as good as another, or that one perspective is as valid as the next. Nor do they require us to say that, since all that matters is that our perspective is good/valid/true for us, there is little point in others trying to budge us or in us trying to budge them, or that all efforts at budging involve insidious grabs at power and control. In fact, these sorts of reductions are misplaced.

Given the broad sweep of the radical pluralist case, I first want to indicate at a general level why I think that its reductions are misconceived, why its insights become too exaggerated. Then I will say something more specific about radical pluralism's case in Northern Ireland. To start with an example far removed from the cultural and political issues at stake in the North, let us briefly consider the fact that there are different descriptions of the universe, which aim to explain its constituent features, causal factors, laws of motion, and so forth. To think of these as incommensurable discourses or as equally valid accounts borders on the absurd, as does thinking that they do not refer to a world independent of our perspectives of it.[4] For instance, most of us would be surprised today to find an adherent of Aristotelian science for the very good reason that post-Copernicus and post-Newton it just is impossible to believe that Aristotle got it right about the universe. This is not to say that we can be sure we have got it entirely right either. As Newton, say, superseded Aristotle, so Einstein in turn has superseded him, and scientific investigation into the constitution of the universe very much remains unfinished business.

The point is that certain types of descriptions open up new discoveries and are in turn refined in the light of them. Old descriptions are discarded because they cannot address the sorts of questions new discoveries raise, because they cease to offer fruitful lines of inquiry and explanation. So in the face of different descriptions of the universe, we are not reduced to saying merely that some post-Einsteinian one is true for us, just as Aristotle's was true for him. Some descriptions prove better than others in the sense that they afford a truer grasp of how the universe works. And this is something that we can expect different perspectives to enter into discussions about and in principle agree on. To suppose that we cannot hope to persuade any would-be Aristotelian that the earth is not the centre of the universe, for example, and that the categories of Aristotelian science have outlived their usefulness, is frankly astonishing.

This example prompts a general counter to the philosophical attack of radical pluralism, one that is close to the intellectual core of what I am calling strong reconciliation. We can admit plurality without forfeiting hope of commonality. And we can do so because it is possible to say that while we inhabit a world that discloses itself differently across cultures and civilisations, these disclosures allow for interaction, adjustment, alteration, abandonment, endorsement, and so forth. We are not destined to understand our world or to define ourselves only in terms of those disclosures, descriptions or perspectives that are most familiar. We may find insights in other disclosures that we wish to appropriate. We may find points of agreement or commonality with other perspectives. Of course, given the sheer variety of available perspectives, others' take on things may at times strike us as strange, if not bizarre. There may be a good deal of misunderstanding, incomprehension and talking at cross-purposes between us. And there may be too a temptation to reduce unfamiliar or uncongenial perspectives to the realm of myth or to depict them as instances of false consciousness, as we move to canonise our own. Indeed, part of the appeal of the radical pluralist argument lies in the reality of such a temptation: precisely because there have been many instances when the perspective of Western science, say, has been canonised and imperialist attitudes, intellectually as well as politically, have been exhibited to others, talk of commonality does appear as a mask for hegemonic control and suppression of difference.

To repeat an earlier point, the mistake is to posit these instances as illustrations of a necessary truth. I have suggested above that there are sound reasons why anyone concerned to grasp how the universe operates cannot reasonably avoid resorting to the discoveries of modern Western science. And it is just misleading to infer that the kind of common mind we may reach here, despite starting from different perspectives, is a violation of plurality or another (surreptitious) imposition of control. The problem with modern science lies elsewhere, namely with various of the items frequently packaged under its name: the pursuit and application of technological innovations regardless of their wider environmental and social consequences; the regulation of international economic development in accordance with the interests of global capital; the infiltration of market rationality into every area of institutional life, and so on. With regard to these, the radical pluralist assault has a lot going for it. There is much (dangerous) hubris that needs to be shed. In terms of how we understand our relation to nature through to how we organise our social and political affairs, we have to be open to insights from non-Western and even earlier Western sources. If, for instance, an Aristotelian approach to science has to give way to modern approaches, it is anything but evident that an Aristotelian approach to ethics has to do likewise.

In short, our current circumstances are characterised by considerable diversity and contestation in matters of politics, ethics and culture, and it is prudent to be wary of those claiming possession of easy, unifying, quick fixes to our disputes. None the less, it is also too facile, and ultimately too reductionistic, to conclude that plurality simply implies incommensurability and that all quests for unity or commonality betray some Nietzschean 'will to power'.[5] It is possible to tread a different path here: one that aspires to a 'fusion of horizons',[6] to use Gadamer's phrase, that is, one that envisages our conversations issuing in a conditional and open-ended reconciliation of our perspectives as we are together broadened out beyond our starting points. This is to anticipate forms of agreement and commonality that derive from taking plurality with the utmost seriousness.

Now, a suspicion may be that, however laudable, the aspiration to fuse and broaden horizons has limited applicability at best, and that it does not resonate in particular circumstances of serious division such as Northern Ireland's. Under these circumstances, indeed, a radical pluralist line may seem more convincing than I have so far allowed. For example, it is possible to read the history of Northern Ireland as an exemplification of the view that a will to power underlies attempts to unify disparate strands of social and political life. Of course, such a reading does not automatically vindicate the further claim that all reconciling attempts must invariably display this will too.

Such a dim assessment of the capacity of human agency to make a difference requires more argument. Among the additional appeals that a radical pluralist line might make here are the following. Unlike the reality of planetary movements, say, which continue on their course irrespective of our descriptions of them, cultural and political reality in Northern Ireland is partly constituted by our perspectives of it. In other words, any adequate account of this reality must accommodate its subject-related properties, namely the assortment of fears, hopes, prejudices, perceptions, analyses and priorities that make up so much of it. Moreover, precisely because the investments involved in our perspectives of cultural and political realities are so intense and because our differences here are often so fractious, the whole business of reaching agreement is altogether more complicated – it just cannot be compared with how we may imagine theoretical physicists settling their disputes. We are confronted, in short, with clashing interpretations that are deeply rooted in ways of life. These reflect different experiences; they invoke different standards; they represent incommensurable discourses. Sure, they may facilitate agreement to a form of mutual co-existence, a *modus vivendi* of sorts (although even here there are no guarantees), but nothing deeper. Attempts to go deeper, to talk of strong reconciliation or substantive commonality, unavoidably entail a diminution of one perspective and an enhancement of another. A will to power is never far away. Or so a radical pluralist argument might go.

I think the thrust of such an argument is profoundly mistaken. For a start, it implies a questionable set of moral priorities. I want to expand on this point shortly. To foreshadow it, I suggest it is troubling when moral hackles are raised at any mention of commonality for fear of a will to power being sneaked in whilst expressions of difference or plurality are given a free ride, even though the divisions that may accompany them are anything but morally benign. Furthermore, a radical pluralist account distorts the nature of our difficulties in the North. It is too easy to latch on to the idea of the alleged incommensurability of unionist and nationalist discourses, to excuse paltry attempts to work through our differences in a way that lessens divisions and permits the articulation of common purposes. At the very least, it is wildly implausible to suppose that reconciliation is impossible in the North because unionists and nationalists are so mysterious to each other that they find each other's interpretations or perspectives incomprehensible, and that they are consequently deprived of the resources that would allow their political and cultural trade to produce a set of common understandings.

This is not to deny that misunderstandings and misperceptions abound, that divisions continue and that shared commitment to common purposes is hard to engender and even harder to sustain. But these problems are more plausibly traced to a relative scarcity of engagement between major sections of our traditions, to the poor quality of the engagements that do occur, and to the fact that unionists and nationalists often disagree. And the crucial point is that these are things we can do something about: disagreements invite further discussion and deliberation, engagements can be increased and their quality improved. Recognising plurality and respecting difference does not have to imply abandoning hope in understanding others or in reaching substantial agreement about how we may together govern ourselves. It is at times a difficult hope to sustain, but that is not because it aims at something that is in principle beyond reach.

TRADITIONS, IDENTITIES AND REASON

This sort of counter to radical pluralism is not, admittedly, enough to see off the claim about incommensurable discourses. This much at least can still be said about it. The claim does not have to suppose that unionists and nationalists are utterly mysterious and incomprehensible to each other. It survives by simply insisting that their disagreements underscore the incommensurability of their discourses: they rely on non-comparable standards, which reflect different cultural–political orientations. Accordingly, it is not just a matter of increasing and improving the quality of engagements between unionists and nationalists in order to reach some common mind. Commonality, rather, can appear here only as an imposition, as the product not of reasoning but of an illicit act of suppression.

To reiterate, a worry with this argument is that it makes dialogue between unionists and nationalists on issues of fundamental concern seem futile. It encourages non-engagement. And if non-engagement is what we have, then it is easy to conclude that our enduring disagreements in Northern society confirm the claim about incommensurability. What continues to be underplayed is the difference that trying to understand each other better can make. Once it is conceded that through dialogue unionists and nationalists may seem less mysterious and incomprehensible to each other, then the prospect of their basic disagreements being resolved does appear in a brighter light than is being implied. But because there is no guarantee that this light will not be extinguished, there is a serious point about the nature of unionist and nationalist disagreements that has to be addressed. Here I want to link radical pluralism's challenge to a broader traditionalist challenge to the possibility of commonality. The point that persistent disagreements indicate incommensurability is profitably considered in conjunction with the familiar claim that divisions between the North's major traditions seem intractable.

With the advent of the Agreement, of course, we may doubt whether we are dealing with sheer intractability here: unionists and nationalists had to shift towards each other to allow it to happen; they had to adjust their traditional stances in a reconciling direction to accommodate changing political realities within Ireland, Britain and Europe. Even so, too many uncertainties afflict the Agreement. Too many divisions remain despite it, not least because antagonistic elements of the historical self-understandings of unionism and nationalism have not been dislodged. As a consequence, cultural tensions with subversive political potential are never far from the surface, as ongoing disputes about flags, police reform and marches illustrate. It is still possible, then, to object that the search for commonality through discussion of our differences in Northern Ireland must end in frustration: our dominant traditions are incompatible in crucial respects and the various identity claims made on their behalf cannot be negotiated. And if incompatibility and non-negotiability are our lot, then talking of the incommensurability of unionist and nationalist discourses seems entirely plausible.

The *incompatibility argument* has impressive credentials. Unequal power relations have constituted the relationship between unionism and nationalism; opposing constitutional priorities have constricted it; and dissimilar historical experiences and memories have stultified it. The Agreement suggests ways around the problems of power and constitutionalism, and I want to leave further consideration of these until Chapters 6 and 7. The remaining historical problem is partly what it is by virtue of its connection to the other two. Unfortunately, that does not mean that their easing implies it can be readily overcome. On the contrary, it is precisely because the North's major traditions have been shaped decisively by dissimilar experiences and memories that cultural apartheid exists between large sections of them. And, as I have been suggesting, it is this that is capable of undoing political progress at other levels.

We are undoubtedly faced, then, with antagonistic historical self-understandings, which strongly infer the incompatibility of the two traditions. Each relies on an exclusive narrative – of siege or of oppression – in which very different dates and events are celebrated. Just as 1690 and 1912 are important dates for unionists, so 1798 and 1916 are for nationalists and, more particularly, for republicans.[7] The meanings carried by the events these dates refer to nourish the dissimilar experiences and memories that reinforce cultural–political divisions in Northern Ireland. They screen out the claims and entitlements of the other tradition. So, if such meanings are constitutive of our traditional identities, how can we avoid conceding their incompatibility?

Possible answers lie in three considerations. First, traditional narratives, like any others, are partial. It is not inappropriate in principle, despite the acrimony any hint of revisionism attracts, to ask whether the meanings of celebrated events are not more complex than each tradition is comfortable admitting, and to probe what the implications of historical complexity might be for how unionist and nationalist identities are understood.[8] Second, it is equally appropriate to raise questions about events omitted from traditional canons, which suggest that antagonism has not been an invariant feature of relations between our main traditions, and which prompt alternative narratives capable of narrowing the divide between unionists and nationalists.[9] Third, it is not clear why we should assume that historical narratives, interpretations and identities that emphasise exclusiveness and antagonism must persist as inflexible fixtures, which cannot be adjusted to suit changing circumstances.

It is the cumulative effect of these three considerations that has the power to wear down the incompatibility argument. This is not to deny that various traditional expressions are incompatible, especially those anticipating the demise of the other. And it is not to say that traditional narratives of siege and oppression lack any credibility, or that there will not continue to be differences of opinion and emphasis between unionists and nationalists on account of their dissimilar historical experiences and memories. But it is to ask by what warrant differences between traditions have to be taken to imply irrecusably antagonistic divisions that must thwart any effort to occupy common ground. The ostensible warrant is that the identity claims made in the name of unionism or Protestantism and nationalism or Catholicism are *non-negotiable*. Conflicts between such claims cannot be resolved by reasoning because they do not appear in terms that permit the sort of reasoning that may be capable of resolving them. Let me say why I do not think those who present or conceive of identity claims in this way are entitled to bypass reason's interrogations.

Identities are not self-referential. They are tied to a variety of

beliefs, practices, institutions, and so on. They are also tied to interpretations of what they are not, that is, they typically define their
distinguishing features in contrast to those of other identities. So
when a tradition, say, calls for respect or recognition of what matters to it, its identity claims cannot be understood independently of
its essential ties or referents. Accordingly, we cannot, as it were,
subtract valued practices and interpretations of others from its
claims and simply respond to what remains. For after such subtrac-
tions there would be no distinctive identity left to make claims or
comments about.

This is all rather obvious, but it is worth reminding ourselves of,
when dealing with the proposition that clashes between competing
identity claims cannot be settled reasonably. The proposition's inescapable implication is that an identity's essential ties are off-limits to
reason too. This is an implication I find almost mystifying and certainly unconvincing.

Take a case where an affirmation of one identity involves a serious misrecognition of another. By misrecognition I mean, following Taylor, where an interpretation of others is projected that they
could not live with, one that distorts their own view of themselves.[10] As a consequence of our dissimilar historical experiences
and memories, there are plenty of such cases in Northern Ireland:
assuming that all Catholics are apologists of republican terror, for
instance, and feckless, untrustworthy subversives to boot; or that
all Protestants are apologists of Orange bigotry if not also loyalist
terror, and mean-spirited, tight-fisted supremacists into the bargain.
Familiar labels of abuse – 'Orangies'/'Jaffas' or 'Fenians'/'Taigs' –
are for many in the North part of an everyday discourse that conveys demeaning images of misrecognition of the other tradition and
locks the language of identity into a deep-seated sectarianism. The
clashing identity claims that feature in disputes about whether Loyal
Orange Order parades should be entitled to proceed along their traditional routes or whether they should be re-routed in the face of
objections from local residents, are infused with such images. The
intensity of these disputes is due in part to the fact that each of the
identities in question thinks it is being damagingly misrecognised

by the claims of the other.

How are we to respond to these types of disputes? My argument is that cases of misrecognition, and with them much else involved in identity claims, properly fall within the domain of practical reason. And since I envisage practical reason operating dialogically, under something like the conditions of fair interactions outlined earlier, I want to suggest that these cases do not prove that commonality is impossible in principle. Through reasonable intercultural debate, for example, it is possible to believe that we will discover grounds for abandoning our misrecognitions of others, altering practices that give unnecessary offence, changing the nature of the identity claims we wish to advance, and making commonality much more accessible. For, among other things, practical reason enables us to say at least the following. Affecting indifference to the misrecognition of others involved in our identity claims is highly irresponsible in Northern Ireland, since it lends spurious justification to sectarian attack, intimidation and murder. Misrecognising others is also unjust, since it inflicts cultural wounds that demean those who are perceived to be different from us. In addition, misrecognition distorts our sense of ourselves: it fails to appreciate our indebtedness to others, it promotes deluded notions of self-sufficiency and superiority, and it condemns us to a narrow, suspicious way of life that renders us incapable of understanding and being enriched by others. Finally, misrecognition entrenches cultural and political divisions and destroys prospects of achieving the sort of togetherness we need if we are to have a decent, workable society to which we all can belong and in which we all can share.

Saying these sorts of things doubtless invites controversy, but controversy of a particular kind: where interlocutors aim to persuade and to be persuaded by reasons. To avoid such controversy, that is, to think that identity claims have to be treated as nonnegotiable is to render reason's voice mute in cases of misrecognition. And this is to risk capitulating to those sectarian interests that refuse to submit identity claims and their alleged entitlements to an intercultural debate, even though doing so might, at the very least, help to resolve tensions over marches. To suppose capitulation can

be avoided by resorting to the old trick of trying to balance competing interests is not much help, since it dodges the issue of misrecognition altogether. Even if on some particular occasion a
compromise of interests is achieved, it is likely to be short-lived
because the root problem remains intact. To declare this problem –
misrecognition – out of bounds to reason assuredly is to dash hopes
of any commonality resulting from discussions of our differences,
but at an extremely exacting price.

This is a price that should give us considerable pause. It is one that
involves us treating existing identities as though they are facts of
nature rather than historical creations, which have emerged over
time and which remain open to change and development. It is also
a price that commits us to a potentially terrifying scenario: if practical reason is impotent here, then anyone may feel at liberty to conclude that misrecognition of others does not matter, regardless of
the consequences; or that what does matter is that one side has the
power to get away with asserting its identity claims at the expense
of another. It is not just that I think such a price is unconscionable: it
is also that I think it is one we should not have to contemplate paying because there is no good reason why we should give up on practical reason. The fact that identity claims are sometimes presented as
non-negotiable demands or entitlements may prove that there is a
lack of civic virtue in Northern Ireland, and that domination and
exclusion remain strong motives of action for some. But it does
not prove that differences of identity are not in principle susceptible
to forms of reasonable interchange that keep alive the possibility of
commonality. Those who think otherwise find themselves in
something of a bind. They risk surrendering to sectarianism, reify-
ing intransigent expressions of identity, and buying into a possibly
dangerous and morally bankrupt scenario. They are caught in the
awful tangles that are part of the price to be paid for pronouncing
practical reason impotent.

Acknowledging the facts of plurality, traditional animosities and
conflicting identity claims poses challenges to the reconciling enterprise of locating grounds of commonality through reasonable discussions of our differences. But it does not wreck this enterprise

altogether, especially since the aim is not to eliminate differences but to overcome the antagonistic divisions that often accompany them in Northern Ireland. Or, more correctly, it does not wreck it unless we push the incommensurability argument to the limit and buy an extreme, virtually anarchic, pluralist line, which holds that plurality is immune from evaluation of any kind. To buy extreme pluralism is, however, extraordinarily difficult. It is hard to imagine a world in which it could hold, namely a world in which differences enjoy unbridled expression whatever the consequence, one in which all thought and action is spared evaluative scrutiny. It is hard to know who would want to live in such a world for very long, and hard to know who would accept the conception of what it is to be a human being (devoid of morality and practical reason) that would be required in order to live in it. And it is not just that an extreme plur-alist line requires extraordinary beliefs; it is also self-defeating. Unbridled pluralism ranks among the least plausible defences of the plurality of human experience against domination, assimilation or eclipse, since it provides no grounds why anyone should respect anyone else's expression of difference and therefore makes enjoy-ment of difference an entirely precarious experience. Discounting this unlikely, and in my view incredible, line on pluralism, there is, I am claiming, no good reason why hopes of commonality emerg-ing through our differences should be abandoned.

COMMONALITY DESPITE DIFFERENCE

I also want to claim that it is possible to conceive of commonality despite our differences. There are a number of ways to advance this claim. We might, for instance, point to our occupation of the same land, to our having a language in common, to our similar social and economic needs, and even to our shared experience of a peculiar Northern culture of conflict, which sets us apart from the cultural experiences of other British and Irish citizens. All of these are important, and perhaps we are too dismissive of their significance in making an impact on how we think about our differences. Even so, none of them is sufficient on its own to give us a sense of commonality that is morally and politically robust enough to call difference's extravagances to account.

Instead I eventually want to make a great deal of the fact that we share a common humanity. If we think about this fact in a particular way, then we have, I will claim, a moral basis for curtailing obnoxious expressions of our cultural differences, and grounds for anticipating a common political life. This is to pursue a contestable line of argument. Even the least contestable core of the argument – namely that we share a common humanity – quickly becomes embroiled in controversy. The puzzle is why it does. For example, it is scarcely a matter of dispute to claim that we are all human beings. Few dispute that this implies more than a biological statement about our membership of the same species. It is widely accepted that the claim carries moral and political significance. Attempting to pin down its significance is, however, another matter. Here dispute seems unavoidable. That is why I am referring to commonality as a *possibility* that exists despite our differences. It is possible for us to agree on what the moral and political significance of our common humanity consists in, but it is not guaranteed that we will. This is partly because there is a tendency to allow our differences to overshadow just how much we do share. In a divided society, particularly, it is easy to lose sight of the obvious, or to reduce it to a banality. Thinking about commonality frequently becomes murky when we are constantly reminded of our differences. Here our points of separation often seem more engaging and readily acquire a disproportionate importance. In such a context, any attempt to restore balance can appear surprisingly controversial, because invocations of a common humanity threaten to depose difference's assumed sovereignty, which many of us have come to take for granted and perhaps to value.

There are, of course, better and worse ways of trying to usurp difference's putative sovereignty in the name of commonality. And discussion of these is unsurprisingly controversial. My attempt to propose what I hope is one of the better ways does not aspire to avoid controversy, especially since it is developed through criticisms of other attempts that I find unsatisfactory. It is expressly intended to serve two purposes: to discover common ground that is sufficiently spacious to accommodate reconciliation's political ideals and so make possible a common political life; and to provide a moral means of keeping difference's excesses in check. A certain way of understanding what we share in common, whatever our cultural differences, indicates what it might mean for these purposes to be realised, and why they deserve to be.

THIN COMMONALITY

Mention of such purposes is instantly controversial. It is, needless to say, likely to set alarm bells ringing among radical pluralists because it may appear to them to signal explicit endorsement of commonality as a device to suppress difference. But this is a misleading appearance. It is one that glosses over a crucial distinction between checking excesses and suppression, and that implies that moral and political discourse can get by without reference to some notion of commonality.

On the latter point, even *radical pluralism* – unless defined in terms that I have suggested are incredible – smuggles in its own, admittedly very thin and limited, notion of commonality. In doing so, it presumes what it denies, namely that despite our different perspectives and allegedly incommensurable discourses, we are capable of being persuaded by arguments and of reaching a common mind about something – even if only the 'approved' truth of plurality. Moreover, plurality is not just presented as a fact of experience about which we can agree in principle, but also as something we should respect. Reconciliation may not be a good thing, on these terms, but plurality is and respecting others and their differences is presumed to be a central good. Apparently, this is something that we as moral beings – in spite of our diverse values and cultures – should be able to agree on and amounts to a moral conviction or standard we may hold in common. Put another way, the standard is this: each culture is entitled to pursue its own way of being human, and this is something we should have no difficulty in accepting. This is an important standard, but (1) it is not clear why, if we are deemed capable of agreeing to it, we are not equally capable of reaching a common mind on much more besides; and (2) there are sound reasons why we need to look for more, since this standard cannot be plausibly regarded as an unqualified moral good or as exhausting the possibilities of commonality.

To restrict commonality's possibility to shared respect of plurality, for example, is to be hamstrung when it is not forthcoming, such as when a particular culture barely genuflects in its direction because moral/cultural superiority is integral to its self-understanding. A range of questions arises here, to which radical pluralism has no obvious answers. Does respect of plurality extend to respecting cultural expressions that treat plurality with contempt? How do we begin to persuade representatives of these expressions to share respect of plurality? Should we even try to persuade them if plurality is foreign to their cultural norms, or is a value that does not rate highly? Can insistence on plurality escape appearing as merely another peculiarly Western value that radical pluralists – in ironical mimicry of their despised cultural-imperialist predecessors – are simply attempting to impose on others? And, if it can avoid this accusation, can it duck the objection that respecting intolerant cultures as they pursue their own ways of being human is tantamount to excusing the (often violent) suppression of difference that occurs within them? The point is that to have anything worthwhile to say in response to such questions requires more than an invocation of plurality as a self-evident good. It requires resorting to deeper sources of commonality than radical pluralists are prepared to allow, but without which even respect of plurality appears as an arbitrary, confused and not always helpful moral value.

Here we need sources that enable us to draw the distinction between checking difference's excesses and suppressing difference. To collapse this distinction is to adopt dubious moral priorities: those that grant free rein to any display of cultural difference and treat any claim of commonality daring to go beyond respect of plurality as reprehensible. The ostensible justification of these priorities is that to allow considerations of commonality to temper or curtail plurality's displays is to commit an unwarranted act of suppression. But this justification is about as convincing as an objection to laws prohibiting murder because they suppress freedom. What gets lost here is that plurality, like freedom, is an important good, but not an unbounded one. And that is why it is crucial to distinguish between checking excesses and suppression.

At a pinch, there may be a case for rejecting this distinction, and for seeing any restriction of plurality in the name of a common humanity as morally inadmissible, if it can be shown that the murder/freedom analogy, or its equivalent, is utterly inappropriate. But this means showing that plurality's manifestations are always morally benign, that there are no excesses of difference that need pruning back. And this seems impossible. In fact, it is difficult to imagine how anyone could propose showing anything of the sort while keeping a straight face, not least in the context of Northern Ireland. As I have been stressing throughout, the reason why reconciliation remains a priority here is precisely because cultural differences often are taken to excessive extremes and exacerbate the sorts of antagonistic divisions that deepen sectarianism, produce violence and make a common political life so hard to achieve.

Radical pluralism cannot in my view successfully hold out against having some check to difference's excesses, or against the need to draw, therefore, on a thicker notion of commonality than that of a shared respect of plurality. But it can rightly counsel vigilance when potential checks and other notions are being considered, since these may too readily grant licence to exercises of suppression. The relevant fear to which radical pluralism gives voice is that moral and political prescriptions of commonality may overreach themselves, by proscribing quite legitimate ways of being human under the guise of merely curbing difference's extravagances. The difficult issue to be decided, then, is not whether it is necessary to distinguish between checking excesses and suppressing plurality – and I am unambiguously claiming that it is – but whether it is possible to articulate an understanding of commonality that respects and does adequate justice to the distinction.

A dominant line in contemporary moral and political thought, pressed most influentially and in different ways by John Rawls and Jürgen Habermas, says that it is possible, so long as we continue to limit commonality's scope. The best way of doing this, we may be told, is by concentrating on questions of what it is right to do, and leaving aside questions of what it is good to be. Three big assumptions are at play here. One is that the omitted questions involve issues that we can never hope to reach a common mind about, since they refer to substantive ethical ideals that are tied to particular ways of life. Commonality is inappropriately sought here, in other words, because what we are dealing with is the very stuff of our cultural (including religious, moral, and metaphysical) differences. Another assumption is that the permitted questions, by contrast, do lend themselves to agreement. This is because their answers can be encapsulated in rationally derived principles that we have access to independently of our substantive attachments. These principles are presumed conducive to commonality either because they are not mired by cultural particularity and are universal in nature (Habermas), or because they reflect a rational consensus within a (liberal democratic) society, one that is not biased towards any particular conception of the good life about which citizens typically disagree (Rawls). A third assumption is that the principles of right or justice that we can hold in common are properly regarded as regulative. They set the normative boundaries within which our various differences and visions of the good life may be freely pursued. Thus we have a proposed resolution of the commonality–difference conundrum: the possibility of commonality is affirmed in a manner that provides the necessary check to difference's excesses without any hint of plurality's suppression.

This resolution promises a neat way around very thorny difficulties, but I am not sure that it works. Considered in relation to societies like Northern Ireland, its limited conception of commonality's possibility arguably is too restricted to check a range of excesses that need checking, and entails a subtle suppression of difference. In other words, although it respects the distinction between checking and suppression, it does so inadequately.

Difference may be subtly suppressed, for instance, even when the intention is to protect it. This may occur when the priority of the right is asserted, even when we are told that principles of justice, say, can and should be decided upon without incurring debts to any substantive conception of the good. An example is when what Rawls calls *'reasonable pluralism'*[11] – which accommodates world-views and ways of life that are substantively incompatible and yet are respectful of a constitutional democratic regime and its legitimate laws – is permitted to flourish in liberal democratic societies, but when the substantive stuff of plurality, namely its various (contestable) reasons, is excluded from public debate or democratic deliberation about the principles that should shape society's basic institutions. Let me indicate why I think that suppression of difference may be involved here by picking up on important facets of Rawls's rationale.

In their personal lives, acknowledges Rawls, citizens may find it hard to conceive of themselves 'apart from certain religious, philosophical, and moral commitments, or from certain enduring attachments and loyalties'.[12] But, he argues, these should be bracketed for political purposes: (1) because they raise controversial issues we cannot expect to reach agreement on; and (2) because by bracketing them we thereby ensure that the basic institutional life of society is not shaped by any particular package of such commitments, attachments and loyalties. Instead this life should be organised in terms of principles of justice we can be expected to hold in common despite our larger differences, since they may be rationally derived independently of the stuff that divides us. By granting a regulative role to such principles, no substantive conception of the good enjoys special favour. Therefore, all of our deepest and principled differences are respected, and 'reasonable pluralism' is safeguarded, as the only constraint on us practising what we believe is having to operate within the terms allowed by those rationally agreed principles of justice that basic institutions of a constitutional democratic polity embody.

Despite its manifest concern to do justice to the plurality of views and identities found within contemporary liberal societies, this Rawlsian rationale entails a subtle and unpersuasive suppression of difference. The fact of suppression on these terms consists in the scarcely acknowledged bias inherent in its attempt to prioritise the right and thereby restrict the range of difference's expression. Take, for example, religious beliefs and values. For many believers faith or commitment is not adequately conceived of in private terms. On the contrary, being true to one's faith means for some striving for public recognition of religiously mandated beliefs and practices. To be excluded in principle from such striving does not signify respect for faith but secular prejudice against it. Accordingly, from the perspective of much religious belief, the attempt to protect society's basic institutions from political bias contains its own kind of bias, and the safeguarding of faith appears as its diminution. In short, what is being presented as a relatively uncontroversial view of society turns out to be a fuller, quite controversial view.

The question is whether there are good reasons to justify this controversial view, which secretes its own sort of bias and implies a certain kind of suppression. There conceivably are if we accept that it is always appropriate for us to do two things: to keep apart our identity as citizens and our identity as persons, and to suspend questions of the worth or truth of the practices and commitments that define the latter – and constitute our substantive notions of what is good – for the sake of agreeing on regulative principles that provide a basis for social co-operation. But neither of these things is always appropriate. If what matters most to a group of citizens is discriminated against on procedural grounds, which preclude even the possibility of a case being put in terms that are authentic to its self-understanding, then it is less than obvious why the person/citizen split in identity would be accepted. It is not clear why its members would prioritise an identity that unavoidably smacked of inauthenticity, or why belief in what is worthy and true would be suspended in deference to principles that deny such belief. It is hard to think that reasons that require these types of major concessions could qualify as good reasons for those who lose out most from them.

As a consequence, we may see the validity in an earlier noted point of Young's (even if it is not quite what she had in mind), namely that certain conditions of democratic deliberation do an injustice to difference in the name of commonality – in this case by precluding the possibility of difference's concerns featuring in the deliberations by which we articulate what we may share in common. To recall Tully's points, which I suggested should be included among the conditions of fair interactions, a just constitutional discussion is one that allows interlocutors to appear in terms true to their cultural identities, and that ensures the language of discussion or deliberation is not already biased to favour certain outcomes. The limited conception of commonality advocated by Rawls cannot meet these conditions of fair interactions, or avoid the accusation that it suppresses difference. And in leaving the reasons for our differences out of public deliberations, it underestimates their potential to undermine any conclusions we might reach. In a society in urgent need of reconciliation like Northern Ireland, where competing identities are vying for public recognition and entrenched differences are poised to wreck political deliberations, it offers an unlikely model precisely because its thin notion of commonality bypasses many of the issues that are at stake in our conflict.

If the quest for a reconciled society remains a priority, other worries emerge too. Whether such a limited conception of commonality, which subordinates concerns of the good to those of the right, is capable of checking all of the excesses that need checking is also a matter of doubt. To air this doubt let me turn from Rawls to Habermas, or at least to that bit of Habermas's complex theory that Shane O'Neill tells us is peculiarly equipped to help us sort out our difficulties in Northern Ireland.

O'Neill makes two fundamental claims of relevance here. The first is that 'we need a universalist standard by which we might evaluate opposed traditions or identities, or assess the extent to which the claims of either community [in Northern Ireland] are legitimate'.[13] Habermas's discourse ethics provides this standard by stipulating 'the procedural conditions by which a normatively justified solution [to conflict] could emerge'.[14] These set a 'procedural test' that substantive claims must pass in order to be normatively valid. They consist in universal rules of discourse – reciprocal accountability, inclusiveness, freedom to question claims and to propose counter-claims, non-coercion – that mark the legitimate procedural constraints on arguments we are entitled to make, that indicate the basis of rational agreement regarding the justness of a given norm. The second claim is that Habermas's contribution is crucial in Northern Ireland because it enables us to tackle the 'main obstacle to a normatively justified solution' to our difficulties – unionist 'blindness' to nationalist rights – by 'helping to discover what could motivate unionists' to reflect on and to transform those parts of their identity that produces such blindness.[15] In the midst of our differences, then, we have a common resort to universal procedural tests – integral to the structure of discourse – that check difference's excesses (such as unionism's typically inflated demands that close off nationalism's rights) by permitting us to say which claims are legitimate and which are not.

In the light of these claims, let's consider the appropriateness of the means being proposed to check difference's excesses. This involves asking how plausible it is to invoke a *universal procedural test* to do the work required in a divided society like Northern Ireland. Three questions seem pertinent.

For a start, why does O'Neill suppose that a universal procedural test, especially Habermas's version of it, provides a motivational key to move unionists to acts of critical reflection and transformation? If we accept the terms of his analysis – which depict a type of unionist blindness as the major source of the excesses that need checking and correcting by a Habermasian device – the supposition seems counterintuitive. It imagines political actors willingly submitting themselves to a test that, on O'Neill's terms, they cannot but fail. This is fanciful, and unionist demotivation seems a much more likely prospect here.

It may, of course, be objected that this is not the point, and that what is crucial is that unionists should be motivated in the way O'Neill prescribes. The second question, then, is why should they? Does O'Neill have compelling reasons why they should? As I understand them, his main reasons are roughly these: it is only by passing a universal procedural test that unionist claims can have normative validity, and it is only by undergoing such a test that unionists can avoid being caught in a performative contradiction – where the universal rules of discourse are relied upon in action even as their implications for action are denied. Now, to be compelling, these reasons have to be capable of trumping other reasons unionists may have for being unmoved by them. And it is unclear to me that they are.

For example, let's suppose that there are unionists, with views similar to Ian Paisley's, who are prepared to concede one of O'Neill's reasons but not the other. Habermas, they may say, is right about the universal rules of discourse, but wrong about these implying uniquely legitimate standards of normative validity. More authoritative standards, they may add, are divinely revealed through the Bible. In denying the normative force of universal proceduralism here, these unionists may allow that they are caught in a performative contradiction, but think that a few logical inconsistencies of this sort are neither here nor there. For what appears as inconsistency on Habermas's standards, appears as a defence of truth on theirs. And truth seems to them incomparably more important. Thus we have an impasse. What is normatively unacceptable according to Habermas's standards – refusing to recognise certain kinds of nationalist rights, for instance – seems justifiable according to a particular brand of unionist standards, since non-recognition of such rights is linked to alleged truths about Catholic error and the political threat it poses, and about how these should be treated. The rub, then, is this: when confronted by reasons for action that claim to be required by faithfulness to an authoritative source, it is not evident that appeals to procedural rectitude or logical consistency can possibly serve as trump cards. O'Neill seems deprived of the compelling reasons that would enable him to show recalcitrant unionists why they should be motivated above all else by universal procedural concerns.

A third question is prompted here: is measuring up to universal procedural criteria really the point in a society in need of reconciliation? The example I have just given indicates why for various unionists it may be anything but the point. One of the example's implications is that it may even be self-defeating to persist in privileging procedural criteria in circumstances of serious division. For doing so downplays the significance of other considerations that are certainly essential to achieving what I am calling a reconciled society, and arguably essential to achieving O'Neill's less ambitious goal of a just constitutional settlement in Northern Ireland.

To explain, let's take it that neither O'Neill nor myself are convinced of the legitimacy of the unionist case alluded to in the above example, and that we both regard it as an illustration of a problem that needs to be overcome, namely what he refers to as unionist blindness to the otherness of nationalists. If progress towards reconciliation or a just outcome in Northern Ireland involves tackling this problem, it seems self-defeating not to avail ourselves of the best means of doing so. One way of tackling it is to take unionist fundamentalists seriously on their own terms. Here we might (reasonably) try to convince them that they had misread their authoritative source; that it is, in fact, a distortion of the message of the New Testament to suppose that it prescribes or requires treating a particular category of human beings in a demeaning manner; that such prescriptions or requirements rely upon esoteric and implausible exegetical techniques. This is to contest the validity of their normative justifications of discrimination by disputing the truth claims on which they are based.

Another way of approaching the problem posed by this kind of unionist blindness is to give substantive reasons against its case for withholding rights on sectarian grounds. These are most likely to be reasons that derive from an inclusive understanding of human dignity. We might want to say, for example, that sectarian violations of this understanding are unacceptable because they offend our deepest moral self-understandings in the contemporary West. They are an affront to our democratic beliefs and practices. Part of the pitch, then, is to contend that sectarian discrimination is intolerable because it does not fit with a democratic way of life we value (and which most unionist fundamentalists claim to value too), because it misrepresents what we stand for. And the pitch may not stop here. Some of us might want to say at least this much more: that reasons for sectarianism that invoke a selective understanding of human dignity cannot match the strength of reasons against sectarianism that invoke an inclusive understanding; that this is the case because, at root, an inclusive understanding of human dignity is ethically superior and counts as a more authoritative moral ideal; and that a society in which sectarianism is denied a toehold is, in one crucial respect at least, better than a society in which it is not.

These ways of dealing with the problem at hand offer substantive reasons why the truth claims and normative recommendations of unionist fundamentalists do not deserve to be accorded legitimacy. They do not guarantee success of course. But by engaging certain unionists' core beliefs they pose difficulties that cannot be as easily shaken off as can charges of logical inconsistency. And yet O'Neill cannot avail himself of these lines of probing. They trespass Habermas's jealously guarded distinction between the substantive and the procedural, and his supporting distinctions between truth and rightness, and between ethics and morality.[16] As a consequence, I think he is in a fix. To repeat, if an important aim is to encourage unionists to reflect critically and to transform their identities, it seems self-defeating to close off these other, potentially very fruitful, lines of inquiry for the sake of procedural fastidiousness. It is also a little odd. For instance, one of the attractions of a good deal of what Habermas and O'Neill have to say about the universal rules of discourse – through their emphases on reciprocity, inclusiveness, freedom and non-coercion – is that they appear integrally linked to an inclusive understanding of human dignity. Indeed, the rules are arguably unintelligible in the absence of such an understanding. To separate these rules from a strong defence of why this understanding is a good thing – by insisting on category distinctions that are anything but obvious – seems more puzzling than illuminating. And, more importantly here, it stifles so many of the appeals that need to be made if unionists and others are to be motivated in ways that enhance the prospects of reconciliation and justice in Northern Ireland. This is to say that a universal procedural test is not the most appropriate means of checking difference's excesses, since it does not provide reasons suited to challenge many of the excesses in question.

In sum, limited understandings of commonality, whether radical pluralist, Rawlsian or Habermasian, do not give much hope of

being able to occupy the sort of common ground that reconciliation requires. Certainly, they point to certain things we may hold
in common despite our differences, most notably a set of basic rights
or principles of justice. But our possession of these is not dependent
on subscribing to the forms of reasoning advised by thin views of
commonality. More to the point, none of these forms adequately
handles the distinction between checking excesses and suppressing
differences. Radical pluralism has difficulty recognising it; Rawls is
open to the charge of subtly suppressing difference by restricting the
range of its voice; and there are any number of excesses that slip
through the net of Habermas's proposed checks. Two larger conclusions emerge from these inadequacies. One is that societies in
need of reconciliation are likely to remain seriously unreconciled if
we operate solely on the basis of any of their terms. Reconciling
ideals cannot operate as priorities here because they are deprived of
a politically significant role. And that, in turn, is because they are
not linked to a full enough view of commonality, since commonality is defined restrictively only in terms of what it is right to do.
We need more than is on offer in these extremely influential schools
of political thought.

THICK COMMONALITY

A fuller understanding of commonality is required to realise the
purposes I indicated were driving my interest here, namely to provide suitable checks to difference's excesses without foreclosing its
legitimate expressions, and to allow reconciling ideals the political
scope they need if they are to function as priorities in a divided
society. I have been hinting that such an understanding is possible.
Let me now build on these hints by explaining what I mean by a
fuller or thicker understanding of commonality, and by elucidating
the central characteristics I associate with it.

A *thick* understanding of commonality implies a certain sort of
content that we are capable of reaching agreement on as certain
sorts of persons. This is content that touches on what it is good to
be and not only on what it is right to do. It is content that we may
hold in common not as hypothetical or truncated selves, but as the

particular persons we are, that is, as persons defined by various commitments and loyalties. The rationale here is quite different from the rationales of the prominent thin understandings of commonality we have just discussed. It is not the Rawlsian one, which infers that in order to agree we may have to suspend consideration of what matters most to us. And it is not the Habermasian one, which presumes that what matters most must be answerable to universal procedural tests. The rationale, rather, is that reconciliation requires appeal to an understanding of commonality that directly engages what matters to us, and that it does so in terms not circumscribed in advance by inappropriate procedural constraints.

The pertinent question becomes, then, what it is that we in Northern Ireland may hold in common despite our differences, given the kind of beings we are, given the histories we have, given the violence we have inflicted and suffered, given the beliefs and practices we value, given, in short, the circumstances in which we find ourselves. Against the cynical view that our circumstances merely serve to underscore our divisions, I want to argue that a thick understanding of commonality is integral to what matters to us, even if it is frequently occluded by many expressions of our differences. By making explicit our reliance on such an understanding, we discover a means of checking difference's excesses and a basis for anticipating a common political life.

Now, it may seem peculiar to claim that a thick understanding of commonality is interwoven in our interpretations of what matters to us in the North, since it sits uneasily with much of our (antagonistic) experience. It appears less peculiar if the claim is linked to what I take to be the moral core of an affirmation of our common humanity, namely that we share a dignity by virtue of being persons. And its oddness continues to diminish if we also think that there is a dignity we share by virtue of being citizens. The notion of a common human dignity is certainly present in how we in Northern Ireland perceive of ourselves and of what is important to us, and the notion of a common citizen dignity is, arguably, implicitly present in our thinking too, although we are perhaps murkier about what it should mean. In both cases, the concept of dignity is imperfectly construed 'thinly', as it has inescapably 'thick' connotations. That is to say, it does not only point to right ways of treating others, but also to good ways of being.

Take the notion of a *common human dignity*, which I have referred to already on a number of occasions. This is a notion that is central to how we understand ourselves not only in Northern Ireland but, more generally, in the contemporary West. It is integral to the moral sources to which we resort in order to make moral sense of our lives, whether religious or secular. For some, probably the majority in Northern society, the notion is rooted in the Judaeo-Christian doctrine that all humans are created in the image of God. For others it derives from a tradition of Western humanism and receives paradigmatic expression in the Kantian view that dignity inheres in rational agency. As I suggested in Chapter 1, the notion inspires talk of human rights. And, as I maintained in discussion of Habermas, it underlies procedural concern with justice. A salutary function of these emphases on rights and justice is that they help to universalise thinking about human dignity; they highlight its inclusive reach. But neither emphasis exhausts the significance of the notion of human dignity. Not only do the religious and humanist sources I have mentioned, and which are explicitly or implicitly drawn upon by Northern Ireland's major traditions, take us deeper by telling us what it is that makes human beings worthy of respect, what it is that entitles them to rights and justice; they also indicate that there is more to affirming human dignity than producing catalogues of rights and procedures of justice. Practices and dispositions that characterise modes of life in which respect of others is deeply ingrained are also called for. Good ways of being are involved in taking seriously an affirmation of our common human dignity.

As noted previously, unease with linking commonality to modes of life and good ways of being springs from fear that some particular cultural/political/religious form will be granted normative privilege and imposed on others. Two responses are germane. The first is that in Northern Ireland there is cross-traditional support for such a link, that is, affirmation of our common dignity is embedded in ways of life with which we are all familiar. Accordingly, the task is not to impose something that will make one or other tradition or way of life resentful; it is, rather, to call upon something that is already shared, but which is sometimes lost sight of. In a sense, doing so poses no great difficulty, but in another sense it does.

The sense in which it is easy to invoke shared understandings here may be seen by reflecting on the rudimentary meaning of what acknowledging a common human dignity entails. Its meaning consists in the conviction that we are the kind of beings in whom dignity inheres and that this must incontrovertibly be the case if our lives are to have any moral contour. That is why it is morally impermissible to withhold recognition of the dignity of other beings of a similar kind. When in practice such recognition is withheld, attempts are typically made to camouflage what is going on. In cases, it may be implied that certain categories of humans – on account of their race, ethnicity, religion, gender, or whatever – are deficient in qualities that entitle them to be regarded as the kind of beings who possess intrinsic dignity. The fateful consequences of this type of thinking are inscribed in memories of the horrors of gas chambers invented in the name of high European civilisation in the twentieth century. Less dramatically, but still poignantly, they are also inscribed in memories of recent events in Northern Ireland, where sectarian-driven denials of the full humanity of others made atrocities easy for some to commit, and made murder almost casual. In recoiling from the barbarity of such acts, as the vast majority of us in the North do, we are saying that it is utterly arbitrary and intolerable to suggest that recognition of human dignity is dependent upon possession of characteristics that differentiate some human beings from others. For the suggestion makes nonsense of the notion of human dignity itself: it has the moral force that it does only because none of the differences that exist between persons are sufficient to deny the dignity of anyone.

It is relatively easy for most of us in the North to agree that our major traditions share a notion of the common human dignity of us all. And it matters a great deal to us that our particular tradition says so. We are rightly uncomfortable with atrocities committed in our name and do not doubt that a notion of our shared dignity should properly act as a moral check to gross excesses of difference. But recognising the dignity of others despite our differences cuts deeper than disowning extreme acts of violence. If most of us agree that such recognition is an important part of what our traditional identities stand for, as I think we do, then we must allow the possibility that it calls into question a 'them and us' mentality, which in practice often makes us less than vigilant in maintaining the dignity of others. Lapses of vigilance occur when we are ambiguous about the use of low-level violence to advance our cause, for example, or when we turn a blind eye to practices of discrimination, or of segregation, or of triumphalism, and so on.

The sense in which it is more difficult to count on shared understandings of a common dignity prevailing emerges here: when the interests of difference appear more pressing than concerns of commonality. This is most likely to be the case when a way of life or tradition is perceived to be under threat. In other words, while there remains in principle an acknowledgement of the dignity of all humans, under certain circumstances its full recognition may be relaxed for the sake of protecting an identity bound up with a cluster of specific differences – of religion, nationality, ethnicity, and so forth. As I have made plain already, and will continue to make plain later, voices of difference should not be prematurely silenced, and the claims of different identities deserve a fair hearing. But that does not mean they should be given licence to suspend recognition of our common dignity except when extreme violations of others' humanness are involved. Here we need to be clearer about what else hangs on an affirmation of a common dignity, regardless of the tensions that may be thereby created within ways of life that want simultaneously to uphold their distinctiveness.

One step towards becoming clearer is to see a connection between human dignity and human flourishing. The connection is this: dignity inheres in the capabilities humans possess – by virtue of their presence being regarded as evidence of our divine image, or our rational agency, or whatever – and flourishing relates to the exercise of these capabilities, or at least to having the opportunity to exercise them. The point of positing such a connection is not to invent another ruse for denying someone's dignity, as though it only applies to those who are exercising their capabilities in a certain way. In terms of dignity, possession of capabilities is what is decisive and not the use to which they are put. The point, rather, is to insist that any affirmation of others' dignity that is unaccompanied by a willingness to allow their flourishing appears too abstract, if not ultimately empty. Otherwise put, concern with dignity implies concern with how humans live; it suggests interest in their living well; it entails some idea of a good life.

Of course, this formulation of the connection between dignity and flourishing, with its specific invocation of a good life, re-introduces the fear that normative bias is unavoidable; that one person's/group's flourishing may be another's repression. A further response to this fear is to say with the North American philosopher Martha Nussbaum that the 'thick' conception of good living or flourishing that is being called upon is also 'vague', and is not loaded in favour of any particular tradition.[17] Two points are immediately important.

First, the emphasis on flourishing relates to what Nussbaum calls the 'basic human functional capabilities', which are recognised across cultures and which enable us to act in ways that are true, say, to our finite, embodied, sentient, reasoning, affiliated, recreational and separate beings.[18] Certain of these capabilities are shared with other species, but they acquire peculiarly human types of expression because of the 'special' and 'architectonic' role played by two capabilities in particular, practical reason and affiliation. As Nussbaum comments, 'all animals nourish themselves, use their senses, move about and so forth; what is distinctive and distinctively valuable to us about the human way of doing all this is that each and every one of these functions is, first of all, planned and organised by practical reason and, second, done with and to others'.[19] To be deprived of the use of some of these capabilities is to be condemned to a sub-human mode of existence, and to be deprived of the use of others may be to live a human life but certainly not a good one.

Second, the moral argument is that these capabilities should be cultivated in people's lives; it is not that they should be cultivated in a specific cultural form. There is deliberate vagueness about the forms in which we should love, grieve, eat, reflect, plan, engage with others, and so on, precisely because there are any number of perfectly acceptable ways of doing so; ways that reflect our different personal and cultural experiences and aspirations. So there is emphatically no agenda to impose the standards of some preferred culture or tradition on another. There is, however, a serious intention to query interests of difference that are disdainful of another group of people's entitlement to live lives in which their basic human functional capabilities may be acted upon and developed. To allow ourselves to feel the force of this query puts us in a position to grasp what else may hang on an affirmation of our common human dignity. That is, once we connect dignity to flourishing we see more clearly that the moral checks to difference's excesses are broadened and tightened. For whatever the value of our cultural differences – and I do not doubt that it is for many genuinely considerable – it is overrated when, as often happens in Northern society, it is coveted at the expense of a common dignity, when its price becomes so exorbitant that it deprives others of an opportunity to flourish. The commonality we share, as bearers of a human dignity, radically questions many of the practices and dispositions of difference that too readily translate into sectarian modes of contempt of others in much everyday life in the North.

It is a short step to move from an emphasis on human dignity, which stresses what we hold in common despite our differences, to an emphasis on *citizen dignity*, which gives anticipation of a common political life. Or at least it is if we continue a thread of thought that suggests something like this: certain of the capabilities conducive to our flourishing as human beings are equally, if not more obviously, conducive to our flourishing as citizens of particular societies. Put another way, it is doubtful whether various of the capabilities that pertain to humans *qua* humans – including crucial elements of the 'architectonic' capabilities of practical reason and affiliation – could be given adequate opportunities to develop in the absence of their application to citizens *qua* citizens. Quite simply, our belonging to societies is an indispensable condition of our flourishing as human beings, but it is a condition that is inadequately satisfied unless members of a society are accorded the dignity of citizens. There are complications with this line of reasoning in the case of Northern Ireland that I want to take up in Chapters 6 and 7. For now I give a quick sketch of what I think recognising the dignity of citizens entails, and of how it throws up the possibility of a common political life unfolding despite the intensity of our differences. The sketch has three main elements.

The first pertains to our commonly shared dignity as individual members of society who are treated as free and equal citizens. This element may be understood in both protective and opportunity terms. To understand it protectively means that citizens must have safeguards that shield them against violations of their dignity (including various forms of discrimination) by other citizens or by the state and its agencies. The language of rights is typically seen as indispensable here, inasmuch as it underscores the equal legal and political status of citizens. To understand citizen dignity in opportunity terms means that all citizens are entitled to live under conditions that make possible their flourishing. To be effective, the opportunity to flourish, to recognise and to choose valued options, must be more than a formal right to which we have a claim. Attention has to be given to inequalities in life conditions, both natural and social, which unfairly inhibit the development of some citizens' capabilities to flourish, and measures need to be undertaken to offset them.

Clearly, trying to do so confronts a problem of scarce resources, which may be particularly acute in certain societies, and which restricts the measures that can be devised. But there is also a problem of priorities, which dictate how a society's resources are used. To prioritise citizen dignity means using available resources to ensure that as far as possible all citizens are brought over a threshold into a situation in which their flourishing is conceivable. Thus we may expect in societies such as Northern Ireland that no citizens will be cut off from adequate health-care treatment, or from necessary social welfare provisions, or from desirable educational opportunities, or from enjoyment of civil and political liberties such as freedom of speech and the right to political participation; and that they will have employment prospects that guarantee non-degrading modes of work. What matters, in short, is that citizens are not denied opportunities to live well because of unfortunate external (material and social) circumstances or because of underdeveloped internal (mind and character) factors. Neither the self-interests of difference nor those of so-called economic rationalism may legitimately deprive any individuals of enjoying those meaningful opportunities to imagine and to pursue a good life upon which their flourishing as free and equal citizens depends.

A second element of citizen dignity involves recognising that citizens are culturally encumbered. Our human capability to form attachments and to affiliate with others very often is expressed through forms of cultural identity, which are crucial to citizens' self-esteem. As I have been stressing, differences between citizens are often at their most acute here and may be exploited to adverse political effect, which in practice denies the dignity of citizens who are perceived as culturally alien. But, as I argued in relation to the accommodating dimension of parity of esteem in Chapter 3, a powerful way of counteracting the divisive tendencies of difference in a society like Northern Ireland is to give equitable institutional and political recognition to our main cultural identities. Not to do so is to continue to privilege a majority identity only, and thereby risk the alienation of a substantial section of citizens. It is virtually to guarantee that society will be radically unreconciled. To speak of a common citizen dignity here may not be as misplaced as it seems. For it does not refer to citizens sharing a common culture, but to them having a common claim to cultural recognition. It is through acknowledging this claim and, in the circumstances of Northern Ireland, giving it institutional and political substance, that the self-esteem and dignity of citizens is affirmed. And this gives culturally different citizens a common stake in a society they can all call their own. Just as it is hard to see a society with worthwhile prospects for citizens functioning in the absence of the first element, so too is it hard to see Northern society overcoming its deepest problems if proper attention is not given to the second.

It is equally difficult to think that we can get along adequately without attending to a third element of citizen dignity, one which focuses on the possibility of a common civic identity developing through the institutions and practices of citizen self-rule and through the qualities of character that are appropriate to them. Understanding political participation as a primary political good is of the essence here, as is developing a sense of concern about the whole of society and its members and forming bonds with other citizens, not least with those who are culturally different. This is to project a political way of life, which requires for its realisation much more than appropriate rights legislation and procedures of justice. It requires too some conception of a common political good and, as I argued in Chapter 4, the cultivation of civic virtues among citizens. It opens up the prospect of us articulating agreed goals through our deliberations, and acts as another constraint on excessive expressions of our differences. No doubt Northern society wants for a shared sense of civic identity, but in its absence our understanding of ourselves as citizens is impoverished and we are missing a crucial element of any serious attempt to develop a common political life. There is, however, no law of nature or of history that denies the possibility of this sense emerging. It is more a matter of what we prioritise and why. Despite our differences, there is no good reason why commitment to a common citizen dignity should not translate into a common civic identity. And if we care about the society in which we live, there are compelling reasons why it should.

The three elements of citizen dignity – which for convenience, even if a little misleadingly (since all have political connotations), I will call the *individual*, the *cultural*, and the *political* – interrelate. Each is necessary to human flourishing and to the creation and maintenance of a decent society. There are, of course, tensions between them, particularly in Northern Ireland. Most conspicuously, problems with the cultural element impinge on aspects of the individual element and significantly stultify the development of the political element. I want to consider some of these problems in the next two chapters. But what these elements, separately and collectively, point to are possibilities of a sense of commonality

eventuating despite our differences and the difficulties they provoke. Grasping our shared human dignity and our potential citizen
dignity, and their relation to issues of how we may all live well,
suggests that if we are prepared to take seriously some of the claims
we make about what we stand for, then the quest for reconciliation
may not always appear elusive. And when commonality is defined
thickly, the ideals associated with this quest are given the political
scope they need to check our excesses of difference and to enable us
to work towards the realisation of a common political life.

CONCLUSION

Talk of reconciliation is idle if we cannot hope to occupy common
ground. I have tried to show that the hope may be reasonably entertained by drawing on two conceptions of commonality, which
enable us to recognise differences without being overwhelmed by
them. In defending these conceptions, and in interpreting them in
the ways I have, my concern has been to answer objections to
reconciliation that either deny it in principle or restrict its scope
unduly. Although, as I have indicated, the two conceptions and
their problems are properly treated separately, they also interrelate.
They may be in play simultaneously.

Take, once again, the issue of misrecognition. I have argued that
through reasonable discussions of our differences we may discover
grounds for discarding our misrecognitions of those who are different from us. If we are engaged in honest encounters with others it
becomes difficult to persist with our distorting stereotypes of them
in good faith, however much revision that implies for positions we
have an interest in maintaining. And it is this sort of consideration
that gives hope of commonality appearing through dialogue about
our differences. Now inasmuch as a consideration of this kind has
any plausibility at all, it is partly because it is also implicitly appealing to the idea that commonality is possible despite our differences.
Specifically, what is being invoked is our possession of a common
dignity as persons and/or as citizens. In other words, many of us are
moved to correct our misrecognitions of others – which we may

become properly aware of only through dialogical encounters, and which we may want to describe as wrong, unjust, or bad – precisely because they violate others' dignity. And, similarly, our concern for the dignity of others is likely to remain abstract until we are made acutely aware through interactions with them of just how damaging our misrecognitions are to their dignity. Thus the argument that commonality's prospects are enhanced through reasonable discussions of our differences is reinforced by the argument that commonality is possible despite our differences, and thus too the force of the latter very often depends on the openings provided by the former. As the case of misrecognition illustrates, the two frequently belong together. And together they reveal reconciliation's efficacy, its ability to erode our destructive divisions when the claims of commonality are permitted to operate as priorities.

These arguments have political salience. I have already indicated as much throughout this chapter. But to sharpen the political point, let me now turn to the final requirement of reconciliation I want to consider and to the political difficulties it faces in the current context of Northern society.

6

NORTHERN POLITICS
OF BELONGING

Belonging is the political requirement *par excellence* of reconciliation. Any society struggles to maintain its cohesion when enough of
its citizens become so disaffiliated that they consider themselves
strangers to its mores, or its laws, its basic institutions, its mode of
government, or indeed other citizens. And a society in which many
disaffiliated citizens are concentrated in tightly knit, relatively
enclosed enclaves, and are organised in their opposition to the state
to the point of trying to subvert it by any means possible, is a society
in serious crisis. For a generation this was more or less the fate of
Northern society. Perhaps it will be its fate again. At the moment,
there is the promise that it will not be, but only if the tentative signs
of an inclusive citizen belonging that have emerged through the
current peace process and political negotiations are permitted more
expansive expression. Citizens who cannot feel at home in the
society in which they live, who cannot say they belong to it in the
strong sense of being at ease within it, of identifying with its defining institutions and practices, or of being prepared to assume the
burdens and responsibilities that its proper functioning requires,
are unlikely to be in any mood for reconciliation. And a society
comprised of enough citizens like that is destined to remain radically
unreconciled for quite some time.

It is not difficult to appreciate, then, that inclusive citizen belonging is a cardinal political requirement of reconciliation. Laying out what its achievement consists in is a little harder to say, however, especially when we include the added complication haunting political deliberations in Northern Ireland, of a political entity whose legitimacy is in dispute. Of course, given the arguments of Chapters 4 and 5, we are not entirely clueless. The requirement of inclusive citizen belonging fits within the structure of what I have called strong reconciliation. It is integral to the goals of healing divisions and articulating common purposes, since in lieu of its satisfaction it is too much to believe these goals could be adequately realised. Moreover, without the requirement being met, any expansion of horizons within a divided society is likely to be limited, as exclusive orientations to belonging are not predisposed to criticise possible excesses in their own claims or to consider generously the claims of others. And inclusive citizen belonging is an improbable prospect if our dealings with one another are not conducted in certain ways and in a certain spirit. Quite simply, it presupposes the possibility of civic virtues being cultivated among citizens and embodied in practices of embrace and engagement that are constitutive of fair interactions.

So what is needed is a politics of belonging that both draws from and extends the arguments advanced thus far. Particular attention is due to the case sketched at the end of the previous chapter for locating common ground in an understanding of our shared dignity as citizens. Or, more especially, further consideration has to be paid to the quandary at the heart of the case: how to ensure that disputes at the level of our cultural dignity as citizens (between apparently conflicting communal/national conceptions of Britishness and Irishness) can be sorted out in a way that also recognises our individual dignity as free and equal citizens, and that facilitates development of our political dignity as self-governing citizens. For it is inconceivable that the requirement of inclusive citizen belonging could be sufficiently met independently of tackling such a quandary. The arguments for strong reconciliation offered already have been of service here. Most importantly, they help to identify that it is a quandary framed in terms of relations between different modes of citizenship, that poses perhaps the greatest obstacle to inclusive citizen belonging. They also give hints about how to resolve it. But they need extending into the contemporary political circumstances of Northern society in order to be convincing. And here fresh challenges have to be met.

These include having to confront opposing tendencies within unionism and nationalism on questions of political legitimacy and political priorities; tendencies that reflect dissimilar experiences and aspirations, and that inspire antagonistic practices. Such tendencies and their associated props are susceptible to a negative spin that makes the challenges here seem too formidable. The spin amounts to saying something like this: the obstacles posed by reconciliation's political quandary cannot be overcome because in the competition between unionist and nationalist politics of belonging – which dominates Northern political life – reconciliation is not rated highly enough to allow it; accordingly, talk of fair interactions, possibilities of commonality, and so forth, are simply confounded by the sheer stubbornness of emphases on communal/national differences and incompatible political outcomes that are integral to Northern politics of belonging; so however philosophically compelling it may seem, inclusive citizen belonging is doomed to remain a theoretical dream.

This negative spin captures part of the political story of Northern Ireland today, but not its whole. The current political circumstances of the North are also amenable to a more positive spin. Its message is simple. The Agreement happened; a majority of parties and a majority of citizens supported it; it ostensibly settles disputes about legitimacy and takes the sting out of other issues of aggravation between unionists and nationalists. The Agreement provides for inclusive citizen belonging and gives hope of its central quandary being resolved. Political reconciliation is, therefore, more than a mere philosophical or pious yearning; its practical possibilities are at hand. Of course, difficulties with the implementation of the Agreement temper confidence in the reliability of this positive spin, but it cannot be dismissed willy-nilly. And, at present, we appear caught between the different scenarios represented by the two spins, as debate continues about the Agreement and its future.

It is in the context of this debate that I want to finish my argument for strong reconciliation, by focusing on the issue of belonging. This argument spreads over two chapters. As I have intimated, within the North belonging appears as a complex cultural and political ideal, which calls upon multi-faceted experiences and aspirations. In this chapter I want to retrace some of the ground already covered from another angle. I also venture into fresh territory and set the scene for the completion of the argument on belonging and reconciliation in Chapter 7. In particular, I now want to suggest that inclusive citizen belonging proves such a difficult requirement to meet partly because matters of belonging are entangled with matters of identity. The forms of their entanglement in the history of Northern society reveal varying experiences of unionists and nationalists, and touch on a raw nerve in relations between them. Conflicting political predispositions are involved in their respective searches for modes of belonging that tally with concerns of identity. These disclose cultural and political barriers, reinforced by considerable emotional and existential investments, to the aspiration of inclusive citizen belonging. But they also manifest hopeful possibilities. I then propose that barriers to and possibilities of inclusivity are further illuminated by attending to aspects of the Agreement and its aftermath in Northern society.

The Agreement attempts to give substance to the prospect of inclusive citizen belonging, but its attempt risks being thwarted through the rejections of its opponents and the conflicting interpretations of its supporters. I maintain that a common way of trying to avert these risks to the Agreement – by adopting what I refer to as a type of pragmatic muddling through – is not sufficient. It pays scant attention to larger problems of different political priorities, views of legitimacy and divisive practices, which are linked to contrasting experiences of belonging and identity, and which cannot be avoided if attaining a reconciled society remains a worthy goal. These problems are taken up in the final chapter.

BELONGING AND IDENTITY

A large part of the reason why questions of belonging assume central importance in the politics of a divided society is because they are closely associated with questions of identity. This may seem an odd claim to those who wear their cultural and/or political identities lightly. It probably raises eyebrows among those cosmopolitans whose identities are ostensibly immune to the pull of attachments to a particular tradition or society. Likewise with thoroughgoing or radical individualists for whom cultural and political allegiances are little more than unwelcome, even if at times necessary, encumbrances. And it is much the same for those post-modern citizens who, according to Young, aspire to be 'strangers' in society, moving without disapproval or hindrance between their various identities.[1] In each of these instances, belonging in the sense of affiliating strongly with the public ethos, practices and institutions of a society scarcely ranks as a political priority, principally because it is not significantly implicated in any of the senses of identity that are valued.

Perhaps Northern society has its share of cosmopolitans, radical individualists and post-modern citizens. But their agendas neither influence the course of Northern politics nor suggest obvious ways through its difficulties. Whether this is regrettable is open to debate, since citizens who are disinclined to develop substantial ties to the common institutions and political life of their society offer unlikely vehicles for healing antagonistic rifts between traditions. And the reality remains that Northern politics is riven by divisions between citizens who want their different identities publicly affirmed and whose sense of belonging is dependent upon this want being satisfied. Unless it can be satisfied, stark divisions will persist. Thus the unavoidable political question that any serious concern with reconciliation must face: how is an inclusive citizen belonging possible?

There are no slick answers to this question. And there is little use in evasive strategies that avoid tackling it head-on in the forlorn hope that Northern society can function effectively regardless. The issues involved run too deep to excuse either slickness or evasion. A glimpse of their depth is afforded by appreciating the nature of the interrelationship between belonging and identity for many citizens in Northern Ireland (and elsewhere), which may be formulated like this: our sense of belonging is incomplete without adequate recognition of our identity in society, and our sense of identity is distorted in the absence of us fully belonging. This formulation invites thinking of our (collective) experiences of identity and belonging in the North in terms of a continuum stretching from the unproblematic at one end to the deeply disconcerting at the other. Our experience is unproblematic when we are self-assured about our identities and fit comfortably within the fabric of society. This is when we enjoy the self-clarity of knowing who we are, when we are oriented to our circumstances in a way that enables us to take a stand accurately reflecting what we are about, and when we find ourselves at home as citizens. Our experience is deeply disconcerting, in contrast, when we are riddled with doubt about our identities and/or are disaffected within society. This is when we suffer the self-confusion of being unsure about who we are, or when we become so disoriented that we are either incapable of taking a stand or uncertain that the stand we do take properly defines what we are about, and when we are alienated as citizens.

In Northern Ireland experience has rarely been entirely unproblematic or deeply disconcerting in the senses I have just described. But, at different times, it has tended more to one pole than the other for both unionists and nationalists. Following partition, and for fifty years of devolved government, unionist experience came close to being unproblematic and nationalist close to deeply disconcerting. Since the conflict, and particularly since the current peace process, there has been a reversal in these experiences. Now it is nationalists who are more upbeat and unionists decidedly more downbeat, even if political arrangements (in the obvious sense that they continue to fall within the ambit of British rule) remain in unionism's favour. But it is the fact that throughout the history of Northern Ireland a gain in one tradition's experience is perceived as another's loss that suggests the difficulty of meeting reconciliation's political requirement of inclusive citizen belonging. A quick glance at each tradition's different plays on central themes of identity and belonging – self-clarity, orientation and being at home – throw this difficulty into sharper relief.

NATIONALIST EXPERIENCE

It may not be too misleading to describe nationalist and republican experience[2] as a movement *from the (almost) deeply disconcerting towards the (almost) unproblematic*. Its initial negative character, in the years following partition, was due to at least three factors, which illuminate nationalists' and republicans' inability to feel at home in society then. First, they were alienated within the North: they opposed and resented partition, they were locked into a state they regarded as culturally and politically foreign, they were politically disempowered, and they suffered social discrimination in areas such as employment, housing, and so forth. Second, Northern nationalists and republicans were relatively estranged from the South. They were reduced to bystanders as their Southern compatriots set about the task of building a new state and society. And whatever the formal consolations of the 1937 Irish constitution's *de jure* claim to the territory of the entire island, it was the *de facto* reality of partition that counted practically, and many felt abandoned by the South. Third, Northern nationalists and republicans had never lived in a society to which they fully belonged, and thus were deprived even of its memory. Pre-partition Ireland was subject to British control, and it was only in the aftermath of partition that the South acquired independence and self-rule.

The aspiration to belong continued to be linked to hope of an eventually united Irish nation. If, as the social theorist Benedict Anderson remarks, the notion of the nation evokes 'an imagined political community',[3] the imaginative creativity required of Northern nationalists and republicans – disaffected with their condition, cut off from their fellow nationals, and dreaming of a political world yet to be born – was considerable. Wistful romanticism may conjure up and occasionally indulge such creativity, but only a robust sense of identity seems capable of sustaining it. Yet prior to the late 1960s there was not much sign of a robust Irish

identity asserting itself publicly in the North. In terms of an orientation to their circumstances, some nationalists justified their relative
absence from public life by invoking a principle of political abstentionism, while others appeared to take a stand somewhere between
resignation and quiet non-conformity. An abortive, poorly supported IRA campaign between 1956 and 1962, and the efforts of a
handful of nationalist politicians aside, little was done explicitly to
oppose the Northern state or to exert influence within it.

Reluctance to take a public stand in Northern political life did
not necessarily imply the disintegration of nationalism, however,
or widespread confusion within its ranks. Sinn Féin chairperson
Mitchel McLaughlin, for example, argues that it 'is a paradox of
the Northern situation that the sense of Irish identity held by the
nationalist community in the North has thrived'.[4] The lack of con-
genial political circumstances may have made its expression and
enjoyment incomplete, but that does not mean that an Irish identity
wanted for self-clarity. Or so it seems now. We may speculate
whether McLaughlin's claim would have looked quite so plausible
in the mid-1960s, say, especially given the dearth of active republican sentiment at that time. And we may wonder what would have
become of it had unionists made greater effort to integrate nationalists within Northern society. None the less, in retrospect the claim
probably had some resonance even during the period of nationalism's bleakest prospects in Northern Ireland. The Irish identity
McLaughlin celebrates has been shaped by adversity and, in the
absence of endorsement in the political structures of the North, has
been nurtured and sustained beyond unionism's gaze through a
range of intracultural practices and institutions.

So in spite of the frustrations and inequalities, not to mention the
humiliations, that many nationalists endured during the years of
unionist rule, their experience, arguably, did not descend utterly
into a deeply disconcerting state because of the cultural resources at
their disposal. The more overtly political harnessing of these
resources in the last thirty years – captured in the demand of parity
of esteem for an Irish identity – together with new forms and
strategies of action have transformed nationalist experience.

Numerous factors left unexplored here are involved in explaining this turnaround, including unionist overreaction to modest requests for equal civil rights, subsequent unionist loss of power and fragmentation, changes in British–Irish political relations and policies, and reassessments of nationalist and republican agendas. The upshot is not that nationalist experience is now unproblematic, but that it has become more self-confident and altogether less problematic than at any time since partition.

Nationalists now adopt a different orientation to their circumstances. Through the Social Democratic and Labour Party (SDLP) and Sinn Féin they are organised into efficient political machines and are devoted to influencing political affairs in Northern Ireland, if not also to hastening the day of the North's incorporation within an Irish republic. Currently, both parties are committed to pursuing their objectives through political means alone. For long years of the conflict, however, it was not always so. Prior to the first Provisional IRA ceasefire in 1994, republicans concentrated their efforts on winning a victory for Irish unity and were quite prepared to use armed struggle to do so. The Northern party of constitutional nationalism, the SDLP, opposed this option of force and its privileging of unity over reform of Northern society. Thus, within the broad family of a re-energised nationalism different orientations were apparent and with them different opinions of what taking a stand should entail. Whereas some (republicans) were prepared to accept that a paramilitary stand against British rule reflected much of what nationalists were about, others (constitutional nationalists) were not. Of course, republicans did not think that this stand reflected everything they were about, but constitutional nationalists thought it distorted what nationalism stood for. With the new consensus that nationalist goals are best pursued through taking an exclusively political stand, the gap between the two sides of nationalism has narrowed: both now stand for immediate reform of Northern society and the longer-term goal of Irish unity. But there still are differences. For republicans, the goal of unity rates more highly and reform of Northern society is often understood more radically.[5]

Overlaps and differences in orientation between constitutional nationalists and republicans are underpinned by their understandings of the identity that their various stands are intended to represent. If nationalists have been relatively untroubled about their sense of an Irish identity – as McLaughlin's claim indicates – it is not because it has not been subject to reinterpretations. Of course, there may well be a residual cultural core that is retained through these reinterpretations, as expressed, say, through music, art and the Irish language. But it is noticeable that the political articulations first of the SDLP and more lately of Sinn Féin attest to a shift away from the image of a Catholic, Gaelic exclusivism that seemed to do so much nurturing work when nationalists were a considerably less visible political force within Northern society. Whatever their membership composition and support base, for instance, neither party officially attaches any political significance to Catholicism *per se*. And even if it is the case that Sinn Féin continues to carry more overt cultural baggage – by utilising cultural symbols for political ends, actively championing renewals of interest in the Irish language, and so on – it rejects suggestions that it is intent on peddling any type of sectarian particularism. Importantly, shifts in Northern nationalists' self-understandings, especially those promoted by the SDLP, coincide with shifts within Southern politics. There the influence of Catholicism has waned considerably, particularly since Ireland's membership of the European Union, and changes to the character of Southern society and the state have seen the South develop into a more fully pluralist liberal democracy.

At present, the identity represented by the SDLP is not only discernibly Irish, but European too. And, crucially, it incorporates pluralist, democratic and egalitarian norms. For Sinn Féin there is less tempering of cultural Irishness through European influences, but there is an increasing play on similar norms, even if they are on occasions taken to have different applications to Northern politics. Interestingly, both parties share the assumption that recognition of an Irish identity in Northern society is entirely compatible with – or more strongly is required by – an affirmation of these norms. And an important part of the confidence and self-clarity of Northern nationalism is revealed here: in the conviction that there is a neat fit between the cultural and political dimensions of nationalists' self-definitions.

Nationalists' confidence and clarity about who they are do not, of course, imply that they are now uncomplicatedly at home as citizens, especially in a divided society with an uncertain political future. And it is questionable if many republicans imagine being properly at home in a society that falls short of a united Ireland. For the SDLP such imagining is a little easier given its emphasis on uniting divided people rather than divided territory. This is an emphasis that is claimed to be suited to the changing political realities of our times. The need to achieve a united and independent sovereign Irish nation state is less pressing than it once seemed because of the growth of integration and regionalism in Europe – which, in conjunction with other global economic factors, is said to make thinking exclusively in terms of nation states increasingly outmoded – and because of what is on offer in the Agreement. The Agreement's promise of a reformed Northern Ireland with institutional links to the South appears to satisfy SDLP aspirations to belong for the moment, while leaving open the possibility of future movement in an all-Ireland direction. Although for Sinn Féin the goal of a united Ireland is not so easily sidelined by developments in Europe and Northern Ireland, republicans too are committed to reform of Northern society and not just its subversion. The fact that both Sinn Féin and the SDLP now are part of the government of the North and are intent on shaping its character in a way inclusive of Irish nationalism and republicanism at once makes nationalists and republicans more comfortable with their circumstances than they have ever been. And for many, especially within Sinn Féin, all of this is merely a forerunner to the eventual completion of their aspiration to belong within a new set of all-Ireland arrangements.

UNIONIST EXPERIENCE

In contrast to the experience of nationalists and republicans, unionist experience reads more like a movement in the opposite direction: *from the (almost) unproblematic towards the (almost) deeply disconcerting.*

Initial reservations about twenty-six counties of Ireland being lost from the Union were quickly overcome when unionist resistance to Irish Home Rule was rewarded through the invention of a polity with an in-built and substantial unionist majority. In 1921 Northern Ireland was created basically in unionism's image and was ruled for five decades by the UUP. During this period, unionists were more or less at home as citizens of the UK and as members of a Northern society whose major institutions reflected their power and an exclusively British identity. Even if this identity came in different brands in Northern Ireland – with some more stridently Protestant than others – such differences were of little consequence until much later.

For the greater part of the period of their rule, unionists were relatively unconcerned by questions of identity, not least because their 'Ulster' variants of Britishness rarely came under external scrutiny. Most got by most of the time with a set of simple reassurances: that they were not part of Catholic, Gaelic Ireland but, rather, were members of a larger British family whose locus of unity was in the Crown; that they had their own parliament in their own society; and that they had the numbers to ensure continuation of their position of security and privilege. These reassurances shaped their orientation to their circumstances. They had taken a stand against incorporation in an Irish Free State, in which they would have been a minority, and would continue to take a stand where necessary to protect their Britishness and the integrity of Northern Ireland.

Unionist experience for nearly fifty years, then, seemed largely, but not wholly, unproblematic. Perhaps it should have been wholly unproblematic given how heavily the dice was loaded in unionism's favour. And, arguably, the problems that prevented development of a relaxed, self-confident unionist mode of belonging were mainly of its own making. These problems, such as they were, congregated around the element of uncertainty that ran through unionist politics. For instance, despite its advantages and guaranteed electoral majority, the UUP contrived to make the border – and therefore the continuing existence of Northern Ireland – the central issue of every election campaign. Thus unionism's renowned siege mentality and fear of Catholic Ireland were never properly put to rest. Thus, too, Northern nationalists remained objects of suspicion, whose minimal claims to equal civil rights – in line with British norms and practice – were perceived to be full of subversive intent. The upshot was that even under optimal conditions there was a twitchy edge to much unionist experience: unionists were never quite as at ease within *their* Northern Ireland as might have been expected.

If they had a mind to (though few it seems do), contemporary unionists could cite good reasons for ruing the short-sightedness of earlier unionist politicians. The latter's failure to integrate national-ists into Northern society, even going so far as to react against the suggestion that they were entitled to equal civil rights, proved the undoing of unionist rule in Northern Ireland when the British gov-ernment prorogued Stormont in 1972. And it also gave ironical substance to unionist fears about the future of their society, as a revi-talised and increasingly radicalised nationalism began to demand much more than fair housing, employment and voting practices. Currently, unionists are expected to accept changes in Northern politics and society that would have been unthinkable to their pre-decessors: sharing power with nationalists and republicans, recog-nising the Irishness as well as the Britishness of the North, allowing that the Irish government is legitimately involved in aspects of Northern political life, co-operating in North–South institutions alongside representatives from the Dáil, and so on. It is not only that many unionists cannot stomach these changes; it is also that they think acquiescing to them signals that Northern Ireland's days as a constituent part of the UK are numbered, that conceding them is tantamount to conceding victory to republicanism.

Other unionists are not quite so apocalyptic in their analysis of what is being required of unionism today. But that does not mean they are not uneasy. There manifestly is a general unease within unionism that is exacerbated by two additional factors: (1) the fact that they have explicitly been at odds with various British govern-ment policies and initiatives since 1972, and have little trust in Brit-ish intentions; and (2) the fact that the unionist majority in

Northern Ireland has been significantly reduced to the point where, although holding overall, it is now decisive in only two out of six counties (Antrim and Down), which themselves include a Belfast that is not at all the bastion of unionism it used to be.[6] In short, unionism's predicament has become sharp, and unionist experience since the outbreak of the conflict in the late 1960s has shifted markedly towards the deeply disconcerting pole.

Take unionism's orientation to its circumstances during this period. Conventional unionist wisdom has it that unionism's strength lies in its unity of purpose: by standing for maintenance of the Union and against perceived threats to it, including diminutions of British sovereignty and of the British character of society. This is what won the prize of a unionist-dominated Northern Ireland in the first place. Since losing an important chunk of that prize in 1972 – domination – unionists have been fighting a series of rearguard actions to shore up their position. But, if there is little doubting their unity of purpose, only rarely have they exhibited unity of action in doing so, and even unified purposeful action does not function as the trump card it once did. For fragmentation is now more typical than unity within unionism and unionist unity is no longer a guarantee of success anyway.

Sure, there is still unity of purpose among unionists, namely to defend the Union. But the political organisation for translating this purpose into concerted action – the UUP – has fragmented. Even if it remains, in the current, diminished form of the UUP, the largest party of unionism, it does so barely and there is now a proliferation of unionist/loyalist parties and paramilitary organisations. Accordingly, there are diverse opinions about how unionism's interests are best served. This loss of political unity has implications for unionism's orientation. The problem is not that there is now such confusion within unionism that the will to take a stand has weakened. It is more that there is confusion about which stands are the most appropriate to take. Many unionists are convinced that the stands of other unionists are misguided if not wrong, that they hinder rather than help the shared purpose of defending the Union.

Paramilitary activities are an obvious example. These typically perplex a majority of unionists because of their propensity to result in atrocities that are morally repugnant and dishonouring to what unionists are about. They also perplex because, in the name of protecting the Union (however indirectly), they threaten to undermine it by implying alternative sources of authority to those provided by British law and forces of the Crown. Various protests against perceived violations of unionist entitlements are another example. Protests taking an expressly sectarian and intimidating form – whether directed against Catholic churchgoers at Harryville in Ballymena, County Antrim, for example, or Catholic schoolchildren in the Ardoyne area of Belfast – appear to scandalise the cause of unionism except in the eyes of unreconstructed bigots.[7] But the most important example, at least politically, is that of the different stands taken over the Agreement within unionism. As I shall make plainer shortly, the differences here are not as great as they sometimes seem. But the confusions are.

The crux issue for unionists is whether the best way to protect the Union is by being for or against the Agreement. Bearing in mind that the Agreement decidedly was not the product of any unionist imagination, even though some unionists were involved in negotiating it, this comes down to asking whether it represents as good a deal as unionism can now hope for. If it does, then it is foolhardy to oppose it, but if it does not, then it is imprudent to give it support. Anti-Agreement unionists appear much surer that they have the right answer, with many of their pro-Agreement colleagues seeming scarcely able to hide their equivocations and misgivings. As a consequence, confusing signals are sent out as to what unionists are about: whether they are properly for or against the Agreement; what it means to be for it if most of the reasons given for being against it are accepted; and what it means for unionists to be against it if they have to share Northern Ireland with nationalists and republicans who are assuredly for it.

It is possible to reduce the range of these confusions by unionists regaining a semblance of unity. They have done so in the past when faced with crises that put their differences in the shade. And they may do so again. At present, and despite Trimble's occasional efforts to claim that the Agreement has strengthened unionism's hand,[8] this seems possible only on anti-Agreement terms. For unionism *en bloc* to take an anti-Agreement stand, however, is not the simple solution that some unionists want to believe. It promises to reduce confusion, but does not eliminate it. Instead, it relocates it in relation to the problem of creating a Northern Ireland capable of winning nationalist and republican support. Given that unionist objections to the Agreement are that it gives nationalists and republicans too much, this is a stiff assignment.

The unavoidable reality is that the old unionist tactic of recoiling from the so-called otherness of nationalists is now much harder to get away with, and nationalists cannot be ignored or treated as lesser citizens without gambling with the future of Northern Ireland itself. And this is largely because unified purposeful action of an anti-nationalist sort has ceased to cut the same ice with the British government as it did previously. It may have delivered partition in the past and have sunk the Sunningdale Agreement, with its proposals of a power-sharing executive and Council of Ireland, in 1974. But it did not sink the Anglo-Irish Agreement in 1985, which only became defunct because it was replaced by the Agreement in 1998. Of course, it is capable of sinking the Agreement, but that does not mean that unionists would emerge as victors. Indeed, on their own terms, displays of united unionist defiance against concessions to nationalism over the last thirty years have failed rather miserably. And adopting a stand that simply pits them against nationalists and republicans, and against the British and Irish governments, gives a very negative image of what unionists are about, as well as ensuring that Northern Ireland is deprived of self-government for quite some time. And whether this course of action would keep confusion at bay, especially among unionists with pro-Agreement sympathies, is very debatable.

It is the image of unionists being at ongoing loggerheads with the British government that has the potential to cause the most confusion in unionist ranks. The fact that their affirmations of Britishness are not reciprocated either by their government or by the bulk of other British citizens is disturbing for unionists. Yet this is the fate of unionist understandings of their identity, which are reflected in the various stands they take to defend the Union. Two contrasting understandings are worth picking out, even if many unionists define themselves through some combination of both. One understanding makes cultural and/or religious Protestantism central to unionism. Elsewhere in Britain, including Westminster, this understanding is greeted with a mixture of incomprehension, disbelief and revulsion, especially when it results in Britishness being associated with paramilitary atrocities and protests directed against Catholic churchgoers and schoolchildren, or, even more widely, with Orange marches and loyalist symbols. Another understanding ostensibly strips unionism of any cultural and religious attachments and reduces a unionist identity to political commitment to a set of pluralist, liberal democratic principles that the British state (unlike the Irish) is presumed to embody.[9] This understanding should be more agreeable in Britain, but it rests on controversial premises: for instance, that unionist political commitments can be acultural; it offers a suspect interpretation of contemporary British and Irish political realities; and its translation into the politics of Northern Ireland effectively denies that nationalists have any legitimate claim to political recognition of their identity in the institutions of the state.[10] It sits uncomfortably with current British thinking.

Discomfort caused by lack of wider British sympathy to unionist identities aside, three other points are pertinent. First, one thing is clear: paramilitary and sectarian stands are intolerable to a political liberal unionist identity, as they may be to versions of a cultural/religious identity also. Second, on the crucial question of how conflicting stands on the Agreement are affected by unionist self-definitions, much less is clear. Two of the most influential advocates of contrasting cultural and liberal identities, Ian Paisley and Robert McCartney respectively, are resolutely anti-Agreement. They and the parties they represent, the DUP and the United Kingdom Unionist Party (UKUP), have little difficulty in finding common cause whatever their other differences. But there is equally both cultural and liberal unionist support for the Agreement, as evidenced in its endorsement by the UUP and loyalist parties associated

with Protestant paramilitaries.[11] There are complexities here that
need further unpacking.

Third, disagreements about identity and orientation within
unionism are more serious than those within nationalism. Within
both there are differences over the relationship between particular
cultural attachments and general political norms, over which
attachments and norms are appropriate, over how they should be
interpreted, and over what sort of stands they warrant. But none
of these prevents nationalists and republicans giving enthusiastic
support to the Agreement, whereas unionists are divided over it.
Moreover, whereas nationalist and republican parties prevent their
cultural attachments from issuing in a political endorsement of
Catholicism, most unionist parties struggle to match their success
with regard to Protestantism. This is particularly awkward for the
UUP, which anxiously tries to project an image of liberal pluralism
even as it retains an institutional link with the Orange Order. No
doubt different unionist groups may feel confident and clear about
who they are and what they are about, but unionism as a whole
seems in a bit of a muddle. For example, Trimble's attempts to sell
the Agreement as primarily a unionist-friendly document have so
far failed to win over doubters in his own party, let alone sceptics
in anti-Agreement unionist parties. And questions that were more
easily treated cavalierly during the years of unionism's rule – such as
the relationship between its liberalism and its Protestantism, including its tendency to find liberal reasons to support Protestant interests, but rarely Catholic ones (in disputes over Orange marches, for
instance) – now demand a clarification that unsettles many unionists' complacently held self-understandings.

Of course, unionists continue to regard Northern Ireland as their
home. And for all their unease about the Agreement, it guarantees
that the North will remain within the British fold for as long as a
majority of Northern citizens consent to it. But unionists feel less
and less comfortably at home in a society that they no longer run
and that no longer bears their exclusive imprint. They crave a security that they think is slipping further from their grasp as they see the
cause of nationalism and republicanism making more and more

progress. Valued practices, such as Orange marches proceeding along traditional routes, cannot be taken for granted any more. Population shifts, brought about by the conflict and ongoing sectarian attitudes and practices, are changing the character of local areas. Increasing numbers of district councils across the North now have nationalist and republican majorities. And so on. Many unionists are disoriented and existentially stretched to cope with changes in their society for which neither their culture nor politics prepared them. If their experience stops short of being deeply disconcerting, in cases it does so barely. Many aspire to belong in a Northern Ireland that is becoming a distant memory. But they remain defiant.

DIFFICULTIES AND HOPES

Given this sketch of the varying fortunes of unionism and nationalism, there is little overestimating the difficulty of satisfying the requirement of inclusive citizen belonging. Its difficulty resides in two major areas. The first is the broad area of what I have called nationalist and unionist experiences. In terms of their own registers, nationalists have experienced enormous gains in recent years and unionists enormous losses. At least at the level of their collective experiences, it is not too much of an exaggeration to say that nationalists have more focused and co-ordinated orientations to circumstances in the North. They exhibit a clearer and more confident sense of who they are and what they are about. And they are better adjusted to, and more at home with, the dawning of new political realities. The impression is that they are moving forward, while unionists are in retreat. Now these contrasts in experience pose the difficulty they do for reconciliation because there is widespread acceptance among nationalists and unionists of the registers that chart changes in Northern society in terms of gains and losses for one side or the other. Precisely because unionists see themselves as losers, they dig in defiantly to hold the line against further erosions of their position. And, for their part, nationalists, thinking that they are on a roll, no longer baulk at what they see as unionist intransigence, and are unprepared to sacrifice gains that are not only considered long overdue but also as just entitlements.

Another way of describing these contrasting experiences of gain and loss is to relate them explicitly to the different types of citizenship that are integral to talk of inclusive citizen belonging. The history of Northern Ireland has witnessed a dramatic shift from a situation in which individual, cultural and political modes of citizen dignity were mostly enjoyed by unionists, to one in which even the British government insists that they are due to nationalists too. Even if their enjoyment of these modes awaits full realisation within Northern society, nationalists' sense of gain is obvious. For those unionists attuned to, or hankering after, dominance and exclusive privileges, their sense of loss is equally obvious. But the tale of gains and losses is not quite this simple. Gains within Northern society, however welcome, do not complete those being sought by some nationalists, and unionists' fear is that their worst losses are yet to come. Told from an anti-Agreement unionist perspective, the missing – and crucial – part of the tale of gains and losses goes something like this.

Republicans will not be satisfied with having their cultural dignity as citizens publicly affirmed in the North, or their political dignity recognised through their participation in a Northern Executive and Assembly, since by their own admission they will never fully belong within Northern Ireland. What they want is a united Ireland, independent of any vestige of British rule, in which their communal/national identity is culturally dominant, and self-government is shared with other Irish citizens. Only then will their desire to belong be satisfied. But this means the demise of unionism, the eclipse of unionists' desire to belong, the denial of their entitlements to cultural and political dignity. Talk of inclusive citizen belonging is not, therefore, what it seems; it is a ruse for an eventual nationalist/republican takeover. Reform of Northern society, along the lines demanded by nationalists and republicans, is its subversion. And, besides, there are principled reasons why it should be opposed. Seen in this light, resistance to rectifying imbalances in Northern society and making it more inclusive is not principally about doggedly clinging to suspect ideals of supremacism and domination; it is ultimately about fighting for unionism's survival.

Needless to say, republicans think such a unionist version of the meaning of change in the North is a distortion, especially in its assessment of what a united Ireland would mean for unionists. But whatever our take on the tale of gains and losses, it might seem to illustrate A.T.Q. Stewart's reading that the Northern conflict 'is about political power and who should wield it', and that, as a consequence, 'each side wastes its breath in trying to persuade the other to adopt its view of the situation, as if all men were reasonable creatures, and none the product of his environment and education'.[12] On this reading, then, the current situation in the North has, as we should expect, all the ingredients of a power struggle between two competing politics of belonging, which much of nationalism thinks it is destined to win, but which unionists are determined never to quit.

If this is the only reading available, then reconciliation's cause is hopeless. But there is another possible reading that, in touching on a second area of difficulty, also offers some hope. The reading is this: unionist and nationalist experiences are mediated through their respective politics of belonging, which entail different ways of acting and thinking, and this is where the conflict between them is primarily located. The second area of difficulty, then, concerns the prospect that we are dealing with politically and conceptually incompatible priorities and frameworks that reinforce antagonisms at the level of experience. And this makes the task of reconciliation seem even more impossible. Or does it? There are two glimmers of hope here.

One is that Northern politics of belonging are not only shaped by the varying experiences of unionists and nationalists, but also by their commitments to norms and principles that admit of reasonable interchange. For example, some of the reasons unionists give against conceding too much to nationalists and republicans in the name of inclusiveness, are not just a reflection of their fears about where such concessions may finally lead, but are based on principles. Not to discuss these reasons in terms of the principles they invoke is demeaning to unionists. And exactly the same can be said for the contrary reasons nationalists give. Stewart's mind-numbing contrast between reasonableness on the one hand and the influence of education and environment on the other, which has it that we in the North are impervious to being persuaded out of any of our prejudices, may pander to our dogmatisms. But it is an arbitrary contrast whose appeal lies merely in the excuse it provides for not having to listen to or think about the reasons others offer. Stewart's advice to jettison hope in reason making a difference is a poor reflection of the similar, but more sophisticated, advice given by radical pluralists. As the arguments developed in Chapter 5 indicate, this is advice that may be safely ignored. In other words, we are not obliged to conclude that practical reason has taken permanent flight from Northern Ireland and that our only option is either to sit back and watch, or to take sides and join in, a power struggle for the North. The priorities, practices and rationalisations of both unionism and nationalism appeal to practical reason, and they are susceptible to forms of evaluation that open the door for reconciling possibilities. At a minimum, there may be grounds for challenging the widespread tendency to judge changes in Northern society only via registers of unionist and nationalist gains and losses.

An additional glimmer of hope is that there are unionists and nationalists who say they have no wish to deny the other's entitlement to belong fully in Northern society. And there was enough in what many on both sides said to deliver the Agreement, which on the face of it is a testament to the seriousness of each's intent to accommodate the other. Problems with the Agreement's implementation, however, cast doubt on how much should be made of this, as we are about to see. It is a puzzle how some pro-Agreement unionists and nationalists can claim to be for inclusive citizen belonging while doing much of what they do and thinking much of what they think. But that is no reason not to take seriously what they claim by scrutinising just how serious they are, that is, by asking whether their practices and the terms of their offers of belonging to the other are at all reasonable. And doing so obviously necessitates considering more explicitly aspects of the Agreement and its aftermath in Northern society.

THE AGREEMENT AND ITS AFTERMATH

The Agreement is a complex far-reaching document that attempts to provide a reasonable balance between the competing claims and aspirations of unionism and nationalism. It redefines relations within the North, between North and South, and between Britain and Ireland. These relations are given form and substance in proposed new structures and institutions, which imply new practices. The Agreement points to a political avenue out of difficulties in the North that is intended to make options of violence moribund. As much as anything, it suggests the opening up of fresh political space within which appear unique and promising opportunities to make Northern society work in ways that have been previously impossible. And yet there is every chance that this space will be closed and the opportunities to renew Northern politics squandered.

Throughout the book, and especially in the first part of this chapter, I have alluded already to aspects of the Agreement and its aftermath. In now focusing more explicitly on these I am not, however, proposing anything like a comprehensive analysis. I offer, rather, a limited snapshot of a complicated document and its reception, which has as its focus those elements that bear directly and most significantly on the theme of inclusive citizen belonging.

THE AGREEMENT

There is a prima facie case for supposing that the Agreement – by virtue of being a product of multi-party negotiations – signifies an improvement in the politics of Northern Ireland. Simply put, a political world in which the Agreement is present is better than the world from which it was absent. I think it represents a welcome and historic change in the public affairs of Northern society in three major respects: by signifying a break from a seemingly intractable political log jam; by intimating a process of change, commanding an unrivalled range of support; and by initiating a shift to arrangements that uniquely reflect the complexity of our Northern cultural and political condition. These are well known, but they are worth rehearsing briefly to remind ourselves in general of the hope the

Agreement epitomises, especially now that much of it has faded, and in particular of how in each of these respects the prospects of inclusive citizen belonging are enhanced.

There are countless ways of describing what the Agreement constitutes a *change from*. But given that its principal concern is to devise new arrangements of government, it is particularly apt to depict it in these ways: as a change from the partiality that characterised Northern Ireland's previous experience of self-government under unionist rule; as a change from the relative unaccountability that has characterised its most recent experience of government in the form of direct rule from Westminster; and as a change from a sterile politics of constitutional standoff that has characterised debate within the North, has stymied earlier attempts at a political breakthrough, and has created a vacuum too easily filled by violence.

A thorough interpretation of the Agreement would read it against the backdrop of earlier initiatives to create new structures of government in the North, including the Sunningdale Agreement of 1974, the Anglo-Irish Agreement of 1985, the Brooke–Mayhew talks of 1991–92, the Downing Street Declaration of 1993, and the Framework Documents of 1995.[13] None of these initiatives, of course, proved capable of commanding enough support within the main political factions in Northern Ireland to give confidence that an end to our political impasse was imminent. Nationalists refused to accept a purely internal solution – that is, a solution involving internal reform of the North without an Irish dimension – and unionists baulked at admitting anything more than an internal solution. Various aspects of the initiatives I have mentioned reappeared in different packaging in the Agreement, but prior to 10 April 1998 it seemed that fundamental constitutional divisions between unionists and nationalists defied reconciliation. And in the absence of constitutional agreement, movement on other issues was halted on the principle that nothing is agreed until everything is agreed. Political stalemate became taken for granted, posturing and grandstanding on apparent trivia appeared normal, and paramilitaries – certainly prior to 1994 and more definitively 1997 – continued to exploit the political gridlock, very often to barbarous effect.

Pitched against such a backdrop, the Agreement suggests change from a situation where basic constitutional agreement seemed impossible, and where progress on a raft of other issues was thereby hindered. It created conditions in which inclusive citizen belonging could be realised.

The *range of support* the Agreement attracted for its programme of change is also welcome and historic. The Agreement owes much to the industry and ingenuity of the British and Irish governments, with the particular help of the American administration under Bill Clinton and the more general good will of international opinion. And, unlike the original decision to partition Ireland, it is not saddled with colonial connotations, nor, despite some republican discontent, has it involved anything approximating a Collins–De Valera type split within Irish ranks. But that is not all. In addition to input from the two governments, the Agreement was negotiated by eight local parties which were specifically elected for the purpose of reaching an agreement: on the unionist side there was the UUP, the PUP and the Ulster Democratic Party (UDP); on the nationalist/republican side there was the SDLP and Sinn Féin; and in between there was the Alliance Party of Northern Ireland, the Northern Ireland Women's Coalition, and the Labour Coalition. Two unionist parties – the DUP and the UKUP – were elected as participants in negotiations but withdrew upon the arrival of Sinn Féin.

What is historic about this range of party support within Northern Ireland, in spite of the withdrawal of two parties, is that not only have constitutional unionist and nationalist parties reached an agreement that previously seemed beyond them, but so too have the major unionist party (the UUP) and Sinn Féin. Even if there is something in Aughey's (unsubstantiated) claims that 'Sinn Féin entered the talks which led to the Agreement in the expectation that unionists could not accept equality and that the Ulster Unionist Party stayed in the talks because it believed that Sinn Féin could never accept a partitionist settlement',[14] it does not make the fact that they signed up to the same Agreement any the less remarkable. And neither does the UUP's refusal to negotiate directly with republicans.

Just as remarkable is the fact that unlike any previous initiative, the negotiations that produced the Agreement included political representatives of the main paramilitary organisations. And from the actions of Sinn Féin, the PUP and the UDP we can conclude that the Agreement (at least initially) had the backing of the Provisional IRA, the Ulster Volunteer Force (UVF) and the UDA. To those with other than extraordinarily short memories, this range of paramilitary support almost beggars belief.

And, not least, the Agreement was overwhelmingly endorsed by the people of Ireland in separate referenda, North and South (with the North registering 71.1 per cent support and the South a massive 94.4 per cent). This was the first time since partition that Northern and Southern citizens had been granted the opportunity to vote on a common proposal affecting the constitutional future of the island of Ireland: an opportunity that was all the more significant because Britain's decision to partition the island, which was given effect through the Government of Ireland Act in 1920, did not seek popular ratification.

So the support the Agreement can call upon is impressive and, some of us might think, democratically compelling. The inclusivity of the opportunity to vote, which gave all citizens in Ireland a say, and the inclusivity of the negotiating process, which involved the two governments and most Northern parties, are achievements of consequence. They allow all of us, and not just politicians of one party or another, to claim ownership of the Agreement. At last a clear majority of those most closely involved in and affected by conflict in Northern society indicated a willingness to chart a new (non-imposed) political future together. And this intimates a substantial investment in the promise of a society to which all Northern citizens can fully and equally belong under the terms of the Agreement.

The Agreement is historic and welcome, finally, in terms of what it represents *change to*. Briefly, it represents change to a political situation in which, to use a buzz phrase, 'the totality of relationships' within the North are arguably given their due for the first time. Institutional facilitation of 'the totality of relationships' in turn reflects recognition of the complex condition of Northern Ireland. Such recognition was essential to a deal being struck between unionists and nationalists; it was indispensable to movement beyond zero-sum politics. And through its incorporation of this sort of recognition, we discern the truly historic and hugely welcome *substantive* achievement of the Agreement: its reimagining of political life in a way that is true to our collective condition in Northern Ireland.

Political reimagining here involves three dimensions, which are taken to reflect 'the totality of relationships' within the North: an internal Northern Irish dimension, a North–South dimension, and an East–West dimension. With regard to its internal government, Northern Ireland maintains its representation at Westminster, but has been also granted a significant measure of self-rule. Various powers, in areas such as health, employment, education and the like, have been devolved to a new Assembly operating on a principle of power sharing, rather than majority rule. The exclusivity of the old unionist domination at Stormont has been replaced by inclusive arrangements whereby unionists and nationalists share governmental responsibilities in accordance with their party strengths. Strikingly, the Agreement has made possible the previously unthinkable: Sinn Féin's membership of a Northern Ireland Executive. A consultative civic forum comprising representatives from business, the trade unions, and the community and voluntary sectors has been established to supplement the power-sharing Assembly. Protection of individual and group rights has been formalised by the incorporation into Northern Ireland law of the European Convention of Human Rights. A Human Rights Commission and an Equality Commission have been also set up. Leading explicit measures of reform of Northern society is that of policing, which I have already commented on in Chapter 3. A commission chaired by Chris Patten recommended changes to the symbols, composition and structures of accountability of policing in Northern Society. A modified form of these changes came into effect from November 2001, most notably with the old name of the RUC being replaced by the new name of the PSNI. Furthermore, paramilitary prisoners whose organisations maintain their ceasefires have secured early releases. And all signatories to the Agreement have committed themselves to normalising life in the North by creating conditions conducive to putting paramilitary weapons beyond use and to demilitarising society.

In terms of the North–South dimension, a new set of institutions has been created to deal initially with twelve areas of common interest and mutual benefit, including agriculture, tourism, social security and education. A North/South Ministerial Council, comprised of ministers from the Northern Assembly and the Dáil, oversees these institutions. Significantly, the Republic of Ireland has altered its constitution to drop its territorial claim to the whole island of Ireland, and to acknowledge instead that Irish unity is an aspiration whose realisation requires the consent of a majority of Northern citizens. On the East–West front, a new British-Irish Council has been invented, involving at least representatives from Scotland, Wales, Northern Ireland, the Republic of Ireland, and Westminster. A new British-Irish Intergovernmental Conference has been also established in place of the intergovernmental council established under the terms of the Anglo-Irish Agreement of 1985. The Agreement replaces that and all previous agreements between Britain and Ireland.

These, then, are among the new structures brought into being by the Agreement. As a safeguard, they are intended to be mutually reinforcing. For example, the Northern Assembly is not allowed to operate in the absence of North–South bodies. But the general point is the one I wish to emphasise: in its attempt to address the 'totality of relationships', the Agreement's proposed structures open up an exciting new political space which seems to give Northern Ireland the sort of chance of working it has not had before.

It has such a chance because the structures integral to the 'totality of relationships' in the North also indicate how it is possible to achieve an inclusive citizen belonging. Put in terms of the modes of citizen dignity I have suggested are of paramount importance in understanding what such belonging means, what they offer is something like this. Our individual dignity as free and equal citizens is dealt with in the Agreement under the section 'Rights, Safeguards and Equality of Opportunity'. As just mentioned, this entails incorporation into law of the European Convention of Human Rights and the establishment of a Human Rights Commission and an Equality Commission to guard against practices of discrimination. Our cultural dignity as citizens is catered for by recognition that Northern society is British and Irish in composition. The Agreement enables us to define ourselves as British or as Irish, or as both. Its North–South and East–West dimensions formalise these definitions through institutional links with the rest of Ireland and the rest of Britain. And through various internal reforms of Northern society based on principles of equality and parity of esteem, and involving policing, symbols, and so on, no tradition is expected to be unfairly advantaged over another. And neither is any one tradition permitted an advantage in government, where equal cultural dignity is politically translated and protected in a number of ways: through a power-sharing Executive, through an Assembly requiring cross-community support in its voting procedures, which incorporate principles of parallel consent and weighted majorities, and through the offices of First Minister and Deputy First Minister, which are accorded identical powers to ensure equal representation from unionism and nationalism at the highest political levels in Northern Ireland. Our political dignity as self-governing citizens is simultaneously affirmed through these political measures, and opens up the prospect of us developing new common commitments and identifications, as we together strive to make Northern society and its institutions viable.

Underpinning these attempts to facilitate inclusive citizen belonging by respecting all citizens' individual, cultural and political dignity is the idea that a Northern Ireland that accommodated them would be generally acknowledged to qualify as a legitimate political entity. This is an idea that has been reinforced by the South's agreement to change the Irish constitution. Sure, its doing so does not preclude the possibility of a united Ireland, but the Agreement makes clear that any legitimate change to the constitutional status of the North requires the consent of a majority of its citizens. Alongside the other historic achievements of the Agreement, then, we must rank the apparent settling of the vexed question of legitimacy, which, in an important way, underwrites their significance.

AFTERMATH

Or so it seemed. The Agreement's achievements may be historic, but not everyone believes they are welcome. They have always had their critics. In addition, disagreements among the Agreement's supporters have increased rather than decreased, and cast doubt on how much they desire to embrace its achievements in their entirety. And the democratic mandate the achievements could rely upon now looks much less impregnable, with unionist support of the Agreement slipping away and anticipations of pro-Agreement politicians fudging their way through their disagreements not inspiring great confidence. The prize of inclusive citizen belonging has gone from appearing almost within reach in 1998 to seeming quite precarious in 2002. In the aftermath of the Agreement, then, three practical problems, with serious ramifications for the future of Northern society, remain: overt opposition to the Agreement; clashing interpretations of its meaning; and the difficulties of trying to muddle through regardless.

The obvious problem the Agreement confronts is that of *overt opposition* from certain republican and unionist factions. The rationale of republican opposition is simple: the Agreement does not deliver a united Ireland, and it does not respect traditional Irish republicanism's fundamental principle, namely that of the Irish nation's right to self-determination. Although everyone entitled to vote on the island of Ireland was given the opportunity to do so on the same day and on the same issue, voters did so in separate referenda and were not deciding their collective fate as one national unit but as two. This suggests that the Agreement's legitimacy rests on something closer to a principle of co-determination than one of national self-determination. Besides, voters were not granted the option of choosing a united Ireland rather than the arrangements of the Agreement. And the upshot is that unionists retain a veto over unity. Republicans reasoning along such lines cannot conceive of belonging fully within the North, or of having their identity claims satisfied in anything other than all-Ireland structures. Those attracted to such reasoning, or, more correctly, attracted to it to the point of actively organising themselves in opposition to the Agreement, are few in number. They are found within the 32-County Sovereignty Movement, the Continuity IRA and the Real IRA, and very often include among their objections to Sinn Féin's support of the Agreement, the belief that armed struggle remains an indispensable component in the quest to end partition.

Unionist opposition to the Agreement is more significant. The core rationale of such opposition has two forms: either it is a protest against the fact that the Agreement signals the final constitutional death knell of Protestant domination in the North (though that is rarely how it is articulated), or it is a complaint against the fact that the Agreement abandons the prospect of Northern Ireland's citizens ever being treated as equal British citizens. What is common to both forms is a refusal to accept the dilution of British sovereignty in Northern Ireland, which is discerned in North–South bodies with their overtones of a pooling of sovereignty. Unacceptable erosions of the British character of Northern society are also detected in the Agreement. Reform of policing, for example, is seen as an unnecessary capitulation to nationalist propaganda, and the release of paramilitary prisoners is viewed as an appeasement of terrorism which plays fast and loose with democratic conventions. The suggestion that unionists should share power with Sinn Féin, without the complete decommissioning of Provisional IRA weapons, is said to be unthinkable, although that has not stopped certain of them accepting ministerial positions in an Executive with republican members.

Unlike anti-Agreement republicans, anti-Agreement unionists enjoy considerable political and cultural clout. From the outset, they included Ian Paisley's DUP, a number of smaller unionist parties, and the Orange Order (whose leadership for the first time publicly broke ranks with the UUP during the referendum campaign). They also included a significant proportion of David Trimble's UUP, which although officially for the Agreement is split down the middle over it, with six of its then ten Westminster MPs openly campaigning against it.

Of course, neither anti-Agreement republicanism nor anti-Agreement unionism have alternatives to the Agreement that are remotely likely to win enough cross-community support to be workable, or that will be seriously entertained by the British and Irish governments. But that does not mean their spoiling tactics can be simply dismissed. They both tap into exclusive notions of belonging and identity that resonate in nationalist and unionist cultures.

The threat posed by anti-Agreement forces has to be judged in relation to the resolution of purpose among pro-Agreement forces. And here the picture is not encouraging. Support of the Agreement appears fragile because there is anything but unanimity among certain of the key parties to it. In a sense this is hardly surprising once we recall that the Agreement was attained without the UUP exchanging so much as a pleasantry with Sinn Féin, let alone entering into political discussions with its representatives. Obviously, in the absence of the sort of communication required to reach a common mind, both parties saw some tactical advantage in signing up to the same deal. But what is considered a tactical advantage for one is typically considered a disadvantage for the other. From the very moment of its inception, in other words, the danger to the Agreement was that it might hang on understandings among its supporters that differed not simply in terms of nuance and pedantic detail, but in terms of fundamentals. And this suggests the Agreement's most persistently nagging problem, namely that of *clashing interpretations*, particularly between Sinn Féin and the UUP; a problem made more acute because reconciling their manifest differences of interpretation is even more difficult when both are vulnerable to charges of ideological sellout from anti-Agreement factions.

Republican and unionist interpretations of the Agreement clash most conspicuously on the constitutional question. For Sinn Féin, the Agreement signals a further step on the road to a united Ireland; for the UUP, it guarantees the Union. For one it is a means to another end; for the other it is the end. North–South bodies represent for Sinn Féin a blurring of the Irish border and a taste of things to come. For unionists they represent an institutional expression of cordial relations between friendly, neighbouring states that makes good political and economic sense. The East–West dimension of the Agreement is emphasised by unionists as strengthening the British tie, whereas Sinn Féin sees it as merely a toothless concession to unionism, the only virtue of which is that it enabled unionists to accept the much more important North–South dimension. In terms of the internal Northern dimension, Sinn Féin stresses the importance of substantial reform: certainly of policing and also of the implementation of an equality agenda which envisages Northern society being stripped of its vestiges of British dominance and parity of esteem being granted to an Irish identity. It also interprets the Agreement as ensuring Sinn Féin's ongoing participation in the government of the North regardless of the fate of silent Provisional IRA guns. The UUP baulks at all of this: police reform should be minimal, Northern Ireland's British character should be maintained, and Sinn Féin's role in government is very much dependent on the continuing decommissioning of Provisional IRA weapons, if not also the disbandment of the Provisional IRA itself.

Given that Sinn Féin and the UUP are supposed to be co-operating in order to make the Agreement work, we are dealing here with interpretive differences of considerable import. What makes matters worse is that the scope for political fudge of such differences is limited by each party's vulnerability to attack from the anti-Agreement factions I mentioned previously. And here is the real sting of the problem of overt opposition to the Agreement: while not in itself enough to impede change in Northern society, it is capable of doing a wrecking job by circumscribing the room for manoeuvre available to certain of the Agreement's supporters. This poses particular difficulties for the UUP, but it also poses difficulties of sorts for Sinn Féin.

With regard to the latter, Sinn Féin is ostensibly susceptible to deeply damaging criticisms: that it is guilty of the ultimate republican heresy by agreeing to work partitionist arrangements; that it is guilty of dishonouring the memory of dead IRA volunteers; that it is guilty of acute naïveté in expecting unionists to soften their intransigence and treat republicans as equal political partners. So far Sinn Féin has managed to escape relatively unscathed from such attacks, not least because it has been able to offer counter-appeals that I mention shortly. But perhaps such attacks restrict its official interpretive flexibility, even if only because they strike chords within its own constituency. For example, in line with its republican critics, Sinn Féin maintains the orthodoxies that all-Ireland support of the Agreement does not constitute an act of self-determination by the Irish people, that Northern Ireland is not a legitimate political entity, that a united Ireland is still a sacrosanct republican goal, and that realisation of the goal is historically inevitable. In maintaining these sorts of things, Sinn Féin continues to make noises that arouse unionist suspicions and fears and so inhibits the possibility of *rapprochement*. But, even so, what is notable is how Sinn Féin has managed to take the Agreement in its stride. Not only has Gerry Adams been able to deflect criticisms from his republican critics, he has also made what seems like a pretty lousy deal for republicanism appear like another notch in Sinn Féin's belt. Sinn Féin remains upbeat, whatever the constraints its critics impose: history is believed to be on its side.

By contrast, unionists whose interests arguably have been better served by the Agreement, at least in the short-term, are conspicuously downbeat despite bursts of bravado from Trimble. Even many pro-Agreement unionists think of themselves as losers and admit to having bought the present deal not because they liked it, but because it was the best they could now hope for. There is, then, a widely shared unionist pessimism, a reasonably common belief among unionists that they are swimming against the tide. A real difficulty here is that pro-Agreement unionism does not possess an interpretive framework that differs markedly from anti-Agreement unionism. At most there are slight differences of emphasis and a greater propensity to pragmatism among pro-Agreement factions. But when we think of what is shared in common and, because of the split in unionist ranks, how little scope pro-Agreement unionism has for making generous overtures to republicans even if it wanted to (which is debatable), then we may appreciate just how serious a difficulty that of interpretive constraint really is.

For instance, on practical issues, pro- and anti-Agreement unionists are opposed to any significant reform of Northern Ireland: both would have preferred policing to remain largely unreformed; both were critical of the early release of prisoners; both dispute the necessity of any public recognition of an Irish identity within Northern society; and both opposed sharing power with Sinn Féin independently of the decommissioning of Provisional IRA weapons. But Trimble is committed to working an Agreement that includes these sorts of provisions, whereas Paisley, for instance, is not. Conceptually, it is hard to spot much difference between pro- and anti-Agreement unionists either. Both uphold as their principal political priority maintaining the Union; both are susceptible to the pull of cultural Protestantism as witnessed in the unified unionist defence of Orangemen's rights; and both are opposed to granting political entitlements to a nationalist identity. But, again, whereas it is easy to move within this sort of conceptual space and reject the Agreement, it is much harder to move within it and somehow make the Agreement work. Pro-Agreement unionism's problem is that the new practices implied by the Agreement do not fit comfortably with the interpretive theories unionists rely upon. Sinn Féin has a similar problem, but it is nowhere near as acute as that confronting the UUP.

One response to this gloomy picture of clashing interpretations, which seems to have been adopted by many in the North who cannot foresee any alternative to the Agreement, is to downplay its significance. This response is similar to what I called in Chapter 3 a realist–optimistic approach, which conceives of reconciliation weakly as a balancing of interests, and pins its hopes of the Agreement's survival on the rational self-interests of pro-Agreement unionists and nationalists. The hunch is that we can ride out differences of interpretation via a type of *pragmatic muddling through*. This makes the fate of the Agreement dependent on a finely tuned balancing act, where perceived gains and losses for unionists and nationalists keep relative pace with each other, and where all parties appreciate the foolhardiness of overplaying their hands. What is immediately worrying about such a state of affairs is that it presupposes the presence of some pretty deft and well-honed political skills, which Northern Ireland's politicians are hardly famous for having perfected.

Pragmatic muddling through is conceivable if we judge that, although limited, the scope for political fudge exists to some extent. In its defence, a rationale with something like the following pitch may be invoked. Of course republican and unionist interpretations of the Agreement clash, but what else would we expect? Pro-Agreement republicans and unionists have to appeal to hardline constituencies and therefore cannot stray too far from their respective orthodoxies if they are to bring enough of their supporters with them. So we should not be too distracted by problems posed by clashing interpretations. What matters is that Sinn Féin and the UUP are committed to working the Agreement, and it is how they do this in practice that counts for more than how they square various of their practices with their theories. Besides, both Gerry Adams and David Trimble can find enough in the Agreement to justify their support of it to relatively orthodox republicans and unionists.

For example, Adams can argue along these lines. Sinn Féin's willingness to embrace the changes outlined in the Agreement should be seen as a continuation of the policies the party has been pursuing to advance republican interests. Unlike the explicit militarism of the 1970s, and unlike the mix of militarism and politics of the 1980s, since the 1990s it has become increasingly obvious that political strategies alone will aid the republican cause. It is now clear that there is no military solution to the problem of the North, and those republicans who think otherwise are kidding themselves. Republicanism is better served by Sinn Féin's participation in mainstream politics. The international support it can draw upon now illustrates the advantage of such participation: Adams and other Sinn Féin leaders such as Martin McGuinness, the current Minister of Education in the Northern Executive, are accepted as statesmen; with the silence

of Provisional IRA guns and the antics of Orangemen and their supporters, it is unionists who appear as the bad guys in the eyes of
world opinion; there is a steady supply of financial support, especially from America; and there are prospects of Sinn Féin becoming
the largest nationalist party in the North and making electoral gains
in the South. And all of these advantages can be enjoyed without
any forfeiting of republicanism's ultimate goals. Besides, since
political realities dictate that there is not going to be a sudden end
to partition, it makes perfect sense to contribute to its elimination
from within the political system: by insisting upon an equality
agenda within the North that makes the nature of society more
republican-friendly; by working to extend areas of North–South
co-operation to the point of making the border irrelevant; and by
deriving hope from the fact that the unionist majority within
the North is being slowly whittled away. These are the sort of
counter-appeals at Adams's disposal, which I earlier suggested
help to explain why Sinn Féin has not been nearly as damaged
by anti-Agreement republican criticism as it might have been.

David Trimble, for his part, has also some arguments to offer to
unionist supporters. The Agreement returns self-government to
Northern Ireland and unionists have a prominent, if no longer a
dominant, role to play in it. The Agreement replaces the loathed
Anglo-Irish Agreement; it has won the kind of change to the Irish
constitution that unionists have been advocating for years; it recognises British sovereignty in the North; and it guarantees that further
constitutional change cannot be legitimately undertaken without
deferring to the principle of consent (in other words, unionists
now have a legally recognised veto). It represents, claims Trimble
to the consternation of non-unionists, 'an internal settlement', and,
he adds for good measure, it enables him to pursue his goal of moving 'unionism closer to the heart of British politics'.[15]

In a sense, then, we might ask who cares whether republicans
believe that the Agreement leads to a united Ireland and unionists
believe that it secures the Union. All that matters is that enough
republicans and unionists consent to work it, for whatever reason.
Keeping going the processes of pragmatic muddling through is

what is of the essence, not becoming fixated on interpretive clashes and ideological incompatibilities. This is enough to aim at for now. The real task, then, is simply to capitalise on the fact that Adams and Trimble have both risked too much to back away from their commitments to making the Agreement work. And this is a task that neither the British nor Irish governments will shirk. We can be confident that both will be praising the virtues of pragmatism at every turn. In addition, the economic carrots being dangled in the event of peace being maintained are very tempting, and there is a growing tiredness in certain previously militant quarters, which makes a return to conflict very unappealing.

Maybe the necessary ingredients are all here to see off the problems of overt opposition and clashing interpretations. Maybe all we should expect is a type of pragmatic muddling through that is able to be sustained by drawing on the sorts of resources I have just mentioned: relatively plausible republican and unionist reasons for supporting the Agreement; the difficult-to-reverse commitments of the republican and unionist leaderships; pressure from the British and Irish governments; economic incentives; and general war-weariness. Maybe the Provisional IRA, by commencing to decommission its arms, has given unionists the sorts of reassurances they needed to enable them to find ways of working with republicans and of treating them as equal political partners, since the price of their not doing so could be otherwise exorbitant. And if hope of lasting peace and political stability in Northern Ireland is realistically to be pinned on the pragmatic muddling through all of this suggests, it may yet prove more durable than the hopes raised by any other initiative in the last thirty years.

But it is hard to believe that pragmatic muddling through does suffice. Three factors count against it. First, it has not yet succeeded in winning over anti-Agreement sceptics within unionism. Or, perhaps more to the point, it appears inherently constricted by virtue of the fact that much politics within unionism has been played on anti-Agreement terms. Take the issue of Provisional IRA weapons which continues to plague unionism, despite the fact that a beginning to their decommissioning has already occurred. This beginning may be enough for now for pro-Agreement unionists, but for how long it will remain enough is open to conjecture. It is not at all enough for those in the anti-Agreement camp, for whom, one suspects, nothing short of the disappearance of the IRA would ever have been sufficient.[16] Prior to republicans' belated move to put weapons beyond use, there had been unanimity among unionists of all persuasions that Sinn Féin must be excluded from the political Executive in the absence of an immediate and verifiable decommissioning of Provisional IRA arms. In October 2002, the call for Sinn Féin's exclusion arose again following allegations of republican misdemeanors, including spying. To prevent a collapse of the Agreement, the British government suspended the Northern Ireland Assembly for a fourth time. Unionist attention has now shifted from the issue of weapons to that of the existence of the Provisional IRA, and even Trimble is making its disbandment a condition of participating in government with Sinn Féin. Whatever about the details of this further unionist demand of republicanism, a worrying consideration here is that anti-Agreement sentiment has grown since the Agreement was first signed, and is possibly now the majority position within unionism. Anti-Agreement unionists have gained at the polls, the UDA has withdrawn its support of the Agreement and its ceasefire has been declared over, there has been an increase in Protestant convictions that the Agreement is depriving them of their rights, and there has been an escalation of sectarian violence among Protestants. The spoiling tactics of the Agreement's detractors within unionism have proved effective. Quite simply, then, pragmatic muddling through does not seem a very reliable guarantor of the Agreement within unionist ranks.

Second, the issues at stake in the clashing interpretations of the Agreement are too fundamental to be glossed over anyway. Behind the strategies of republicans and pro-Agreement unionists, which make it advantageous for both to muddle through pragmatically at present, lurk substantive disagreements over such matters as political priorities, legitimacy and the character of society. Only a remarkably short-sighted view of politics, or a very weak version of reconciliation, would imagine that we can get by indefinitely without having to face up to these. Their capacity to undermine a delicate balance of interests should be never underestimated.

Third, such a restricted, pragmatically inclined approach to politics and reconciliation short-changes us on the possibilities the Agreement makes available for inclusive citizen belonging. By not exploring the substantive disagreements inherent in unionist and republican interpretations of the Agreement, it also fails to challenge their deleterious implications for the cultural and political dignity of some set of citizens or another. This is because on the terms of this approach a range of crucial questions is simply bypassed for reasons of convenience. For example, neither unionist nor republican interpretations are interrogated with a view to determining whether they offer reasonable conditions of belonging to non-unionists and non-republicans respectively. Rather, it is deemed sufficient if their interpretations provide grounds for peaceful unionist and republican co-existence. Thus interpretive biases reflecting the interests of a particular (unionist or nationalist) politics of belonging, including certain exclusive tendencies on matters of citizen dignity, are untroubled by scrutiny. But skating over such awkward issues of contestation is equivalent to allowing problems such as sectarianism to fester. As a consequence, a pragmatic response to disputes of substantive politics and interpretation asks us to settle for considerably less than the Agreement promises. Troubling aspects of conflicting politics of belonging are left unresolved, and the unhelpful register of gains and losses for one identity or another is left intact. More than pragmatic muddling through is required.

This is not at all to deny that pragmatic compromises have their place in the politics of a divided society. It is simply to say that for important reasons these are not enough. To be told that wanting more smacks of impractical overreaching rings a little hollow given the precariousness of underreaching pragmatic attempts to salvage the Agreement. Weak reconciliation is better than no reconciliation, but it is an inadequate substitute for strong reconciliation. And strong reconciliation is impossible without probing issues that pragmatism leaves aside. Although it may be frowned upon by those whose political wisdom tells them that this is an inopportune moment to rock the boat of either pro-Agreement unionism or republicanism, the logic of strong reconciliation insists that both have to be held accountable for placing cultural and political obstacles in the path of a reconciled society.

THE UNION, UNITY
AND A RECONCILED SOCIETY

A political argument for strong reconciliation suited to the con-temporary conditions of Northern Ireland has to point to ways through cultural and political barriers that inhibit the realisation of inclusive citizen belonging. Of course, if even a weak line on recon-ciliation has its work cut out trying to negotiate compromises between competing politics of belonging, it does not appear to augur well for the prospects of a strong line. Present conditions in the North may seem more like a cynic's delight. Perhaps it is cynics who have the last laugh. This is a conclusion that I evidently want to hold out against. But, in addition to the well-rehearsed and bleak views of an anti-reason that reduces politics to a power struggle, and an anti-Agreement unionism that anticipates republicanism's defeat and nationalism's taming, another cynical view of the Agreement . that debunks the rationale I am advocating rates a quick mention. In other words, before trying to improve upon the pragmatic politics of weak reconciliation – by delving into substantive contro-versies that are of little concern when the point is just to muddle through – it is germane to discuss one further assault on the very possibility of what I am aiming for.

To reiterate, I am claiming that the possibilities of an inclusive citizen belonging suggested by a notion of strong reconciliation

are encouraged by the Agreement, and yet also discouraged by conflicting understandings of its meaning and resistance to its implementation. But, it might be retorted, discouragement traces back to
the Agreement itself inasmuch as it institutionalises sectarianism –
through such devices as the voting mechanisms in the Assembly –
and so dampens any reasonable expectation of a common political
life developing. This retort has a point, since, as we have seen, the
Agreement has not succeeded in taking us beyond sectarianism.
And the voting mechanisms – which stipulate that a motion may
be carried in the Assembly only when supported by majorities
within unionism and nationalism – helped to create a moment of
near farce when, on account of disagreements within the UUP,
members of the non-aligned Alliance Party and Women's Coalition temporarily had to redesignate themselves as unionists in order
to have David Trimble re-elected as First Minister.

None the less, neither the retort nor this complication with the
Assembly's voting procedures need be considered fatal. For example, in recognising that Northern Ireland's citizens mostly define
themselves as unionists, nationalists and republicans, the Agreement
simply reflects prevailing realities and tries to find a way of shaping
them in a reconciling direction. In doing so, it holds out the
prospect that these definitions may be capable of reformulations
that take us beyond the intransigent images they frequently suggest.
And it is this prospect that enables us to project a future that is not
confined to the antagonistic relations that have historically stymied
attempts to articulate common projects in which unionists, nationalists and republicans can share. Admittedly, this remains a considerable challenge, and one that is unlikely to succeed without the
disposal of much cumbersome baggage. And if it proves impossible, then the cynical retort about the Agreement underwriting
sectarianism may be difficult to dismiss. Even so, it is hard to know
what plausible alternative there is to working with existing political
self-definitions. For to imagine another agreement that bypassed
the realities of how most Northern citizens currently define themselves politically is to imagine a different society with different concerns and problems, and with different citizens. And reconciliation's

hope in the Agreement remains undiminished here because the institutional arrangements it contains suggest political levels of co-operation that are designed to facilitate the development of a common political life, and that, if fully operationalised in an appropriate spirit, are conducive to the emergence of a common citizen identity. Or so I want to argue.

Since cynicism in any of its guises offers no way of tackling our most important questions in the North, it may now be left aside. The challenge that remains is to prevent the Agreement's achievements, which bear decisively on the modes of citizen dignity crucial to inclusive belonging, from simply ebbing away. And this means attending to basic disagreements involved in the clashing interpretations of the Agreement's meaning offered by the UUP and Sinn Féin, as it is these that have imperilled its future from the outset. As we have noticed, issues of decommissioning, paramilitary disbandment and reform of Northern society are the immediate focus of their disagreements. But it is what these represent that is most interesting, namely larger disputes about priorities and practices that are rooted in their respective politics of belonging. An illuminating way of getting a handle on what is going on here is to probe how unionists' and republicans' views of their political priorities lead them to treat the question of legitimacy. For it is competing understandings of legitimacy, which are bound up with conflicting priorities, that are at the heart of their disagreements on decommissioning, disbandment and reform and that lie behind their antagonistic practices.

In the Agreement *legitimacy* applies to constitutional and institutional matters, and different standards are invoked in each. The constitutional standard is that of majority consent. Just as majority consent was required to legitimise the Agreement, so it is required to effect legitimate constitutional change in Northern Ireland. The difference is that whereas the South's consent was involved in vindicating the Agreement, only the consent of Northern citizens is valid for constitutional change. Since this provision was in the Agreement, it is not seen as problematic: in effect Southerners, in endorsing the Agreement, consented that future constitutional change in the North is primarily a matter of Northern consent.

The institutional standard is not majoritarian; it is, rather, that of cross-community agreement underwritten by norms of justice and fairness. The idea here is simple enough. Whatever about recognition of its formal legitimacy, Northern Ireland can work properly as a democratic society only when its institutions attract the allegiance of all of its citizens. And much more than the consent of a Northern majority is needed for this to occur. As Joseph Ruane and Jennifer Todd point out, these two senses of legitimacy with their different standards are part of the same package, which 'implies recognition of the legitimacy of Northern Ireland as a political entity is contingent on the justice and fairness of its governing institutions'. Therefore, if 'Northern Ireland cannot function in an egalitarian manner, the question of its constitutional legitimacy and legitimacy as a political entity will again come sharply into question'.[1] For quite different reasons, neither unionists nor republicans properly respect the totality of the package within which legitimacy appears in the Agreement, a fact that goes a long way to explaining why Northern politics remains in a parlous state that inhibits the realisation of inclusive citizen belonging.

I now want to argue that unionists' and republicans' restrictive treatments of legitimacy reflect inadequacies, if not also (in the case of republicans) confusions, in their political priorities, which give unwarranted licence to dubious practices. The point I am driving at is this: proper realisation of inclusive citizen belonging, that is, a realisation that incorporates individual, cultural and political modes of citizen dignity, is stunted by a cluster of beliefs and practices associated with unionist and republican priorities and conceptions of legitimacy. The aim is to clear a path through these seemingly formidable obstacles in order to illuminate the priorities, practices and understandings of legitimacy required by a reconciled society, namely one in which all citizens are able to enjoy a sense of belonging by having their dignity affirmed at individual, cultural and political levels of their lives. I start the argument with a discussion of unionism.

THE UNION AND LEGITIMACY

It is the constitutional part of the Agreement's package on legitimacy that counts for unionists. It represents, for the UUP, a final deal that secures the Union and recognises Northern Ireland as a legitimate political entity. For unionists it gives pre-eminence to the principle of British sovereignty in the North, with the consequence that matters of institutional reform are properly interpreted in its light. That is why, says Trimble, 'the flying of the Union is of crucial importance to all unionists. It is the ultimate visible symbol of sovereignty flowing from the Agreement, reaffirming as it did that Northern Ireland's constitutional future lies in the hands of her own people.'[2] Or, as he put the point when opposing symbolic changes to the RUC, the principle of sovereignty is of the essence: the RUC's 'name and badge... are critically important as a clear reflection of the fact that the police are enforcing the laws of the United Kingdom and that the Agreement did not create some bi-national state, but recognised the continuing sovereignty of the Westminster Parliament'.[3] And precisely because the Patten Commission did not make sovereignty a guiding first principle in its recommendations of police reform, its report is dismissed as 'a product of third rate academic theorising about the best model for achieving a politically correct police force'.[4]

CONSTITUTIONAL PRIMACY

So unionists believe it is entirely appropriate to prioritise British symbols in Northern Ireland. From their perspective, the problem with much nationalist and republican pressure for reform is that it does not grasp the primacy of the principle of sovereignty the Agreement established. It fails to face up to the logical consequences of admitting Northern Ireland's legitimacy as a political entity that falls under the aegis of British sovereignty. By contrast, a unionist orientation to reform is shaped decisively by these consequences. And it is the unrelenting determination to press home this point about sovereignty that underpins unionism's decision to make the decommissioning of Provisional IRA weapons a make or break issue for the Agreement, and that purportedly vindicates its treatment of Sinn Féin.

Given that for the UUP the justification for negotiating the Agreement in the face of criticism from other unionists was to win the 'one great prize' of nationalist Ireland's acceptance of 'the legitimacy of Northern Ireland's place within the United Kingdom', Trimble insists on knowing where republicanism stands. 'Either Republicans have given their consent to the political and constitutional arrangements of Northern Ireland or they have not.'[5] Sinn Féin's participation in partitionist arrangements is not a sufficiently unequivocal response, since the Provisional IRA's refusal to accede to unionist demands for decommissioning until October 2001 inferred that republicans were continuing to withhold recognition of Northern Ireland's constitutional legitimacy. The tactic, then, was to squeeze republicans on this issue of capital importance, either to force their capitulation or to have them ostracised as the recalcitrant offenders who reneged on the deal they signed up to. Unless republicans buy into a reading of the Agreement that concedes the primacy of British sovereignty, there is no prospect of doing business with them. Either the Agreement underwrites this primacy or it does not. If other parties are prepared to act as though it does not then it is not worth saving, for it ceases to be of value to unionists. That is why unionists made (and until it is completed, may continue to make) decommissioning a crunch issue for the future of the Agreement. And it is only a small extension of this logic to make the disbandment of the Provisional IRA a crunch issue too.

What we see here is how the Agreement's standard of constitutional legitimacy is presumed to underwrite the priority of defending the Union and to shape the practices and attitudes unionists adopt in relation to the contested topics of decommissioning, disbandment and reform. But unionism's case is problematic. Unionists overplay the significance of the principle of sovereignty in a way that stretches the spirit, if not also the letter, of the Agreement and makes life difficult for all non-unionists; they require the principle to do more work than it is cut out to, most notably by employing it as a check on institutional reform in a divided society;

and they indulge shoddy politics in their handling of the issue of decommissioning. As a consequence, the terms of their offer of inclusive belonging to nationalists and republicans are deeply flawed and serve as a barrier to political reconciliation.

CONSTITUTIONAL OVERKILL

Unionists overplay their hand by applying a lexical ordering to the two standards of legitimacy in the Agreement: *the constitutional always has priority over the institutional*.[6] This means in effect that the standard of institutional legitimacy (cross-community agreement based on justice and fairness) is circumscribed in advance by the constitutional standard (majority consent) and its principle of British sovereignty. This lexical ordering reflects the UUP's priority of defending the Union and protecting the Britishness of Northern Ireland. It enables pro-Agreement unionists to accept certain sorts of institutional reform but not others. For example, they do not have to rail, as all unionists once did, against the replacement of a majoritarian principle by a principle of power sharing in the institutions of government. The following remarks of Trimble explain why. 'In the Executive we are acting under authority that we receive from Her Majesty. When the Sinn Féin Chairman of an Assembly Committee reports on a piece of proposed legislation he is part of a process that ends with the Royal Assent.'[7] In other words, cross-community agreement on institutional reform is an acceptable standard inasmuch as it works under the principle of British sovereignty. And since power sharing poses no threat here, unionists can live with it in principle. But the same cannot be said for any understanding of the standard of institutional legitimacy that shows disregard for the sovereignty principle's primacy. That is why Trimble rejected Patten. And it is also why, given his conviction that the standard of constitutional legitimacy is trumps, he can consistently boast that he has 'secured an internal settlement'.[8] If we buy unionism's lexical ordering of the two standards of legitimacy, that is a plausible reading of the Agreement.

As I said, however, it is a reading that stretches the Agreement's spirit, if not also its letter. And it is one that guarantees a clash with non-unionists. Whatever nationalists and republicans imagined they were signing up to in the Agreement, it was certainly not an internal settlement grounded in a lexical ordering of the standards of legitimacy that makes institutional reform subject to a principle of British sovereignty. By insisting on this reading Trimble is on a collision course with nationalism in general, and not only republicanism. To sustain it, he simply has to drain many of the Agreement's provisions of their intended content. For example, recognition of the formal principle of British sovereignty is expressly qualified by at least these measures: the Irish state's formal involvement in Northern affairs through the intergovernmental conference, and informal involvement in the Agreement's implementation; institutional links between North and South, which, if allowed to develop their own dynamic, are unlikely to be contained within the bounds of British (or Irish) sovereignty; an equality agenda that bears on the culture of Northern Ireland's institutional life without perpetual deference to any sovereignty principle; and anticipation of a diminished role for the British state in the North, especially once demilitarisation has fully occurred. These measures neither add up to an 'internal settlement' nor guarantee the primacy of a constitutional standard of legitimacy.

It is, moreover, a curious thing to suppose that a formal principle of constitutional sovereignty should serve as a check on institutional reform to the extent indicated by unionists. Part of what underlies the supposition is the view that upholding British sovereignty is intimately connected to maintaining the British character of Northern Ireland, particularly of its public institutional life. Accordingly, there is resistance to permitting the institutional standard of legitimacy to apply autonomously, to go unchecked by the constitutional principle, most of all when it is taken to include granting parity of esteem to an Irish identity. So when cross-community agreement based on norms of justice and fairness is presumed to be tied up with an equality agenda involving parity of esteem, Trimble is effectively saying that it is unacceptable, that there is no cross-community agreement here, since unionists regard this understanding of the institutional standard as unfair. The tie with parity of esteem must be broken through resort to the constitutional standard of legitimacy. Otherwise the sovereignty issue will be fudged. There are problems here with the unionist line: a selective invocation of fudge, a tendency to give licence to objectionable unionist/ Protestant practices, and obliviousness (real or feigned) to the partiality of British symbols. Together these suggest strongly that a formal principle of constitutional sovereignty is not cut out to do the work unionists expect of it in a divided society.

For example, to insist on constitutional exactitude in the name of minimising fudge is to overlook the fact that Northern Ireland only exists because of a fudge of the standard of constitutional legitimacy that unionists demand must be rigorously applied to the North. Sure, unionists can plausibly talk of partition being a reflection of division in Ireland rather than its cause. Or they can talk persuasively of their right to self-determination, and of Northern Ireland's eighty years' existence as a separate political entity being sufficient to confirm recognition of the legal status it already enjoys in international law. But none of these ways of talking disguises the fact that partition did not satisfy the standard of constitutional legitimacy required by the Agreement. And neither, of course, did the decision to draw the border between North and South along its present lines, since it reflected little more than a capitulation to unionist interests. In other words, if constitutional exactitude is the determining factor in political deliberations, nationalists are perfectly entitled to object that unionists are assuming a legitimacy for Northern Ireland that has no grounding in justice, whatever the range of prudential and legal positivist arguments that can be marshalled in its support. And, they might add, this continues to matter because unionists have consistently failed to show any interest in creating the sort of Northern Ireland to which nationalists could give unswerving allegiance.

Now, if nationalists had chosen to press their own version of constitutional exactitude, by wanting the currently accepted standard retrospectively applied to the question of partition, there would not have been an Agreement, and Northern politics would remain stuck in a zero-sum game with competing sovereignty claims to six counties of Ulster inflexibly pitted against one another. The genius of the Agreement was to make possible political movement beyond such an impasse: by nationalists conceding the sovereignty issue to unionists, at least in the short-term, in the expectation that Northern reform and North–South institutions would operate on a different rationale. And yet it is just this possibility that is jeopardised by an overzealous demand that reform and North–South co-operation must be conducted within parameters prescribed by a strict application of the principle of British sovereignty.

The potential for jeopardy is exacerbated by possible ramifications of unionist zeal in pinning everything on its version of constitutional exactitude, and by the political blindness it encourages. The ramifications are evident in a chain of reasoning that is familiar among unionists and loyalists, even if it is not comprised of logically necessary links, and which underscores the entanglement of much Britishness with Protestantism in Northern Ireland. It might go like this: (1) upholding British sovereignty entails protecting the British character of Northern society; which partly means (2) insisting on the rights of Orangemen to march along their traditional routes irrespective of any other consideration; which often involves (3) protesting vigorously against those decisions of the Parades Commission that do not find in Orangeism's favour; which, when unsuccessful, (4) reinforce the perception that the Britishness of the North is being eroded because Orange/Protestant entitlements are being denied; and which (5) either justifies or casts in a sympathetic light various acts of law-breaking among unionists, if not also an increase in sectarian practices and tensions that threaten or produce violence.

Now, of course, constitutional unionists are to varying degrees uneasy with the final link in this chain of reasoning. But their criticisms even of its excesses are tame by comparison to their condemnations of any sort of republican misdemeanour. They are also relatively meek compared to their defiant outbursts against attempts to qualify Orangemen's right to march wherever they want, or against arguments why the institutional character of society should reflect Irishness as well as Britishness. Whatever the pluralist noises made by more liberal elements within unionism, the task of safeguarding the Britishness of the North remains closely associated with that of protecting traditional Protestant practices. This association escapes serious political challenge on account of the conspicuous reluctance of any unionist/loyalist party to oppose the Orange line on marching.

The rub, then, is that in practice commitment to the overriding priority of British sovereignty in matters affecting reform of Northern society, is a culturally encumbered act: it creates cultural conditions and expectations that, when unfulfilled, give rise to Protestant discontent, if not also unrest. It is a commitment that raises the stakes for unionists generally, so that when it is rebuffed it engenders a feeling of loss, a conviction that society is being shaped independently of unionist control and in ways that are contrary to the interests of its senses of belonging and identity.

The refusal among liberal unionists to acknowledge unionism's cultural attachments suggests their affliction by a peculiar form of blindness. At any rate, they seem to join in a chorus of praise to the unsullied liberal pluralist virtues of making constitutional considerations primary with their eyes firmly shut. For the symbols of Britishness – the Union flag, the name of the RUC, and so on – that are, according to Trimble, indispensable to an affirmation of sovereignty, are not culturally neutral in the context of Northern Ireland. Nor are they presumed to be by anyone outside liberal unionist ranks. The blithe assumption that non-unionists who voted for the Agreement are somehow obliged to concur that symbols of British sovereignty are impartial representations of institutional justice and fairness in a divided society is unconvincing. What does not seem to register is that the name RUC carries connotations of unionist domination; that the Union flag has been used on countless occasions for sectarian purposes, and so forth. For unionists to imagine that all they are proposing here is innocent and in keeping with liberal democratic practice elsewhere is to ignore how and why Northern Ireland was created, why its institutions failed to win nationalist allegiance, why it has been divided (often violently so), and why it has been an abnormal society by typical liberal democratic standards.

To fly in the face of such realities is virtually to act as though the conflict never happened, or as though it served merely to vindicate the cause of unionism. It suggests that the main lesson to be drawn from the last thirty years is one that non-unionists have been slow to learn: that nationalist cloth must be cut more modestly and that republican cloth must be discarded completely. This is, however, a form of make-believe that ignores the composition and nature of Northern society today. It is, unfortunately, a form that is nurtured by the supposition that it is both possible and desirable to employ the principle of British sovereignty to check Northern reforms and types of North–South co-operation that do not fit within the agenda of defending the Union. In short, blindness to what dealing seriously with rifts between citizens requires in Northern Ireland accompanies preoccupation with the constitutional standard of legitimacy. To overextend the reach of any sovereignty principle here guarantees only ongoing divisions.

So too does the way in which unionists have played the issue of *decommissioning*. This is not to infer that everything they say about it or, indeed, about paramilitary disbandment, is invalid. There are democratic considerations here that pose acute difficulties for republican views of legitimacy. I return to these shortly. For the moment, it is sufficient to say that there is prima facie plausibility to a number of unionist objections: that without Provisional IRA weapons being put beyond use it is not possible for the kind of relations of trust to be developed that enable Northern society to achieve a level of workable decency; that it is unacceptable to have a party in government with a private army behind it; that this constitutes an implicit threat to unionists that is intolerable in a democracy, and so forth.

These sorts of objections, however, would carry more authoritative force if they were not isolated from other problems in Northern society, and if they were detached from the unionist agenda of prioritising the principle of British sovereignty. Part of the problem here is that unionists tend to disregard the larger context within which discussion of decommissioning, disbandment and the application of democratic principles find their place. Northern Ireland is an abnormal society that has been racked by conflict and division, and by competing sovereignty claims. The issues of decommissioning and disbandment are properly seen in the light of the bigger project of the implementation of all aspects of the Agreement, including reform of Northern society, demilitarisation, and fully functioning North–South institutions. The Agreement indicates how we in the North may win through to democratic achievements. And, since it is far-fetched to suppose that these will happen overnight, it is implausible to insist on an immediate and mechanical application of abstract democratic principles independently of other changes to practices and institutions. Democracy's achievements require a considerable amount of good will from unionists, loyalists, nationalists and republicans in order to be realised.

Here unionists attached too little weight to concessions republicans had already made through Sinn Féin's participation in partitionist arrangements, for example, and through movement towards decommissioning that the Provisional IRA initiated even prior to putting some of its weapons beyond use. With regard to the latter, it is worth recalling that the Provisional IRA remained on ceasefire and had not turned its weapons on British forces for years. Moreover, international arms inspectors verified that its weapons were in dumps, and it indicated a willingness to decommission them to the satisfaction of the Independent International Commission on Decommissioning set up under the terms of the Agreement. Indeed, there is every reason to believe that if unionists had been prepared to trust the judgement of General de Chastelain and his colleagues, decommissioning may have occurred earlier.

Unionists also seem inclined to forget that there is an equal onus on loyalists to decommission their weapons, not least since it is their ceasefires that are most doubtful (a fact confirmed by the British government's decision in October 2001 to declare those of the UDA and Loyalist Volunteer Force (LVF) over). The readiness of (some) unionist politicians to offer half-hearted criticisms of loyalist violence is at best unhelpful. When they infer that loyalist paramilitary activities are ultimately the fault of the IRA because of its failure to decommission, they are indulging bad politics, even worse morality, and for those religiously disposed (as many are), appalling theology. And, not least, with the start to IRA decommissioning and the breakdown of the UDA's ceasefire, the inference is also plainly absurd.

Against this backdrop, Trimble's persistence in exerting pressure on Sinn Féin over the decommissioning issue – by resigning as First Minister, threatening to withdraw unionist ministers from the Executive, vetoing the official participation of Sinn Féin ministers in North–South meetings (despite two legal findings against him), and continuing to operate in a confrontational mode – was hardly conducive to resolving outstanding difficulties. His justification for such persistence and conduct – 'it's the only language republicans understand' – would be laughable (after all, how would he know since he has never tried using any other language in his dealings with Sinn Féin?) if it did not have potentially serious negative ramifications. These are ramifications that are likely only to be exacerbated by Trimble's continued use of confrontational language in his current demand for an immediate disbandment of the Provisional IRA.

I have already commented in Chapter 4 on the views of language at work within unionism that explain part of what is going on here. What we are dealing with are anti-dialogical practices that run counter to any idea of fair interactions and rule out any possibility of a sense of commonality emerging through a reasonable discussion of unionist and republican differences. But to change these practices would mean that unionists would have to listen to republican understandings of the Agreement, of how decommissioning and disbandment fit with other reforms that have not yet occurred, of how unionist practices are an obstacle to their achievement, of why it is not only Sinn Féin's responsibility to create the conditions that make them likely but the UUP's as well. This is not to exonerate republicans' line on decommissioning and disbandment – I am shortly going to be sharply critical of it – but to suggest that there was space for a serious unionist–republican dialogue over arms and related issues that never occurred because of unionism's confrontationalist tactics. And it is immensely naïve for pro-Agreement unionists to believe that having (apparently) got their way over decommissioning by acting as they did, they have the winning recipe for dealing with any future dispute with Sinn Féin, such as one over the conditions and timing of paramilitary disbandment. But this is not a message they are keen to hear. The trouble is that unionists retain an incentive for sticking with their divisive tactics and practices, namely protecting the invulnerability of their interpretation of the Agreement with its pristine line on the primacy of British sovereignty.

It is a mistake to underestimate the problem this incentive poses. Trimble has risked his reputation within unionism, and his party has embarked on a strategy with potential electoral pitfalls, on the judgement that anti-Agreement unionists got it wrong, that the Agreement secures the Union. The terms of this judgement are such that it can be vindicated only in a way that even anti-Agreement unionists should be obliged to accept. And that means by Trimble's lexical ordering of the standards of legitimacy winning the day. Not least because anti-Agreement unionists do not believe that two acts of decommissioning by the Provisional IRA constitutes evidence that this has yet happened, the pressure on Trimble not to relax his narrowly procedural interpretation of the Agreement's constitutional checks on reform and requirements on arms is considerable. Accordingly, there is little motivation to make the reading of the Agreement, on which so much hangs, a hostage to fortune. On this logic, in the absence of decommissioning that is what counting republicans among the class of political actors to whom reasonableness is due would amount to, since it would involve entertaining an interpretation of the Agreement that downplays the sovereignty principle the UUP has made decisive.

It is true that the SDLP is also a threat on this point, but the main tactic so far has been to avert potential trouble from that source by playing hard ball with Sinn Féin first on the question of decommissioning and now on that of disbandment. What matters most is not relinquishing the primacy of the sovereignty principle. Prior to the explicit demand for disbandment, Provisional IRA decommissioning could be construed as unionism's victory here, as could Sinn

Féin's abandonment by other parties and the two governments. Failing either of these outcomes, upping the stakes by gambling with the future of the Agreement itself was the next best outcome. It is unionist interests, which Trimble has tied indissolubly to the determining role of the constitutional standard of legitimacy, that are of the utmost importance to the Agreement's unionist supporters and opponents alike. And with a commencement to decommisssioning by the Provisional IRA, Trimble could for a while overlook the spin republicans put on it by satisfying himself that it implied acquiescence to his reading of the overriding constitutional ramifications of the Agreement. Now that disbandment of the Provisional IRA has replaced decommissioning as the primary condition of political progress, Trimble has simply reverted to his pre-decommissioning logic: until republicans comply with the condition (once decommissioning, now disbandment) that is taken to underwrite the primacy of the standard of constitutional legitimacy, there can be no sharing government with Sinn Féin.

To sum up, by prioritising defence of the Union, pro-Agreement unionists offer an often tendentious interpretation of the Agreement. This is one that, in its insistence on the centrality of a formal principle of sovereignty, is prepared to excuse tactics and practices that do nothing to improve relations within a divided society. The twists and turns of Trimble's strategic manoeuvrings to outflank his unionist and republican opponents, and his gambles with the future of the Agreement have ensured that Northern politics lurch from one near-crisis to another. They also add to the uncertainty that afflicts a unionist politics of belonging. At one level, they suggest that unionists are most at home when politics follow a set of clear procedures underpinned by first principles that guarantee Northern Ireland's Britishness. At another level, they indicate that many unionists also require political endorsement of cultural practices and symbols that carry unmistakably Protestant connotations. Unionists' security may lie principally at the first level, but for many it seems to need reinforcing at the second. But in playing politics at both these levels, a unionist politics of belonging betrays exclusive instincts that virtually dictate that unionist experience, like Northern political experience in general, will be crisis-ridden and uncertain. And this is something that neither Trimble's bluster about achieving 'an internal settlement', nor calculative moves to squeeze nationalists and republicans into accepting his version of constitutional exactitude, can succeed in hiding.

The difficulty for unionists is that they can no longer get by without non-unionist support. And that is precisely what is missing, since the procedures and principles on which they rely at one level, and the practices and symbols they want underwritten at another, are unacceptable to nationalists and republicans. They unduly restrict the scope available to non-unionists' cultural dignity as citizens by continuing to privilege unionist and British identities in the institutional life of the North. They do not come close to satisfying nationalist and republican aspirations to belong. The twist now is that as a consequence unionists' aspirations are doomed to be similarly frustrated. If Northern Ireland does not work for nationalists, it will not work for unionists either. Circumstances in the North today are such that (full) belonging is a mutual achievement or it is nobody's. And pragmatic muddling through can only hide this uncomfortable reality for so long. That is why reconciliation's requirement of inclusive citizen belonging does not only make moral sense, it makes compelling practical sense too. In failing to appreciate this, Trimble's endeavour to win victories for unionism that nationalists find unpalatable only serves to increase unionists' sense of loss when they are not forthcoming. The tragedy is not that Trimble's reading of the Agreement is not finding the support he seeks – it does not deserve to – but that it heightens tensions and divisions. The politics of belonging that runs through the mix of constitutional exactitude and cultural practices unionism advocates, are in many respects inimical to reconciliation and do not do citizens any favours by making its task more difficult than it need be.

BETWEEN UNITY AND REFORM

For republicans what counts about the Agreement is that it initiates a process that involves reform, if not transformation, of Northern society, and opens the door to a united Ireland. For them the key to legitimacy is the entire package of measures involved in this process. There are ambiguities here. One thing is clear though: an unreformed Northern Ireland is an illegitimate political entity. Whether a reformed/transformed one would be legitimate is a more difficult matter to decide. But if unionism's emphasis falls on the constitutional standard of majority consent, republicanism's falls on the institutional standard of cross-community agreement informed by norms of justice and fairness. Seeing this institutional standard properly applied without undue constriction by the constitutional standard is evidently a priority for Sinn Féin. But so too is achieving a united Ireland. The relation of these priorities to each other raises interesting questions about a republican politics of belonging that bear upon various practices and understandings of legitimacy.

Let's take three possible readings of the relationship between the priorities. On one, the priority of a united Ireland is uppermost and that of institutional reform (which, for convenience, I now want to understand broadly to include changes to the character of Northern society and the development of North–South bodies) is subservient to it. Here the appropriate way of describing the connection between these priorities is to say that reform is important for the sake of unity, since it is through reform that Irish unity is now best pursued. Sure, reform may have its own benefits in improving the current lot of republicans within Northern Ireland, but its principal value consists in its ability to serve the ultimate purpose of achieving an all-Ireland republic.

On another reading, however, there has been a mostly unadvertised adjustment to the weightings of republicanism's priorities, with more emphasis falling now on institutional reform. Here reform is more unambiguously considered a good thing in its own right and its value is not measured in terms of its service to the cause of unity. In other words, reform cannot be scuppered for unity's sake, since on this reading it cannot be reduced merely to a strategic ploy. Irish unity remains a strongly desired outcome, of course, but it is no longer an overriding determinant of republican policy and tactics.

It is possible to find support for both of these readings in recent statements from Sinn Féin leaders.[9] But, since it is unclear that either properly captures the current position of Sinn Féin, I want to leave them aside for the moment. For it seems that republicans regard treating them as distinct readings, which imply potentially conflicting rankings of their priorities, as certainly inconvenient and possibly distorting. It suits Sinn Féin to collapse the two into one and thereby to offer a third reading, which encourages thinking of its *priorities as complementary*, as merely different sides of the same new coin with which republicanism is presently trading. For instance, republicans are now saying that since the road of reform still keeps hope of reaching the destination of Irish unity very much alive, it is perfectly plausible to exploit reform's immediate advantages without diminishing the ongoing importance of unity. And, as both priorities can be affirmed simultaneously, there is no need to explore possible tensions between them.

Or, better, this third reading appears to make the priorities of reform and unity co-equal and, therefore, denies the appropriateness of ranking them. It may be taken to do so on the grounds that they are interlocking or co-dependent. Reform is unity's equal because it is integral to unity's realisation. This is to say that reform is incomplete without unity, because unity is its *telos*. And, likewise, it is to say that unity is dependent upon reform, since without it, the dawning of a thirty-two county Irish republic will be postponed, perhaps indefinitely.

UNITY AND REFORM

The claims deemed capable of backing up this view of the interlocking nature of unity and reform include at least the following. (1) A proper extension of the norms of justice and equality, upon which reform is based, delivers a compelling case for unity. (2) Besides, given that thoroughgoing reform achieves much that was traditionally expected of unity, it is a short step to complete it through a constitutional change that makes all-Ireland arrangements comprehensive. (3) It is easier to anticipate unionists taking this step as they become more accustomed to reform, not least to its North–South component, and so realise that their fears of unity were unfounded. (4) It is also a step that, in the context of a shift of emphasis from militarism to reform, is made increasingly imminent by demographic changes in the North, which will soon see a nationalist majority there. (5) Unity remains historically inevitable and reform, unlike militarism whose course is run, now hastens its arrival by creating conditions that facilitate a smoother transition to its achievement.

The final claim, which is presumed to be reinforced by the other four, is pivotal. To clarify, its invocation of a long-standing republican thesis of historical inevitability is traditionally understood to mean that there is an intrinsic purpose in Irish history, which will be fully revealed when it is brought to realisation through an appropriate form of agency. And, strikingly, when militarism and then a mix of militarism and political action proved to be inappropriate forms – as their failure to deliver a united Ireland attests – republicans were disinclined to question the thesis itself. Instead, after paying due homage to the contribution made by militarism to the cause of Irish unity, they latched on to another form of agency, namely a republican-driven process of political reform. As a consequence, Sinn Féin replaced the Provisional IRA as the central actor within republicanism.

Three points are instantly significant here. First, even with this change of agency, the current republican position keeps faith with the structure of the traditional formulation of the inevitability thesis: it is through a suitable form of agency that Ireland's historic destiny will be fulfilled.

Second, the change of agency has, nevertheless, important ramifications. The change casts Sinn Féin in a catalytic role as reform's champions and overseers. But this new form of agency does not just consist in the activities of Sinn Féin, however indispensable they are taken to be. It encompasses the entire process of reform, including, therefore, those activities of unionists that aid, rather than obstruct, the process. Thus looms what must seem to republicans as a delicious irony: the prospect of pro-Agreement unionists serving as unwitting agents of Irish destiny. New practices also accompany agency's change, most notably those bound up with ongoing attempts to woo unionists to the cause of reform, and with a determination to save the Agreement from collapse in order to keep the reform process alive, even at the price of decommissioning Provisional IRA weapons under less than optimal conditions. Of course, decommissioning is not such a massive price to pay once reform dislodges militarism as the principal form of agency. And, besides, although the timing of decommissioning was doubtless influenced by unprecedented US pressure following the terrorist attacks in New York and Washington DC on 11 September, it proceeded on the back of assurances of British moves on demilitarisation and pro-Agreement unionist willingness to allow the institutions set up under the Agreement to function without further blocks. In other words, enough was guaranteed in the name of reform to permit more concessions on militarism. Thus we may understand the extent of Sinn Féin's enthusiasm for an Agreement that Trimble thinks safeguards the Union.

Third, we may also observe more clearly the distinctive angle of Sinn Féin's focus on the institutional standard of legitimacy in the Agreement. This standard assumes such importance among republicans because it is seen as integral to a process of reform that now enjoys a privileged role as the agent of Irish destiny. This does not mean that they view the standard of constitutional legitimacy as utterly irrelevant. It is more that it should be sidelined until reform has achieved its goal through the emergence of a new Irish republic, for only then will it be linked to a principle of Irish, and not British, sovereignty. On the question of legitimacy, then, the dispute between republicanism and unionism is not only about different emphases on the institutional and constitutional standards contained in the Agreement. It is also about a traditional clash over sovereignty, which remains muted at present because it suits Sinn Féin not to highlight it for fear of jeopardising the process of reform.

If this is Sinn Féin's preferred reading of the relationship between its priorities, it is faced with formidable problems: reform is an improbable agent of destiny; belief in destiny is hugely problematic;

and, as a consequence, the question of legitimacy cannot be handled so neatly. For example, reform's credentials as an agent of Irish unity as laid out in claims about norms, potential achievements of reform, overcoming unionist fears, and demography are quite uncertain. The crucial feature of claims such as these is that they deal with contingent factors that might or might not yield Irish unity. It is a massive, and an unwarranted, assumption to believe that they must. Indeed, each claim can be taken quite plausibly to indicate the sufficiency of reform as an end in itself.

Take the claim (1) about norms of justice and equality extending beyond reform into a case for unity. At best, this claim convinces in highlighting the difficulty of offering a normative justification for partition. If norms of justice and equality, together with the Agreement's standard of constitutional legitimacy, had been adhered to in the early decades of the twentieth century, it is unlikely that Ireland would have been divided into separate jurisdictions. But post-partition, it is not a simple matter of undoing what republicans perceive as eighty years of injustice through a retrospective application of such norms (just as it is similarly not a simple matter of undoing the injustice caused by colonisation through retrospectively applying contemporary norms in countries such as the USA, Canada and Australia, where indigenous populations ended up with much rawer deals than nationalists did in Ireland). Under prevailing circumstances, North and South, the normative case for unity is more complex, though certainly not discredited. But to be persuasive it has to involve reference to a range of complicating considerations, including the prudential and legal reasons unionists cite in support of Northern Ireland's legitimacy; the various agreements reached on the North between democratically elected British and Irish governments; the substantial investments citizens, North and South, have made in their respective polities, and so on.

If it were merely a matter of deciding whether partition was normatively justified in the first instance, these sorts of complications could be screened out and the normative case for unity decided more easily. It is, however, an act of supreme political naïveté to suppose that such complications can be ignored, and it is also dubious to imagine that they do not raise morally significant questions that affect our normative deliberations. Accordingly, those who conclude that it is enough to set our sights on a reform process, thoroughly informed by norms of justice and equality, which is allowed to run its course without the additional promise of unity, are not necessarily employing morally deficient reasoning. At the very least, the normative cases for reform and unity invite further reflection and debate. Unity is not the only normatively valid option here.

Nor is it when we consider the claim (2) about the potential advantages of reform making easier the transition to a united Ireland. If the realisation of the reform process envisaged by the Agreement already entails satisfaction of various traditional aspirations of unity – closer integration of North and South, the end of unionist rule, changes to the character of Northern society – then looking for a further transition may seem superfluous; and all the more so if the prize of leaving it aside is significant unionist approval of reform. Sure, as claim (3) anticipates, experience of reform might overcome unionists' fears of unity, and even put some of them in the mood for it, but it does not guarantee their enthusiasm to break the tie with Britain as republicans would wish. To imagine unionists opting for unity is to project a scenario that has no basis in historical experience. And to think that unity is feasible without unionist consent may be something that republicans are content to live with, but it is not something that any Irish government is likely to welcome. So, again, getting unionists to go along with reforms that satisfy much that was associated with unity may seem to many as more than enough for the time being.

If republicans have no compelling reasons for envisaging unionist consent to reform's extension into unity, then the claim (4) about demography indicates little more than a willingness to short-circuit the onerous task of persuading unionists of unity's benefits. At heart, it is a very crude claim: whether unionists like it or not, Irish unity is going to happen because Catholics are outbreeding Protestants in the North. But if or when Protestants become a minority in Northern Ireland is a matter of conjecture, and the assumption that a Catholic majority would be enough to secure unity ignores what every opinion poll has shown, namely that a sizeable minority of Catholics have consistently expressed a preference for remaining part of the UK[10]. And, anyway, to win unity on a sectarian head-count bequeaths to a future Dublin administration the disquieting prospect of an aggrieved Protestant minority that would prove very difficult to mollify. A reform process that relies ultimately on demographic change to effect its translation into unity is on shakier ground than republicans are happy to admit. It anticipates a potentially uncongenial political situation that many proponents of reform regardless of unity may be inclined to sidestep, not least because instead of completing a process of reform that carried extensive unionist support, it might undo it.

To repeat, the four claims above may give substance to hope in unity's eventual arrival, but they need not. And, as I have tried to indicate, there are serious reasons why it should not be assumed that they will. The upshot is that reform is an unreliable agent of unity. To suppose that the inconvenience of this upshot can be overcome by reiterating the claim (5) that unity is destiny is easily the least defensible move of all. No doubt belief in destiny has been a sustaining myth for republicanism, which has fuelled its ethos of resistance to British and unionist rule through difficult times. But in the absence of a divine, historical or natural law that necessitates a united Ireland, there is little else to be said for it. The inevitability thesis or belief in destiny is nothing more than a hoary republican fiction; and one that has not always had benign implications.

The line on legitimacy suggested by this third reading of the relationship between republicanism's priorities also is hard to sustain. Forestalling on the issue of constitutional legitimacy until the process of reform delivers the right constitutional outcome is at once a disingenuous strategy. It is one that puts a cynical gloss on the rationale of currently focusing on the institutional standard of legitimacy alone. But if the approved constitutional result is not a foregone conclusion, and if there are reasons to doubt whether reform will produce it, then both the strategy and coherence of the position on legitimacy implied by the third reading become suspect. In short, the attempt to posit the priorities of reform and unity as co-equal begins to falter noticeably.

It falters rather more decisively when we face the fact that, on the terms of the third reading, the priorities are not co-equal at all. Unity continues to be treated as an inviolable republican principle, while reform enjoys its elevated status only due to a belated rethinking of agency. So, whereas the goal of unity is immune from scrutiny, reform remains in principle vulnerable to another shift in republicanism's strategic planning. And, if the grounds for buying the third reading are as slippery as I have argued, some sort of shift is always on the cards – if not from the current leadership of the republican movement, which has probably invested too heavily in reform to back away from it and save face, then from a subsequent leadership.

UNITY OR REFORM?

One way out of the quandary here is to revert to the second reading of the relationship between republicans' priorities, by making reform unreservedly primary. This would enable republicans to pursue a strategy that appeals at every turn to normative justifications, that frees their commitment to the Agreement's standard of institutional legitimacy from cynical connotations, and that reflects more comfortably the democratic self-image that Sinn Féin is cultivating. Of course, it would also mean that the goal of unity becomes susceptible to revision. In effect, it implies republicans having to settle for whatever reform proves capable of delivering, even if that falls short of a thirty-two county Irish republic.

The difficulty is that, in a sense, the second reading points to an even greater transformation of republicanism than that called for in the change of agency's form from militarism to reform. It projects the republican movement down an exclusively political path without the aid of a consoling belief in unity's inevitability. And, for all the adjustments that republicans have made, this explicitly asks more of them than they have ever been prepared openly to give. To explain, it is naïve to suppose that republicans would have agreed to a shift of agency, which made decommissioning of

Provisional IRA weapons possible, if they did not believe that Sinn Féin's political gains were a sure indicator that reform was the most effective route to unity. That is why what is being requested in the second reading cuts more deeply into the heart of republicanism: it requires (at least a tacit) willingness to sacrifice the very belief that made it possible to effect a change of agency.

This is a requirement that the third reading tries valiantly to avoid by tying reform inextricably to unity. But if, as I have suggested, this reading is not viable, then the best way of escaping it is to resort to the first reading, which leaves intact the traditional ranking of unity over agency. This means of escape from an unpalatable requirement remains a powerful temptation within republicanism. Accordingly, even if it is scarcely acknowledged, and even if self-confident rhetoric often disguises it, republicanism faces a predicament. Deprived of a plausible refuge in the reassuring evasions of the third reading, it is caught between the other two, with *unity and reform competing for the primary role* in shaping republicanism's orientation to post-Agreement politics.

There is quite a lot at stake in this competition. The question of republicanism's relation to its past, which brings into focus the lingering influence of militarism and its connotations, is at its centre. Here, the first reading still exercises a hold over republican imaginations that goes unchallenged by Sinn Féin and that the second has difficulty breaking. This is due in large measure to the value placed on continuity within republicanism, which an affirmation of unity's primacy appears to facilitate, but which a prioritisation of reform potentially disrupts. For example, existentially speaking, the first's attraction compared to the second may be summed up in these simple propositions: (1) the goal of unity was traditionally pursued through armed struggle; (2) ditching armed struggle in favour of reform is bearable for the sake of unity; (3) but ditching it for the sake of reform itself, with unity relegated to an uncertain aspiration, is close to unbearable (for many republicans).

To press further, when propositions (1) and (2) are taken together, as the first reading recommends, it is easier to spin the line that only an astute tactical change at the level of agency has occurred. More than that, the first reading also permits referring to reform as building on the achievements of militarism, and to Sinn Féin as benefiting from the ground-clearing work of the Provisional IRA. Far from seeming futile, then, militarism can be presented as virtually anticipating its own transcendence by creating conditions that made reform possible. Continuity within republicanism is thereby maintained. And in allowing that reform merely promises to complete a process, already begun by militarism, that reaches its *telos* in unity, the first reading discourages debate about potentially difficult issues such as the legitimacy of the Provisional IRA and its activities.[11]

The second reading, which is associated with the proposition (3) that loosens reform's attachment to any pre-given outcome, does not guarantee continuity. Indeed if, as it implies, the goal of unity is no longer privileged, then policies and tactics that appeared justifiable (however debatably) when unity's primacy was unproblematically accepted suddenly appear in a different light. The second reading threatens to open precisely that door on republicanism's past that the first keeps firmly shut. It has no reason aside from convenience for wanting to prevent awkward questions being asked of militarism and its legacy within republicanism. If anything, it is better served by having them raised, since the greatest obstacle to an unrestrained embrace of reform's priority comes from the pull of the first reading. Not only does the first restrict reform to an instrumental role; it also indulges a romanticisation of republicanism's militaristic past. In doing so, it leaves undisturbed attitudes and assumptions that are hard to defend in general and impossible to square in particular with an ambition to achieve a reconciled society.

The troubling aspects of the first reading are linked to beliefs and practices associated with the alleged legitimacy of the Provisional IRA. Maintaining the primacy of the goal of Irish unity as a guide to action does not, of course, necessarily entail such beliefs and practices. But they have been a distinctive feature of republicanism's commitment to unity's primacy. No doubt, with the shift from militarism to reform, many former practices have been abandoned, but others persist, as does belief in the Provisional IRA's legitimacy. Even so, making an issue of these may be judged a mistake. Perhaps, given the change of agency, a version of pragmatic muddling through is the best way of handling tensions within republicanism over unity and reform, including questions about the Provisional IRA.

For instance, it might seem imprudent, if not also an act of bad faith, to interrogate beliefs and practices that principally refer to a pre-ceasefire and pre-Agreement Northern Ireland. After all, it is these that the republican movement has determined through its actions, if not yet through its creed, to leave behind in its current pursuit of political reform. Therefore, rather than draw attention to worries about beliefs and practices that echo in the present but belong essentially to a past that republicanism is already moving beyond, it might seem better to shrug at the occasional commotion they cause and let them fade gradually into the background undistracted by critical comment. Holding to the conviction that discomfiting items of republican baggage can be quietly discarded as future circumstances dictate, the pragmatic point is to encourage its new reformist inclinations and leave its views on unity and the Provisional IRA – much like unionist views of the Union – to take care of themselves. The line is that all of these bones of contention will eventually be resolved if we spare ourselves from ongoing rancour and simply ignore them for now.

As with most versions of pragmatic muddling through, there is merit in such reasoning. In the context of a divided society, where no side has clean hands, it is frequently impolitic to insist on political actors purging themselves of all vestiges of questionable beliefs and practices before progress is allowed to occur. The issue of decommissioning is a good example. For reasons already aired, I think unionists were wrong to risk the Agreement itself on this issue. It just is fortuitous for Trimble that events in the USA on 11 September made possible what his confrontational pressure had failed to deliver, but which might have been possible much earlier through dialogue. And whether the Provisional IRA's acts of decommissioning prove sufficient to keep further crises at bay remains to be seen. As I have noted already, they have not proved nearly enough for anti-Agreement unionists to throw themselves into the project of fashioning a new Northern society. But to say that political progress has been unwisely held up for more than three years because of unionism's preoccupation with constitutional exactitude (which republicans still do not believe they have conceded, whatever Trimble chooses to believe to the contrary) does not mean that the republican movement should be let off the hook for its stance on decommissioning and other issues.

Put succinctly, I am claiming three things here. First, in line with the above rationale of pragmatic muddling through, there are persuasive political reasons in the context of Northern Ireland for not allowing an issue such as decommissioning to block reform, even if the reasons for retaining weapons are dubious. But, second, this does not mean that those invoking dubious reasons should not be answerable for them. And, third, in the absence of reasonable debate about the sources of our divisions, of which weapons are a product, pragmatism can only take us so far. It cannot deliver a reconciled society, since it glosses over precisely what needs sorting out if we are to achieve it, and at best serves only to create certain conditions that contribute to its possibility.

Extending beyond the issue of decommissioning, it is important for the sake of reconciliation to probe more deeply than pragmatism advises those tensions between republicans' priorities that potentially hamper reform. And that means here attending to controversial connotations of the first reading. As I now want to argue, the terms on which republicanism clings to the *primacy of unity* involve views about the Provisional IRA's legitimacy that are not only a massive problem for unionists and other non-republicans, but are also incoherent, implausible and conducive to divisive practices. These views should not be ignored precisely because they are a serious impediment to reconciliation and to republicanism's full acceptance of the Agreement, including its constitutional provisions.

The Provisional IRA is deemed an illegal organisation in Britain and Ireland. Yet, on the issue of decommissioning, for example, the

Provisional IRA reserved the right to take its own counsel and to decide on its own terms if, when and how arms would be put beyond use. Its arrogation of such a right, which indicates that it does not consider itself subject to the authority of the British or Irish governments, is grounded in traditional Irish republicanism's opposition to partition. It is based on three premises. First, since partition violated the Irish nation's right to self-determination, it is illegitimate, as are the governments, North and South, created as a result of it. Second, until the injustice of partition is corrected, the Army Council of the IRA is the legitimate heir of the last pre-partition Irish government and the Provisional IRA is the legitimate Irish army. Third, the current Provisional IRA, formed in 1969 following a split in the republican movement, properly appropriated these mantles of republican legitimacy and was justified in declaring war on Britain in the name of the Irish people and for the sake of righting the wrongs inflicted on Ireland by partition. Given such premises, the Provisional IRA, which announced a ceasefire as an undefeated army, is entitled to rely on its own authority in all matters pertaining to decommissioning.

It has been some time since republican practice has meshed with this form of reasoning. Put simply, it is incoherent to endorse a change of agency from militarism to reform and yet continue to accept that, pending unity, the Provisional IRA represents legitimate authority in Ireland. Reform necessarily entails practices that recognise anything but such a view of the Provisional IRA. Otherwise expressed, faithfulness to the legitimacy claims of the Provisional IRA requires strict anti-partitionist or abstentionist policies that the republican movement abandoned in the 1980s. And, equally, faithfulness to the path of reform requires giving up these legitimacy claims. From one angle, then, much republican practice now subverts its traditional theory about the Provisional IRA, and, from another, commitment to this traditional theory restricts the outworking of practices of reform. Not to admit the incompatibility of traditional republican theory and new republican practice is incoherent.

Consider how it is that reform-oriented practices no longer fit with traditional theory. For instance, the claim that the Provisional IRA has the right to call its own tune on decommissioning by virtue of representing authentic Irish authority makes sense, however perversely, if a stringent anti-partitionist line is upheld (even though it would hardly be contemplated short of a united Ireland on these terms). At least when the primacy of armed struggle is asserted and the temptation of becoming entangled in partitionist structures, North or South, is resisted, the claim is not compromised by republicans' complicity in their dealings with alternative institutions of authority. The same cannot be said when republicans – sitting as members of the Dáil and the Assembly and serving as ministers in the Northern Executive – are involved in working partitionist arrangements in both jurisdictions in Ireland. For then they are open to the charge of undermining the basis of the Provisional IRA's putative authority: by implicitly acknowledging the legitimacy of partition and by operating under political authorities that find the Provisional IRA's claim to authority intolerable. Certainly, there is a good case for saying that republican abstentionism makes unity's achievement highly unlikely, that it makes impeccable pragmatic sense to pursue unity through reform rather than through armed struggle, and that doing so means participation in partitionist arrangements is unavoidable. But the case that compels eschewing abstentionism for the sake of unity also implies dumping the authority claims of the Provisional IRA. Traditional republican theory is out of kilter with republicanism's change of agency.

That is not the whole story, of course. To intimate a line I want to press shortly, the persistence of the theory also circumscribes the space available to reform, and not all of republicanism's contemporary attitudes and practices mirror its change of agency. The salient point now is that republicans' belief in the intrinsic dignity of their brand of militarism – reflected in their theory of the Provisional IRA's privileged status – still impinges on the present in ways that put the process of reform under pressure. This is evident in the expectation that others should respect entitlements claimed by republicans on decommissioning, say, that ultimately invoke the legitimacy of the Provisional IRA. There is a limit to how much any form of democratic politics, and especially one in a divided society, can bear the strain caused by such a presumptuous expectation. Even if we allow, as I have argued we should, that there are extenuating circumstances in Northern Ireland that do not warrant collapsing the Agreement over issues such as decommissioning, it does not wash for republicans to pursue reform but still keep the Provisional IRA's legitimacy claims in reserve until the goal of unity is reached.

The attempt to have it both ways – and so dodge facing the incoherence of a position that undercuts and clings to traditional legitimacy claims – is not convincingly pulled off by distinguishing between republicanism's political and military wings. To suppose it is sufficient to refer to Sinn Féin and the Provisional IRA as different organisations with their own rationales implies a distinction of substance that may be suited to international consumption, but not domestic. It is understandably rejected as a cynical joke by unionists. This is not to deny that there are separate republican organisations with different structures and ways of doing things. But what irks about the distinction is that it invites us to turn a blind eye to the problem of overlapping political and military memberships within republicanism. And it also asks us to buy an image of symmetry, whereby a supposedly unified republican movement operates unproblematically with its political and military wings adhering to conflicting standards of legitimacy. This demands too great a suspension of critical judgement. The fiction of republican symmetry can be maintained only by Sinn Féin declining publicly to distance itself from the Provisional IRA's legitimacy claims, as its orientation to reform suggests it should.

These are very implausible claims to remain silent about. It is little wonder that Sinn Féin does not advertise them, but it is unimpressive that it does not do more to distance itself from them. For a start, the basic premise upon which the Provisional IRA's claims relies arguably no longer holds. To recall, the premise is that the legitimacy of democratically elected Irish and British authorities is justifiably not acknowledged because partition violated the Irish nation's right to self-determination. But this is hard to sustain given that an overwhelming majority of citizens on the island of Ireland endorsed the new arrangements of government outlined in the Agreement. This should count decisively for Sinn Féin, especially since it helped to negotiate these arrangements and presents itself as a democratic party. And assuming the realisation of the Agreement's reform package, it has no excusable reason for not accepting the legitimacy of the constitutional provisions that accompany reform. The point is that the Agreement, including its reform and constitutional stipulations, has all-Ireland support. Post-Agreement Northern Ireland is regarded as a legitimate political entity by the bulk of citizens, nationalist, republican and unionist.

Yet it is precisely this point that Sinn Féin is curiously reluctant to concede. Despite the Agreement, the tug of traditionalism has not disappeared. All-Ireland support of the Agreement may be welcome but it does not constitute an act of national self-determination. Therefore, republicanism's basic premise has not been invalidated, since the principle of legitimacy enshrined in it has not been satisfied. Or so the argument in defence of reluctance might go. But, whatever about republicans' pragmatic tactical flexibility, it is an argument that appeals only to an unbending, fundamentalist mentality. Three things about it are quite extraordinary: first, the hubris involved in discounting the moral and political weight of citizens' unequivocal verdict in favour of the Agreement; second, the assumption that the principle of self-determination admits of only one canonical interpretation – which draws on a pre-partition ideal – in the circumstances of a divided society eighty years after partition; and third, the failure to grasp the democratic significance of the fact that beyond the confines of the republican movement there is no sympathy for the view that republicanism's canonical interpretation should trump the citizens' verdict. It is difficult not to conclude that disregard of democracy is at work here. Certainly, it is a conclusion that is encouraged by talk of the Provisional IRA not being bound by the terms of the Agreement, since only Sinn Féin was a signatory to it. Besides hinting at the schizophrenic condition of republicanism, such talk suggests that democracy is fine only when it delivers the right constitutional result, namely one extending Irish sovereignty into the North.

Lack of democratic credibility has, of course, always been the problem with the Provisional IRA's legitimacy claims. Admittedly, the claim of its first premise protests against partition's violation of a core democratic principle – national self-determination – but the claims of its other premises pay scant regard to democratic considerations. For even if partition was illegitimate, and even if there had not been an Agreement endorsed by citizens in both jurisdictions in Ireland, it scarcely follows that the Provisional IRA is the legitimate voice of Irish authority. Its self-appointed role as custodian of Irish sovereignty and democracy appeals to a certain notion of tradition, and not democracy, for its justification.

To explain, accepting the Provisional IRA's legitimacy claims is equivalent to believing that democracy in post-partition Ireland is in such a state of corruption that it requires the guidance of republican tradition, not to mention the interventions of the Provisional IRA. The tradition of physical force republicanism is presumed to be a repository of superior wisdom and authority that cannot be matched by democratically elected governments, North or South. Or so the other premises of the case for Provisional IRA legitimacy seem to infer. These speak of the IRA embodying proper political–military authority under conditions of partition, and of the Provisional IRA as this authority's current representative. The specific point about the Provisionals may be left aside here, since it refers to an earlier period when there was inter-republican rivalry for the mantle of legitimate heir of the republican tradition. The central question that remains concerns the basis of the legitimacy claimed for a tradition that permits the Provisional IRA to assume an authoritative role, entitling it to declare war on Britain in the name of the Irish people.

Its basis is transparently not democratic. Dissatisfaction with partition has never come remotely close to translating into majority support of republican militarism in either jurisdiction in Ireland. The Provisional IRA simply arrogates the authority to represent the will of the Irish people in ways that manifestly defy the wills of most people living in Ireland, North and South. The fact that it feels justified in doing so indicates that the basis of its alleged legitimacy lies in the tradition it supposedly embodies. Accordingly, it is in the light of republican tradition that corrupt (partitioned) democracies are judged. This implies that the privileged tradition functions like an authoritative metaphysical source to which only the faithful (physical force republicans) have proper access. Thus the Provisional IRA, on the pretext of returning true (unpartitioned) democracy to Ireland, considers itself warranted in ignoring what citizens actually say they do and do not want done on their behalf.

Perhaps the most charitable thing to say here is that the Provisional IRA is displaying an antiquated pre-modern and pre-democratic attitude. 'God, nature and immemorial tradition,' said Arendt, were treated as the ultimate sources of legitimate political authority prior to acceptance of popular consent as the standard of democratic legitimacy.[12] And an Irish republican twist on the third of these sources is arguably involved in the extravagant, non-democratic claim to legitimacy the Provisional IRA is making. This could be regarded as a quaint and tolerable belief within contemporary liberal democratic societies if it served merely as a vehicle of consolation and edification among republicans. But when it is used to usurp democratically based authorities to the point of declaring war in the name of a superior traditional authority then it is a different matter altogether.

It is a serious problem that the basis of the Provisional IRA's claim to legitimacy has no justification that is recognisable in democratic terms and is difficult to concede without the aid of republican faith. And the fact that the Provisional IRA has proved more than ready to override the views of the vast majority of citizens who lack the requisite faith reveals that its claim is not only arrogant, but dangerously so. That is why Robert McCartney is entitled (for once) to use Isaiah Berlin's concept of positive freedom to explain what the Provisional IRA is effectively saying: in the name of a higher freedom, which popular will is too fickle or too ignorant to understand, but which the Provisional IRA represents, the liberation of Ireland from all traces of British rule shall be effected whether that is what citizens want or not.[13] The point is that this is intolerable in a democracy, however imperfect it may be. And the outworking of the Provisional IRA's belief about itself has certainly had terrible consequences in Northern Ireland.

It is perhaps worth adding that republicans cannot plausibly escape responsibility for such consequences by falling back on a weaker form of justification of the Provisional IRA's actions. That is to say, it is unconvincing for republicans to plead exemption from democratic accountability on the grounds of the abnormality of Northern political life or the dubious practices of unionists. There are other and better ways of dealing with these than by expecting citizens to excuse republicans' decision to prosecute an armed struggle. Given its disdain of their democratic rights, the Provisional IRA has no right to expect citizens to regard its claim to legitimacy as anything other than bogus nonsense. And the republican movement as a whole invites ridicule for endorsing, through its support of the Provisional IRA, a conception of legitimacy that scorns deferring to the democratic entitlements of citizens, even as Sinn Féin demands that unionists recognise its democratic mandate and stop treating it like a political pariah. Maybe their self-confidence is so great that republicans believe they can simply gloss over awkward questions about their beliefs and actions, but there is no disguising the fact that talk of the legitimacy of the Provisional IRA today is plagued by incoherence and implausibility.

It is also plagued by the difficulty of divisive practices. Talk of the Provisional IRA's legitimacy dates back, of course, to when militarism was the principal form of agency within the republican movement. And divisive practices are integral to militarism in the very strong sense that, as I argued in Chapter 4, it effectively defines unionists out of existence. As I also pointed out there, a crucial implication of the change of agency from militarism to political reform (which I referred to as a change from a language of violence to a language of dialogue and reconciliation) was that divisive practices were dislodged from the heart of republican activity and unionists were able to be recognised in a new way. Inasmuch as republicans continue to cling to belief in the Provisional IRA's legitimacy, however, their recognition of unionists remains qualified and the problem of divisive practices persists, albeit in less extreme forms. Two of these forms stand out.

First, the legacy of the problem of divisive practices haunts the language of reconciliation republicans feel at liberty to employ. Certainly, Gerry Adams, for example, is right to say that both sides in the North have inflicted terrible pain on the other and that both need to be forgiving if we are to move forward together and create a better society.[14] But there is a limit to the kind of culpability republicans are prepared to admit to here. If it is still believed that the Provisional IRA was justified in waging a war against Britain for a generation, then particular responsibility for various of its deeply divisive practices is evaded in the broad sweep of Adams's language. For example, many innocent victims of the Provisional IRA's activities are reduced to the status of unfortunate, but inevitable, casualties of war. Moreover, there is conspicuous silence on the fact that the Provisional IRA committed sectarian murders, which it has never officially owned up to as sectarian acts.[15] And many of its so-called legitimate targets, whether in the RUC, the Ulster Defence Regiment (UDR), or in industries that serviced them, were also Protestants, and, whatever the niceties of its ideological justifications, it is immensely naïve of republicans not to think that unionists would see the killing of these targets as sectarian to the core.

Second, practices considered constitutive of a republican culture that celebrates the honour of dead Provisional IRA volunteers also appear divisively sectarian to unionists. Much of the cultural–religious imagery drawn on initially to justify and then to commemorate the Provisional IRA's struggle has been expressly Catholic. The sacrificial strand in militant republicanism embodied earlier in the century by Padraig Pearse was fully in play in all its Catholic overtones in the hunger strikes of 1981, and remains evident in how they are remembered today.[16] And, more generally, just as the Union flag has been used by unionists and loyalists with sectarian intent, so has the Irish flag by republicans. If it is grossly a case of special pleading by unionists to exempt British symbols from sectarian connotations in the context of Northern Ireland, it is every bit as bad for republicans to suppose that Irish symbols are free from such connotations when used in displays of triumphalism and defiance here too. For a self-proclaimed non-sectarian movement, republicanism attracts remarkably few Protestants to its ranks. Almost all unionists just do not buy Provisional republicanism's non-sectarian claims about itself; of those from republican backgrounds, only the remnants of the Official IRA that now comprise the Workers' Party are believed on that score. The upshot is that it is make-believe for republicans to think that their practices, especially those attached to affirmations of the Provisional IRA's legitimacy, have not contributed to the problem of a sectarian malaise in Northern society. Sectarianism is not only the fault of unionists/Protestants.

Only a full-blooded *prioritisation of reform*, which expressly relegates unity to an aspiration, seems capable of overcoming the problems associated with the continuing influences of militarism within republicanism. This brings us back again to the second reading of the relationship between republicanism's priorities. As I have already suggested, this reading facilitates unqualified republican appeals to democratic and normative considerations and permits recognition of the entitlements and dignity of unionists. In addition, the decisive departure it indicates from militaristic nationalism can resort to another reason that is intrinsically republican in kind. If it is a classical republican priority – and it has been in the broader Western tradition of republican thought and practice – that citizens identify with the institutions of their society, then it may be questioned why the concept of republicanism should be as closely tied to traditional nationalism as it clearly has been within the Irish republican movement. A concept more attuned to classical republicanism and not so intimately defined in nationalist terms might be expected to emphasise the cardinal importance of institutional legitimacy based on cross-community support and norms of justice and fairness. It is such an emphasis that has the potential to accommodate the cultural dignity of all Northern citizens and make much more likely their allegiance to common institutions.[17] And, partly as a consequence, it is one that also holds out more promise of citizens' political dignity being fulfilled, through their participation in the processes of self-government that are available in a society to which they are all committed.

A further point of attraction here is that the unqualified emphasis on the standard of institutional legitimacy that accompanies prioritising reform calls upon an unambiguously non-sectarian version of republicanism. This is a version that is closer to the spirit of 1798 and its emphasis on the 'unity of Protestant, Catholic and Dissenter', and that, given present circumstances, has greater scope than versions preoccupied with a united Ireland for facilitating citizens' different cultural attachments, even as it stresses the political benefits of a common citizenship.

On the issues of political priorities and understandings of legitimacy, then, the position of republicanism is much more complex than that of unionism. What is obvious, though, is that the three possible readings of republicanism's current position I have discussed are incompatible with unionism's fixation on the principle of British sovereignty derived from the constitutional standard of legitimacy. But whereas two of these – the first and the third – make inconceivable any recognition of Northern Ireland as a legitimate political entity, another – the second reading – does not. It suggests that an institutionally reformed Northern society may be enough to win republican allegiance. With the exception of this reading, which can hardly be taken as established within republican circles, there remains much to be disturbed about in republicanism's current equivocal stance. When unity retains the upper hand in republican thinking, as it does in the first and third readings, a conflict with unionists over sovereignty that can admit in principle of one winner only lies just below the surface, however much attention is directed at the standard of institutional legitimacy. And the impulse of an old republican politics of belonging, which unionists fear as signalling an irreparable rupture of many of their constitutive attachments in Northern Ireland, is also in play.

To prioritise unity under present circumstances means that the dominance of an Irish cultural/national identity simply counts more than anything else; that a republican politics of belonging will not be satisfied with anything less. Trimble may think he is winning now, but republicans think they will win in the long run. The game of gains and losses for one identity or another thus continues despite the Agreement and despite republicans' reconciling noises. And the clash of political priorities and views of legitimacy, along with the persistence of divisive practices, suggest that achievement of inclusive citizen belonging is some way off. Or it does if we think there is little alternative but to work around highly debatable forms of republican and unionist reasoning and simply seize whatever pragmatic opportunities open up.

BELONGING AND A RECONCILED SOCIETY

I have been trying to indicate that there is an alternative and that unionist and republican interpretations of the Agreement should be challenged. The challenges I have offered are intended to suggest what a plausible alternative might look like. To recap, I am claiming that a reconciled society, unlike a perfect one, is a reasonable possibility; that it is a possibility that hangs on the realisation of inclusive citizen belonging; that such a realisation is best understood in terms of recognition of individual, cultural and political modes of citizen dignity; and that these modes are the entitlements of all citizens rather than the exclusive or privileged preserve of members of one tradition or another. As I have been stressing during the last two chapters, however, a conception of a reconciled society, which links inclusive belonging to a multi-faceted understanding of citizenship, has to prove itself in the specific divisive conditions of Northern Ireland. And that means having to encounter difficulties thrown up by contrasting experiences and aspirations of belonging and by the politics that reflect them, especially in the context of opposition to the Agreement and disagreement among its supporters. One point is clear, namely that anti-Agreement unionists and republicans offer no hope of a reconciled society. Another is now almost as obvious: pro-Agreement unionists and republicans offer limited hope of it too.

Concerning the latter point, the problem is that attention is not sufficiently focused on political reconciliation because other unionist and republican interests operate as powerful distractions. As a consequence, many of the particular sources of division in Northern society remain relatively undisturbed and continue to obstruct attempts to meet the requirements of inclusive citizen belonging. These sources are evident in the views of legitimacy and political priorities, as well as in various divisive practices, that are involved in competing politics of belonging, and that still significantly shape unionist and republican interpretations of the Agreement. Part of pursuing the goal of a reconciled society, then, entails showing, as I have been trying to do, why these interpretations are deeply problematic.

It is not enough, in other words, to pay lip service to the claims that all citizens are entitled to belong in their society and that their doing so entails respect of their individual, cultural and political dignity. Taking these claims seriously implies being prepared to tackle impediments to their realisation. As I have been arguing, this means curbing the influence of exclusive unionist and republican politics of belonging. And that in turn suggests revising received political priorities, views of legitimacy and divisive practices. Under the conditions currently prevailing in Northern Ireland, reconciliation's political requirement of inclusive citizen belonging cannot be met without different priorities, views of legitimacy and practices. If this sounds like an impossibly tall order, then, arguably, it is no more than the Agreement anticipates. But this anticipation may be kept alive only by refusing to accept the interpretive constraints of unionism or republicanism. On the crucial questions of legitimacy, priorities and practices, I take such refusal to have something like the following implications.

To start with the vexed question of *legitimacy*, it is sufficient to stick with the reasonable balance the Agreement strikes by distinguishing between its constitutional and institutional senses. Indeed, it is potentially a far-reaching and an inspired move to tie one sense to the standard of Northern citizens' consent and the other to the standard of a cross-community agreement based on norms of justice and fairness. Although this is a move that unionists and republicans helped to negotiate, it is one they seem disinclined to be bound by.

Unionists explicitly and republicans implicitly place inordinate weight on the constitutional standard of legitimacy. For unionists it is immediate recognition of the primacy of this standard that matters, since it currently underscores the Britishness of the North. And it matters so much that it overshadows the institutional standard to such a degree that much proposed reform of Northern society – which goes beyond what is deemed constitutionally permissible – predictably meets with opposition. For republicans, at least on two readings of their present strategy, the constitutional standard matters eventually, that is, once a reform process drawing on the institutional standard of legitimacy has achieved its putative goal of Irish unity.

An inescapable implication of these different emphases on the constitutional standard is that, appearances to the contrary notwithstanding, the old competition between British and Irish principles of sovereignty remains alive and the reasonable balance proposed by the Agreement is subverted. Thus an Agreement that Declan Kiberd, for example, thought left 'behind concepts of sovereignty and nationhood' and provided a 'common bond' among its supporters that 'will probably override their actual relation to their respective powers',[18] is twisted into meaning the opposite as unionists and republicans pursue conflicting constitutional outcomes.

To restore reasonable balance, it is necessary to recover the institutional standard of legitimacy from its position of subservience to the constitutional. This means stating unequivocally that it is neither merely a tool of some future constitutional arrangement nor the poor cousin of some present one. In a divided society, institutional legitimacy should never be forced to play second fiddle, as a reform-oriented reading of republicanism potentially grasps better than any other unionist or republican position we have discussed. The point is straightforward: without institutions that attract the allegiance of citizens, any society, whatever its constitutional arrangements, is in serious trouble. Accordingly, striving for institutions that are just and fair and are perceived to be by citizens from all traditions is indispensable to overcoming divisions in society. But trying to tailor such striving in accordance with a supposedly overriding constitutional imperative is misconceived. Constitutional security has little worth without legitimate institutions, and just how much security there would be in their absence is debatable.

Released from the yoke of constitutional domination, an emphasis on institutional legitimacy puts the issue of sovereignty and its relation to belonging in a different perspective. The hold of thinking that our sense of belonging is impoverished unless linked to a principle of British or Irish sovereignty is broken; instead, belonging is tied to institutions with which all citizens can identify. Accordingly, the question of constitutional belonging is left open. An institutionally reformed Northern Ireland with developed North–South links remaining, as the Agreement initially envisages, within the UK may turn out to be the best possible arrangement for the foreseeable future. Or it may not. Perhaps joining a united Ireland may come to seem an eminently reasonable move. Maybe in a changing European environment neither will be eventually seen as of major consequence. What matters is that in the context of pursuing institutional legitimacy, the most appropriate constitutional outcome for Northern society is that which proves most conducive to uniting divided people, as in their different ways the Alliance Party, the SDLP, the Workers' Party and, more recently, the Northern Ireland Women's Coalition seem to have understood longer and better than most other political actors in the North. The mistake is to attempt the short cut of putting a constitutional outcome ahead of institutional reform, since it succeeds only in reinforcing divisions.

This is a mistake that is easily avoided if the *priority* is to achieve a reconciled society. But it is one that is typically committed if the priority is to defend the Union or to press for a united Ireland. This is not to say that a reconciled Northern society is impossible within either a United Kingdom or an all-Ireland framework; it is in principle possible within either. It is, rather, to say two main things. One is that to prioritise a constitutional outcome, to insist upon the primacy of a British or an Irish framework, is to put reconciliation in a subordinate position; it is to place it at the mercy of unionist or nationalist/republican interests.

As I have been emphasising, reconciliation's subordination to a preferred constitutional arrangement is as foolish as it is familiar. In a polarised society like Northern Ireland, such subordination plays to exclusive aspirations of belonging; it underwrites fixed and privileged notions of British and Irish identities; it panders to registers of gain and loss that operate in terms of sectarian indices. For, however much the rhetoric of inclusion is employed, it is clear that the contest between competing constitutional outcomes involves a contest for cultural domination. And when a particular constitutional outcome is seen as a victory for one cultural/national identity, it is unsurprising that serious resistance is encountered to suggestions that more than the dominant identity should be represented in public institutions. The unfortunate situation in Northern society is that much post-Agreement politics continues to reflect pre-Agreement concerns and the goal of inclusive citizen belonging remains almost as elusive as ever.

Its elusiveness is guaranteed whenever it is considered unproblematic to prioritise a constitutional contest, which engenders the intense cultural antipathies that contribute to appalling community relations and inhibit political co-operation. For the combination of constitutional and cultural differences at work here militate against the achievement of reconciliation's political goal of inclusive citizen belonging, principally because they are contemptuous of the individual, cultural and political modes of dignity of many citizens. This is obviously the case with cultural dignity inasmuch as its full enjoyment appears to depend upon a constitutional victory of one national identity or another: it is then assured that some citizens must lose out. But it is also the case with the individual and political dignity of citizens. Sure, there may seem ample liberal protection of individuals' dignity as free and equal citizens under British and Irish law, but it has been easy in practice for unionists and republicans in the North to justify sacrificing the dignity of certain individuals for the sake of the (supposedly) overriding priority of defending the Union or of advancing Irish unity.

We may, of course, doubt the validity of justifications that entail demonising others in order to excuse mistreating them. Just what sort of conditions have to exist to warrant sacrificing some individuals' dignity, how it could be plausibly maintained that such conditions ever existed in Northern Ireland anyway, and why we should even contemplate thinking of victims of violence as unfortunate, but inevitable, casualties of war are questions that still beg convincing answers from the North's major protagonists. Even in post-Agreement Northern society, there is sufficient sectarian prejudice to enable various unionists and nationalists to act as though the dignity of some individuals is properly treated as subservient to larger cultural/constitutional causes.

In such a society, citizens' political dignity is also precarious. The Agreement has, of course, precipitated increased experience of political dignity by introducing new institutions and practices of self-government. But this experience is limited because it can draw only on a very thin notion of political commonality, namely one which suits competing cultural interests and yields merely uneasy, provisional alliances between them. The point is that even the minimal amount of commonality necessary to sustain a semblance of self-government is perpetually vulnerable to rearticulations of unionist or nationalist interests. Accordingly, political dignity, which is tied to citizen self-rule, always risks being diminished for the sake of cultural/constitutional purposes.

So a central question that is properly asked of unionist and republican priorities of defending the Union or pursuing Irish unity is not why these should matter, but why they should matter *most*. If the costs of making them matter supremely are a continuation of antagonism, fear, suspicion, contempt, misrecognition, and so on, it is entirely germane to wonder about the wisdom of prioritising either. And they appear as utterly misconceived priorities if we think that the individual and political dignity of citizens is important, and that there is something troubling about a mode of cultural dignity that inclines to exclusivity and domination. Quite simply, in the current context of a post-Agreement, yet still deeply divided, Northern Ireland neither unionism's nor republicanism's typical priorities commend themselves if our chief concern is reconciliation.

The other main thing to say here is that once reconciliation is prioritised, it is important to depict Northern society in a way that does not undermine the political ambition of creating a society in which all citizens may belong. It is unhelpful, therefore, to think of the North merely, or even primarily, as a site of the Union or as the lost green field awaiting return to its proper owner. A more suitable depiction arguably thinks of Northern society as a site where British and Irish factors intermingle, sometimes clash and, when not sectarian in nature, warrant mutual recognition, and as a site of civic possibilities. Working on the conviction that the most appropriate constitutional arrangements are those that succeed in uniting divided people, this depiction deliberately plays down the overburdened issue of constitutional sovereignty so crucial to the competitive contest between traditional unionism and nationalism. It suggests that Northern Ireland may become a reconciled society only to the extent that the non-sectarian aspects of its major cultural identities are respected and fairly represented in institutional life and a common civic identity begins to develop. For the point of this depiction, to repeat, is to allow the modes of dignity that constitute inclusive citizen belonging and therefore political reconciliation, to enjoy uninhibited expression.

Thus there can be no question of any individuals being used as fodder for dominant cultural interests. And thus, too, concern for individuals' dignity is not restricted to ensuring their protection against violence and discrimination; it is also about creating opportunities for their flourishing as free and equal citizens: opportunities that are explored in areas of health, education, welfare, employment and so forth. There are signs of the Assembly and the Executive turning attention to enhancing individuals' opportunities to flourish in these areas. A significant part of reconciliation's brief is to encourage the development of such signs, not least by insisting that all citizens are entitled to decent opportunities to flourish and that their entitlement should not be set aside for the sake of cultural/constitutional battle. A depiction of Northern society that facilitates reconciliation also opens up another perspective on the cultural dignity of citizens, by enabling us to think of our major cultural identities as complementary.

Accordingly, a full conferral of dignity does not hang on the outcome of an antagonistic struggle for constitutional victory and cultural domination; it depends more on an embrace of our cultural interrelatedness, which is feasible when satisfaction of the standard of institutional legitimacy is not impeded by constitutional overkill. Appreciating interrelatedness, in other words, implies the presence of institutions that reflect the complexity of our cultural condition in the North and so may command the allegiance of all citizens. Under such circumstances, the cultural dignity of all citizens is catered for because, to borrow from Tully, it comes 'not only from public recognition of one's culture, but also because one's culture is respected among others and is woven into the public fabric of the association, gaining its strength and splendour from its accommodation among, and interrelations with, the others'.[19] This perspective is almost impossible to attain if politics remain stuck in the oppositional game of chasing incompatible constitutional priorities. But it is entirely possible once Northern society is depicted in a way that gives reconciliation its due position.

This is a perspective that also rates highly the political dignity of citizens, which is bound up with self-government. By contrast, once self-government in Northern Ireland is made contingent on the narrow interests driving the divisive cultural manoeuvrings of much unionism and nationalism, citizens' political dignity is severely underrated. That is why the provisional, calculative alliances that the North has experienced since the Agreement are inadequate to the longer-term needs of Northern society, even if they have made a measure of self-rule possible and are an improvement on what went before. The needs that are poorly served here include those focusing on eradicating sectarianism: the dismantling of sectarian structures, the abandonment of sectarian practices and the deconstruction of sectarian mindsets; needs that cannot be met if political dignity is vulnerable to sectarian whims or interests; needs that require much stronger forms of togetherness, namely forms that may endure through the emergence of a common political identity among citizens who are committed to working institutions that do not involve the cultural domination of one tradition by another. Indeed, it is probably true to say that the best way of breaking down antagonism at the cultural level, of fostering thinking of the North's cultures as complementary and interrelated, is by cultivating citizens' identification with the common institutions and practices of self-rule. This is unambiguously to promote the political dignity of all citizens. And the point of doing it is not because it serves or undermines the Union, or because it hastens or delays Irish unity, but because it is now a common political good for Northern citizens. So in the current context of Northern society it is important to take citizens' cultural entitlements and civic possibilities together. If we do not, the danger is that the cultural dimension will spin out of control, despite the Agreement, and wreak a divisive havoc that threatens the individual dignity of citizens, gives only selective regard to their cultural dignity, and plays fast and loose with their political dignity. Prioritising the reconciling ambition of inclusive citizen belonging continues to make compelling political sense.

Now, pressing for reconciliation's priority evidently involves advocating suitable *practices*. To recall the arguments of Chapters 4 and 5, this minimally means opposing the instrumental machinations of many politicians in favour of fair interactions between citizens. It means seeing civic virtues as crucial and the encouragement of dialogue as indispensable rather than optional. No doubt doing so encounters difficulties, because some entrenched cultural practices are obstacles to reconciliation and it may seem impolitic to point this out. But, to repeat, Northern society is hardly going to become less sectarian if people are never challenged to change any of their attitudes or actions. From the angle of reconciliation, it is imperative to work for the transformation of those views and practices that are offensive to others and misrecognise who they are. And this means striving to achieve forms of commonality both through and despite our differences, as the arguments of Chapter 5 suggested.

It is bogus to think that attending to the peculiarities of Northern society somehow invalidates these arguments or makes them less relevant or pressing. It is when we conceive of a reconciled society as a goal that is possible through fair interactions and through pursuit of a commonality that respects our non-sectarian differences, that we have reasons besides mere pragmatism for criticising the lingering influence of militarism in republicanism and loyalism; it is then that we equally have reasons for insisting that dialogue is the way to offset this influence and not counterproductive and often hypocritical threats to collapse the Agreement. The interesting thing here is that in terms of what is necessary to achieve inclusive citizen belonging, various accepted practices in post-Agreement Northern Ireland – where pro-Agreement parties continue to vie for supremacy – appear not only ill-advised but silly. For example, even if Trimble is, as he and his supporters controversially think, playing an astute calculative political game within unionism that serves also to put republicanism on the back foot, it is little more than a misguided distraction if the practices accompanying his political priorities contrive to impede the goal of a reconciled society and reduce it to a distant dream.

CONCLUSION

The various historical experiences and memories of unionists and nationalists make it easy for many of them to conceive of belonging in terms that are most advantageous to their tradition. Whatever sympathies these experiences and memories evoke, they are not sufficient to justify any exclusive conception of belonging. Following the Agreement it seems that most of us agree about that. And yet closer examination reveals that exclusive tendencies are not just restricted to anti-Agreement circles, but that they continue to shape much pro-Agreement politics. The fact that this is so indicates again the sheer difficulty of reconciliation's quest in Northern Ireland. Achieving the goal of inclusive citizen belonging is no easier than achieving fair interactions or a sense of commonality among citizens. There are stubborn cultural and political obstacles here that cannot be effortlessly swept aside. I have tried to show how we might go about tackling these obstacles, and two points about the arguments I have been developing are worth concluding with.

The first is a general one: sensitivity to reconciliation's difficulties in the context of Northern society does not diminish the case for strong reconciliation; the moral and political considerations that informed discussion of fair interactions and commonality, and that continued to inform discussion of inclusive citizen belonging, are not invalidated just because they are unpopular among those pressing an exclusive agenda. In other words, there is no good reason why Northern politics is exempt from standards that are accepted in other Western democracies, even if there is a lot to be said for attending to how these standards are interpreted and implemented in a particular context. The stark upshot is that special pleading for sectarianism ought to fall on deaf ears if we purport to take reconciliation remotely seriously.

The second point is more specific: it is only as we call into question the primacy attributed (explicitly or implicitly) to principles of constitutional sovereignty that there is much hope of attaining an inclusive citizen belonging in the North. As I have been at pains to stress, this is to think about politics differently, but in a way that seems at least in tune with the spirit of the Agreement. It is hard not to believe that anticipation of a prospering, reconciled post-Agreement Northern society requires thinking that runs along lines something like these.

CONCLUSION

Three broad outlooks on reconciliation have cropped up throughout the book. One views *reconciliation as being beyond reach*. This amounts to a dismal view, even when it appears as a celebration of difference and not as a bundle of sectarian prejudices. For it has nothing constructive to say about how the deep problems of division in Northern society may be seriously tackled, and it is ill-equipped to call apostles of division to account. Or so I have argued. Its main contribution is to pose questions that any decent approach to reconciliation has to wrestle with. Another outlook is slightly more upbeat and sees the possibility of balancing the interests of unionism and nationalism in a manner both may find acceptable. I have called what is on offer here a type of *weak reconciliation*. This is a position that is not without merit, both philosophical and political. But it fails to make a sufficiently vigorous assault on the sources of our destructive divisions in the North, and asks us to settle for less than we should. For all the so-called real world wisdom that instructs this view, I have argued that it is short-sighted.

I have contended that we require the outlook of what I have named *strong reconciliation* in order to make up for the deficiencies in the other two. Strong reconciliation is intended to serve three purposes above all others: first, to spell out an ideal that shapes what our priorities should be in Northern society; second, to show how the ideal (or something like it) is implicit in important things we say about ourselves and what we stand for; and third, to indicate why it should not be allowed to slide into the background or be over-ridden by other things we say or stand for, particularly those things that create sharp divisions between us and play to our narrow cultural and political self-interests. Taking these purposes seriously dislodges our prejudices. It involves asking whether many of our divisive priorities and practices are worth the investments that have been made in them. It opens us up to possibilities of change and co-operation for the sake of making Northern society a decent place to live in for all citizens.

The Agreement gives heart to this notion of strong reconcilia-tion, but its aftermath in the North does not. Resistance to recon-ciliation, weak or strong, is enormous, despite much talk to the contrary. But to give in to the anti-reconciliation forces in North-ern Ireland is to pay them a compliment that is undeserved. It is worth bringing the argument of the book to a close by reiterating this point, since it unearths possibly the greatest prejudices against reconciliation's prospects.

Strong reconciliation may indeed seem too demanding in a society that is accustomed to cultural and political attitudes being shaped by the habits of self-interest, suspicion and contempt of the 'other'. And it may also seem odd. It is certainly more customary for many Northerners to settle for A.T.Q. Stewart's view that 'uncertainty about real estate'[1] is what divisions in our society boil down to, and that here it is simply a matter of sticking to the prop-erty claims of our particular tribe, which most of us have learned from birth. And it probably suits many of us to be told by Stewart again that 'there is no misunderstanding between Catholic and Pro-testant in Northern Ireland, none whatsoever. Nor do they need to get to know each other better. They know each other only too well, having lived alongside each other for four centuries, part of the same society yet divided by politics and history.'[2] This is a familiar and convenient view, which, in addition to providing no reason why we should even expect the antagonistic relations on display in North Belfast and Drumcree to be any different, takes the demand out of many of my arguments by making them seem irrelevant, if not bizarre.

On Stewart's terms there is no such thing as misrecognition in Northern Ireland, political dialogue is beside the point, and anyway strong reconciliation may have dangerous implications. The drift of my emphases on cultivating fair interactions, searching out common ground, and seeking inclusive belonging, encourages citizens in the North to believe that instead of slotting into a friend/enemy distinction based on squabbles about real estate, intertraditional co-operation, if not indeed fraternity, is a better option. Stewart is alert to the mischief in this sort of drift. Quoting Joseph Conrad, he offers the following advice: 'There is already as much fraternity as there can be – and that is very little and that very little is no good. What does fraternity mean? Abnegation – self-sacrifice, means something. Fraternity means nothing unless the Cain–Abel business. That's your fraternity.'[3] Among other things, this advice implies a misanthropic view of political relations. And not least because I think such a view is profoundly misplaced and serves only to reinforce divisions in Northern society, I believe that strong reconciliation, however odd or demanding it appears, matters enormously.

NOTES

INTRODUCTION

1 Michael Ignatieff, *Virtual War: Kosovo and Beyond* (London: Chatto and Windus, 2000), p. 212.

2 The marching season in Northern Ireland occurs during spring and summer. Although not exclusively Protestant, the vast majority of marches held during this period commemorate and/or celebrate important events in Protestant history. The most numerous and popular of these marches are organised by the Orange Order. Most pass off peacefully, but a few are deeply contentious and frequently provoke sectarian clashes and standoffs. Controversial marches invariably involve disputes over routing, namely when Orangemen, for example, propose to parade through an area whose (predominantly Catholic) residents do not welcome them and wish them to take an alternative route.

3 Those interested in compensating for these deficits may profitably consult on theology Miroslav Volf,

Exclusion and Embrace: A Theological Exploration of Identity, Otherness, and Reconciliation (Nashville: Abingdon Press, 1996), and Michael Hurley (ed.), *Reconciliation in Religion and Society* (Belfast: Institute of Irish Studies, 1994); and on politics Paul Arthur, *Special Relationships: Britain, Ireland and the Northern Ireland Problem* (Belfast: Blackstaff Press, 2000), and Dermot Keogh and Michael H. Haltzel (eds), *Northern Ireland and the Politics of Reconciliation* (New York: Woodrow Wilson Center Press and Cambridge University Press, 1993).

CHAPTER 1

1 See, for example, Ronald Beiner, *What's the Matter with Liberalism?* (Berkeley, CA: University of California Press, 1992), and Alasdair MacIntyre, *After Virtue: A Study in Moral Theory* (London: Duckworth, 1981).

2 This is not to say that there are not continuing disagreements about what facing up to reconciliation should entail in Australia. See, for example,

Michelle Gratton (ed.), *Reconciliation: Essays on Australian Reconciliation* (Melbourne: Blackwell, 2000).

3   See Fred Argy, *Australia at the Crossroads: Radical Free Market or a Progressive Liberalism?* (Sydney: Allen and Unwin, 1998), and, more generally, Peter Self, *Rolling Back the Market: Economic Dogma and Political Choice* (London: Macmillan Press, 2000).

4   Ken Maginnis quoted in Duncan Morrow, 'Suffering for Righteousness' Sake? Fundamentalist Protestantism and Ulster Politics', in Peter Shirlow and Mark McGovern (eds), *Who are 'The People'? Unionism, Protestantism and Loyalism in Northern Ireland* (London: Pluto Press, 1997), p. 55.

5   Ian Paisley quoted in Dennis Cooke, *Persecuting Zeal: A Portrait of Ian Paisley* (Dingle: Brandon, 1996), p. 99.

6   *Ibid.*, p. 134.

7   A.T.Q. Stewart, *The Shape of Irish History* (Belfast: Blackstaff Press, 2001), p. 182.

8   A.T.Q. Stewart quoted in Susan McKay, *Northern Protestants: An Unsettled People* (Belfast: Blackstaff Press, 1999), p. 294.

9   Norman Porter, *Rethinking Unionism: An Alternative Vision for Northern Ireland*, new updated edition (Belfast: Blackstaff Press, 1998).

10 Arthur Aughey, 'Norman Conquered', *Fortnight*, no. 355 (November 1996), p. 31.

CHAPTER 2

1   Colin Coulter, 'Direct Rule and the Unionist Middle Class', in Richard English and Graham Walker (eds), *Unionism in Modern Ireland: New Perspectives on Politics and Culture* (Dublin: Gill and Macmillan, 1996), pp. 174–6.

2   Volf, *Exclusion and Embrace*, p. 116.

3   Hannah Arendt, *The Human Condition* (Chicago: University of Chicago Press, 1959), p. 216.

4   This is Volf's gloss on Arendt in *Exclusion and Embrace*, p. 121.

5   Michael Ignatieff, *The Warrior's Honor: Ethnic War and the Modern Conscience* (London: Chatto and Windus, 1998), p. 34. Of interest here is the play made on the same idea of 'minor difference' to illuminate relations between Catholics and Protestants in an earlier period of Irish history in Donald Akenson, *Small Differences: Irish Catholics and Irish Protestants 1815–1922* (Dublin: Gill and Macmillan, 1991).

6   Charles Taylor, 'Nationalism and Modernity', in Robert McKim and Jeff McMahan (eds), *The Morality of Nationalism* (Oxford: Oxford University Press, 1997), p. 33.

7   Ernest Gellner, *Nations and Nationalism* (Ithaca, NY: Cornell University Press, 1983), p. 18.

8   I have briefly discussed another kind of cosmopolitanism – one based more on universal moral values, than on the bureaucratic imperatives of the modern state, which can be reconciled with particular identities – in 'The Republican Ideal and Its Interpretations', in Norman Porter (ed.), *The Republican Ideal: Current Perspectives* (Belfast: Blackstaff Press, 1998), pp. 1–33.

9   Claude Lévi-Strauss quoted in Volf, *Exclusion and Embrace*, p. 75.

10 Iris Marion Young, *Justice and the Politics of Difference* (Princeton, NJ: Princeton University Press, 1990), p. 179.

11 *Ibid.*, p. 180.

12 Alan Finlayson, 'The Problem of Culture in Northern Ireland: A Critique of the Cultural Traditions Group', *Irish Review*,

no. 20 (winter/spring 1997), p. 86.

13 Aletta S. Norval, 'Identity and the (Im)Possibility of Reconciliation: The Work of the Truth and Reconciliation Committee in South Africa', *Constellations*, vol. 5, no. 2 (1998), p. 261.

14 Richard English, 'Unionism and Nationalism: The Notion of Symmetry', in John Wilson Foster (ed.), *The Idea of the Union: Statements and Critiques in Support of the Union of Great Britain and Northern Ireland* (Vancouver: Belcouver Press, 1995), p. 136.

15 *Ibid.*, p. 138.

16 Richard English, 'The Northern Ireland Peace Process Reconsidered', *Eire-Ireland. An Interdisciplinary Journal of Irish Studies*, vol. 31, nos 3 and 4 (1997), p. 275.

17 Arthur Aughey, 'A State of Exception: The Concept of the Political in Northern Ireland', *Irish Political Studies*, vol. 12 (1997), pp. 1–12.

18 Arthur Aughey, 'McCartney in the Wings', *Fortnight*, no. 340 (June 1995), p. 12.

19 While still writing respectfully of Schmitt, Aughey has recently discerned in the Agreement possibilities of a new politics of civility. See Arthur Aughey, 'A New Beginning? The Prospects for a Politics of Civility in Northern Ireland', in Joseph Ruane and Jennifer Todd (eds), *After the Good Friday Agreement: Analysing Political Change in Northern Ireland* (Dublin: University College Dublin Press, 1999), pp. 122–44.

CHAPTER 3

1 I have already discussed this concept at length in *Rethinking Unionism*, pp. 41–52; 165–7; 187–90. My remarks here are intended neither to repeat nor replace that discussion, but to supplement it.

2 See, in particular, their suggestions in *Frameworks for the Future* (Belfast: Her Majesty's Stationery Office, 1995).

3 For an illuminating discussion of the distinction between self-respect and self-esteem along the lines I am following here see Axel Honneth, *The Struggle for Recognition: The Moral Grammar of Social Conflicts*, trans. Joel Anderson (Cambridge: Polity Press, 1995).

4 Young, *Justice and the Politics of Difference*, p. 179.

5 See, for example, the Faith and Politics Group's pamphlet, *Doing Unto Others: Parity of Esteem in a Contested Space* (Belfast: Faith and Politics Group, 1997).

6 James Tully, *Strange Multiplicity: Constitutionalism in an Age of Diversity* (Cambridge: Cambridge University Press, 1995), p. 54.

CHAPTER 4

1 This is a view discernible in Hegel's early writings. See Honneth, *The Struggle for Recognition*, pp. 12–13.

2 Michael Sandel, *Democracy's Discontent: America in Search of a Public Philosophy* (Cambridge, Mass.: Harvard University Press, 1996), p. 6.

3 Will Kymlicka and Wayne Norman, 'Citizenship in Culturally Diverse Societies: Issues, Contexts, Concepts', in Will Kymlicka and Wayne Norman (eds), *Citizenship in Diverse Societies* (Oxford: Oxford University Press, 2000), p. 6.

4 William Galston, *Liberal Purposes: Goods, Virtues, and Diversity in the Liberal State* (Cambridge: Cambridge

University Press, 1991), p. 220.

5   Hannah Arendt, *Men in Dark Times* (Harmondsworth, Middlesex: Penguin, 1973), p. 245. Arendt's highlighting of this implication of forgiveness occurs in the larger context of her analysis of the life and work of Bertolt Brecht, and pertains in particular to the relationship between judging and forgiving. She writes: 'the equality before the law whose standard we commonly accept for moral judgements as well is no absolute. Every judgement is open to forgiveness, every act of judgement can change into an act of forgiving; to judge and to forgive are but two sides of the same coin. But the two sides follow different rules. The majesty of the law demands that we be equal – that only our acts count, and not the person who committed them. The act of forgiving, on the contrary, takes the person into account; no pardon pardons murder or theft but only the murderer or the thief. We always forgive some*body*, never some*thing*.' *Ibid.*

6   Honneth, *The Struggle for Recognition*, p. 129.

7   Tully, *Strange Multiplicity*, p. 205.

8   Iris Marion Young, *Inclusion and Democracy* (Oxford: Oxford University Press, 2000), p. 59.

9   Tully, *Strange Multiplicity*, pp. 34–5.

10 Hans Georg Gadamer, *Truth and Method*, trans. G. Barden and J. Cumming (London: Sheed and Ward, 1975), p. 386.

11 Padraig O'Malley, *Biting at the Grave: The Irish Hunger Strikes and the Politics of Despair* (Belfast: Blackstaff Press, 1990), p. 185.

12 On 15 August 1998 the Real IRA – a breakaway from the Provisional IRA that disapproved of the latter's ceasefire – detonated a bomb in Omagh, County Tyrone, which killed twenty-nine civilians. This was the single deadliest atrocity in the history of conflict in Northern Ireland.

13 See, for example, Mitchel McLaughlin, 'The Irish Republican Ideal', in Porter (ed.), *The Republican Ideal*, pp. 62–84.

14 Gerry Adams quoted in Brendan O'Brien, *The Long War: The IRA and Sinn Féin from Armed Struggle to Peace Talks* (Dublin: O'Brien Press, 1993), p. 98.

15 John Dunlop, *A Precarious Belonging: Presbyterians and the Conflict in Ireland* (Belfast: Blackstaff Press, 1995), p. 84.

16 David Trimble, *To Raise Up a New Northern Ireland: Articles and Speeches 1998–2000* (Belfast: Belfast Press, 2001), p. 144.

17 Aughey, 'McCartney in the Wings', p. 12.

18 Trimble, *To Raise Up a New Northern Ireland*, p. 58.

19 Dunlop, *A Precarious Belonging*, p. 84.

20 *Ibid.*

21 *Ibid.*, p. 99.

22 See further Charles Taylor, 'Language and Human Nature,' in his *Human Agency and Language: Philosophical Papers, 1* (Cambridge: Cambridge University Press, 1985), pp. 215–47.

23 Dunlop, *A Precarious Belonging*, p. 84.

24 Trimble, *To Raise Up a New Northern Ireland*, p. 114.

25 Thomas Hobbes, *Leviathan* (Harmondsworth, Middlesex: Penguin, 1968), p. 106.

26 Any number of philosophical approaches to language give impeccable reasons for scepticism here. As effective as any are those found in the celebrated discussion of language's relation to 'forms of life' in Ludwig Wittgenstein,

Philosophical Investigations, trans.
G.E.M. Anscombe (Oxford:
Blackwell, 1976).

CHAPTER 5

1   Iris Marion Young, *Intersecting Voices: Dilemmas of Gender, Political Philosophy and Policy* (Princeton, NJ: Princeton University Press, 1997), p. 66.

2   I propose commenting here only on one of the senses attached to the notion of incommensurability, namely that it is impossible to share meanings and understandings across traditions and cultures. The case I develop against this sense does not necessarily imply that it is misplaced to speak of incommensurability in other senses – for example, when we have to choose between different goods we value because there is no standard measure by which we can weigh them up.

3   This type of reasoning is frequently associated with so-called post-modern and/or post-structuralist authors. In the text below, I prefer to describe it as a species of radical pluralism. Among its influential sources are the works of the French thinkers Michel Foucault and Jacques Derrida. Another important source, especially for my depiction of radical pluralist reasoning, is the North American philosopher Richard Rorty. See, for example, his *Philosophy and the Mirror of Nature* (Princeton, NJ: Princeton University Press, 1979), and, more especially, *Philosophy and Social Hope* (Harmondsworth, Middlesex: Penguin, 1999).

4   Two clarifications are needed here. (1) My claim, expanded in the text below, is that incommensurability is a misnomer when different discourses are trying to explain the workings of the universe, not when only one is and the other is trying to do something else. (2) In saying that there is a world independent of our descriptions of it, I am not retracting my earlier point that we do not have access to such a world independently of our descriptions. It is perfectly plausible to hold both points. For discussion of these sorts of clarifications see the debate between Richard Rorty and Charles Taylor in James Tully (ed.), *Philosophy in an Age of Pluralism: The Philosophy of Charles Taylor in Question* (Cambridge: Cambridge University Press, 1994), pp. 20–36; 219–22.

5   Friedrich Nietzsche, *The Will to Power*, trans. Walter Kaufmann and R.J. Hollingdale (New York: Vintage, 1967).

6   Gadamer, *Truth and Method*, p. 273.

7   These dates are shorthand references to significant events in Irish history. They partly matter as much as they do to unionists and nationalists/republicans because they are taken to indicate important attempts to relieve either a sense of siege or a sense of oppression. Thus the years 1690 and 1912 recall events valued by unionists because they gave promise of liberation from the worst fears of a Protestant siege mentality, namely the Protestant William III's victory over the Catholic James II at the Battle of the Boyne, and resistance to Irish Home Rule demonstrated in the signing of the Ulster Covenant and Declaration by 471,000 people. Similarly, the years 1798 and 1916 recall events valued by nationalists and republicans because they attest to efforts to end English rule – considered by many as the

source of oppression – in Ireland, namely the United Irishmen's Rebellion and the Easter Uprising.

8 For an example of what I mean by this consideration see Norman Porter, The Ideas of 1798', in Mary Cullen (ed.), *1798, 200 Years of Resonance: Essays and Contributions on the History and Relevance of the United Irishmen and the 1798 Revolution* (Dublin: Elo Press, 1998), pp. 105–12.

9 See, for example, Frank Wright, 'Reconciling the Histories of Protestant and Catholic in Northern Ireland'; and Joseph Liechty, 'History and Reconciliation: Frank Wright, Whitley Stokes and the Vortex of Antagonism', in Alan D. Falconer and Joseph Liechty (eds), *Reconciling Memories* (Dublin: Columba Press, 1998), pp. 128–48; 149–76.

10 Charles Taylor, *Multiculturalism and the Politics of Recognition* (Princeton, NJ: Princeton University Press, 1992).

11 John Rawls, *Political Liberalism* (New York: Columbia University Press, 1993), p. xvii.

12 *Ibid.*, p. 31.

13 Shane O'Neill, 'Pluralist Justice and Its Limits: The Case of Northern Ireland', *Political Studies*, vol. 42 (1994), p. 369.

14 *Ibid.*, p. 373.

15 *Ibid.*, pp. 372ff.

16 See Jürgen Habermas, *Justification and Application: Remarks on Discourse Ethics*, trans. Ciaran Cronin (Cambridge, Mass: MIT Press, 1993).

17 Martha Nussbaum, 'Human Functioning and Social Justice: In Defence of Aristotelian Essentialism', *Political Theory*, vol. 20, no. 2, (May 1992), pp. 214–15.

18 Nussbaum's list of basic human functional capabilities runs as follows:

1 Being able to live to the end of a complete human life, as far as is possible; not dying prematurely or before one's life is so reduced as to be not worth living.

2 Being able to have good health; to be adequately nourished; to have adequate shelter; having opportunities for sexual satisfaction; being able to move from place to place.

3 Being able to avoid unnecessary and nonbeneficial pain and to have pleasurable experiences.

4 Being able to use the five senses; being able to imagine, to think, and to reason.

5 Being able to have attachments to things and persons outside ourselves; to love those who love and care for us, to grieve at their absence, in general, to love, grieve, to feel longing and gratitude.

6 Being able to form a conception of the good and to engage in critical reflection about the planning of one's own life.

7 Being able to live with and for others, to recognize and show concern for other human beings, to engage in various forms of familial and social interaction.

8 Being able to live with concern for and in relation to animals, plants, and the world of nature.

9 Being able to laugh, to play, to enjoy recreational activities.

10 Being able to live one's own life and nobody else's; being able to live one's own life in one's very own surroundings and context. *Ibid.*, p. 222.

19 *Ibid.*, pp. 222–3.

CHAPTER 6

1 Young, *Justice and the Politics of Difference*, pp. 226–56.

2 I treat republicanism here as part of the family of Irish

nationalism. This is because I am dealing mainly with Sinn Féin's version of republicanism. Other Irish republicans, most notably those with backgrounds in the Official IRA and/or with current associations with the Workers' Party, dispute that republicanism is properly related to nationalism. See, for example, Des O'Hagan, 'The Concept of Republicanism', in Porter (ed.), *The Republican Ideal*, pp. 85–112.

3 Benedict Anderson, *Imagined Communities: Reflections on the Origins and Spread of Nationalism* (London: Verso, 1983).

4 McLaughlin, 'The Irish Republican Ideal', p. 78.

5 For a discussion of similarities and differences between Sinn Féin and the SDLP here see Jennifer Todd, 'Nationalism, Republicanism and the Good Friday Agreement', in Ruane and Todd (eds), *After the Good Friday Agreement*, pp. 49–70.

6 Much to the chagrin of unionists, this point was underscored by the election in June 2002 of Sinn Féin councillor Alex Maskey as Lord Mayor of Belfast.

7 In recent years loyalists have organised protests, which have invariably been abusive and occasionally violent, against Catholic churchgoers (Harryville) and schoolchildren (Ardoyne), whose routes to church or school have taken them along roads that are presumed to be part of Protestant territory.

8 See Trimble, *To Raise Up a New Northern Ireland*.

9 This is a view pushed by Arthur Aughey in his *Under Siege: Ulster Unionism and the Anglo-Irish Agreement* (Belfast: Blackstaff Press, 1989) and by Robert McCartney, *Liberty and Authority in Ireland*, Field Day Pamphlet no. 9 (Derry: Field Day, 1985). It

is a view echoed recently by David Trimble in a speech to the UUP's ruling council when he invited his audience to 'Contrast the United Kingdom state – a vibrant multi-ethnic, multinational liberal democracy, the fourth largest economy in the world, the most reliable ally of the United States in the fight against international terrorism – with the pathetic, sectarian, mono-ethnic, monocultural state to our south.' Quoted in the *Observer*, 10 March 2002.

10 For more on liberal and cultural unionism, see Porter, *Rethinking Unionism*.

11 The parties associated with Protestant paramilitaries are the PUP, which is close to the UVF, and the Ulster Democratic Party (UDP), which is close to the UDA. Or at least that was the case until November 2001 when one of the parties – the UDP – was dissolved.

12 A.T.Q. Stewart, *The Narrow Ground: Patterns of Ulster History* (London: Faber and Faber, 1977), p. 180.

13 For a good discussion of these earlier initiatives and their bearing on the Agreement see Arthur, *Special Relationships*.

14 Aughey, 'A New Beginning? The Prospects for a Politics of Civility in Northern Ireland', pp. 138–9.

15 Trimble, *To Raise Up a New Northern Ireland*, p. 125.

16 The following sorts of comments from anti-Agreement unionists greeted news of a second act of decommissioning by the IRA in April 2002. It was a 'stunt' that 'no one will be fooled by', announced Peter Robinson of the DUP. And within Trimble's own party, UUP MP Jeffrey Donaldson remarked that this 'further IRA gesture has more to do with the Irish general

election and deflecting attention away from the break-in at Castlereagh Police Station than it has to do with a commitment to peace and democracy'. Quoted in *Belfast Telegraph*, 8 April 2002.

CHAPTER 7

1 Joseph Ruane and Jennifer Todd, 'The Belfast Agreement', in Ruane and Todd (eds), *After the Good Friday Agreement*, p. 21.
2 Trimble, *To Raise Up a New Northern Ireland*, p. 125.
3 *Ibid.*, pp. 130–31.
4 *Ibid.*, p. 130.
5 *Ibid.*, p. 134.
6 I am following the North American philosopher John Rawls's use of the term 'lexical order' here in an attempt to elucidate the way in which unionists, influenced by David Trimble, interpret the Agreement. Rawls applies what he calles a lexical order to principles of justice. As he explains, this 'is an order which requires us to satisfy the first principle in the ordering before we can move on to the second, the second before we consider the third, and so on. A principle does not come into play until those previous to it are either fully met or do not apply. A serial ordering avoids, then, having to balance principles at all; those earlier in the ordering have an absolute weight, so to speak, with respect to later ones, and hold without exception.' John Rawls, *A Theory of Justice* (Oxford: Oxford University Press, 1972), p. 43. A key to understanding Trimble's reading of the Agreement, it seems to me, lies in grasping that for him the two standards of legitimacy are not equal and do not have to be balanced with respect to each other. As I try to show in the text

below, the constitutional standard always has an absolute priority for him and the institutional standard only comes into play when it does not imply any constitutional compromise. In this sense, then, I am claiming that in a Rawlsian use of the term, a lexical ordering is being applied to the standards of legitimacy contained in the Agreement.
7 Trimble, *To Raise Up a New Northern Ireland*, p. 129.
8 *Ibid.*, p. 144.
9 See, for example, Todd, 'Nationalism, Republicanism and the Good Friday Agreement', pp. 49–70.
10 See, for example, the results of a recent academically conducted poll for the *Belfast Telegraph*, which had 16 per cent of Catholics preferring to remain within the UK and only 44 per cent of Catholics even thinking that a united Ireland was likely during the next twenty years. *Belfast Telegraph*, 22 February 2000.
11 Thus Gerry Adams, in a speech anticipating the IRA's decision to engage in an act of decommissioning arms, states that 'the IRA is genuinely committed to building a peace process in which the objectives of Irish republicanism can be argued and advanced. The Army has repeatedly demonstrated leadership and patience and vision and I respect absolutely its right to make its own decision on this issue [decommissioning].' Quoted in the *Irish Times,* 23 October 2001. These remarks indicate not only that the military agent of republicanism shares the objectives of the political agent, but also that the legitimacy of the IRA, even under conditions of reform, remains beyond question: thus

Adams respects 'absolutely its right to make its own decision'.

12 Hannah Arendt, 'What is Authority?', in her *Between Past and Future* (London: Faber and Faber, 1961), pp. 91–142.

13 See McCartney, *Liberty and Authority in Ireland*. I am severely critical of other uses to which McCartney puts Berlin's concept of positive freedom, and of Berlin's understanding of the concept. See Porter, *Rethinking Unionism*, pp. 146–56.

14 See, for example, Gerry Adams, 'Transforming Hope into Reality: Negotiating a New Beginning', in his *Selected Writings*, new expanded edition (Dingle: Brandon, 1997), pp. 342–9.

15 Adams details the categories of persons deliberately killed by the IRA as follows: 'members of the crown forces'; 'loyalist activists'; and 'persons working in direct support of British crown forces'. See Adams, 'Towards a Lasting Peace', in his *Selected Writings*, p. 284. The latter category in particular raises eyebrows given its susceptibility to a very broad definition. Provisional republicans should not be surprised if others see here an attempt, and a very unconvincing one at that, to disguise the sectarian nature of various Provisional IRA killings.

16 See, for example, O'Malley, *Biting at the Grave*.

17 See further my discussion in 'The Republican Ideal and Its Interpretations', pp. 1–33.

18 Declan Kiberd, 'Romantic Ireland's Dead and Gone', *Times Literary Supplement*, vol.12 (June 1998), p. 14.

19 Tully, *Strange Multiplicity*, p. 205.

CONCLUSION

1 Stewart, *The Shape of Irish History*, p. 184.

2 *Ibid.*, p. 185.

3 *Ibid.*, p. 183.

BIBLIOGRAPHY

Adams, Gerry, *Selected Writings*, new expanded edition (Dingle: Brandon, 1997)

Akenson, Donald, *Small Differences: Irish Catholics and Irish Protestants 1815–1922* (Dublin: Gill and Macmillan, 1991)

Anderson, Benedict, *Imagined Communities: Reflections on the Origins and Spread of Nationalism* (London: Verso, 1983)

Arendt, Hannah, *The Human Condition* (Chicago: University of Chicago Press, 1959)

   Between Past and Future (London: Faber and Faber, 1961)

   Crises of the Republic (Harmondsworth, Middlesex: Penguin, 1973)

   Men in Dark Times (Harmondsworth, Middlesex: Penguin, 1973)

Argy, Fred, *Australia at the Crossroads: Radical Free Market or a Progressive Liberalism?* (Sydney: Allen and Unwin, 1998)

Aristotle, *Ethics*, trans. J.A.K. Thompson (Harmondsworth, Middlesex: Penguin, 1966)

Arthur, Paul, *Special Relationships: Britain, Ireland and the Northern Ireland Problem* (Belfast: Blackstaff Press, 2000)

Aughey, Arthur, *Under Siege: Ulster Unionism and the Anglo-Irish Agreement* (Belfast: Blackstaff Press, 1989)

   'McCartney in the Wings', *Fortnight*, no. 340 (June 1995)

   'Norman Conquered', *Fortnight,* no. 355 (November 1996)

   'A State of Exception: The Concept of the Political in Northern Ireland', *Irish Political Studies*, vol. 12 (1997)

   'A New Beginning? The Prospects for a Politics of Civility in Northern Ireland', in Joseph Ruane and Jennifer Todd (eds), *After the Good Friday Agreement: Analysing Political Change in Northern*

Ireland (Dublin: University College Dublin Press, 1999)

Beiner, Ronald, *What's the Matter with Liberalism?* (Berkeley, CA: University of California Press, 1992)

Cooke, Dennis, *Persecuting Zeal: A Portrait of Ian Paisley* (Dingle: Brandon, 1996)

Coulter, Colin, 'Direct Rule and the Unionist Middle Class', in Richard English and Graham Walker (eds), *Unionism in Modern Ireland: New Perspectives on Politics and Culture* (Dublin: Gill and Macmillan, 1996)

Dunlop, John, *A Precarious Belonging: Presbyterians and the Conflict in Ireland* (Belfast: Blackstaff Press, 1995)

English, Richard, 'Unionism and Nationalism: The Notion of Symmetry', in John Wilson Foster (ed.), *The Idea of the Union: Statements and Critiques in Support of the Union of Great Britain and Northern Ireland* (Vancouver: Belcouver Press, 1995)

'The Northern Ireland Peace Process Reconsidered', *Eire-Ireland. An Interdisciplinary Journal of Irish Studies*, vol. 31, nos 3 and 4 (1997)

Faith and Politics Group, *Doing Unto Others: Parity of Esteem in a Contested Space* (Belfast: Faith and Politics Group, 1997)

Finlayson, Alan, 'The Problem of Culture in Northern Ireland: A Critique of the Cultural Traditions Group', *Irish Review*, no. 20 (winter/spring 1997)

Frameworks for the Future (Belfast: Her Majesty's Stationery Office, 1995)

Gadamer, Hans Georg, *Truth and Method*, trans. G. Barden and J. Cumming (London: Sheed and Ward, 1975)

Galston, William, *Liberal Purposes: Goods, Virtues, and Diversity in the Liberal State* (Cambridge: Cambridge University Press, 1991)

Gellner, Ernest, *Nations and Nationalism* (Ithaca, NY: Cornell University Press, 1983)

Gratton, Michelle (ed.), *Reconciliation: Essays on Australian Reconciliation* (Melbourne: Blackwell, 2000)

Habermas, Jürgen, *Justification and Application: Remarks on Discourse Ethics*, trans. Ciaran Cronin (Cambridge, Mass.: MIT Press, 1993)

Hobbes, Thomas, *Leviathan* (Harmondsworth, Middlesex: Penguin, 1968)

Honneth, Axel, *The Struggle for Recognition: The Moral Grammar of Social Conflicts*, trans. Joel Anderson (Cambridge: Polity Press, 1995)

Hurley, Michael (ed.), *Reconciliation in Religion and Society* (Belfast: Institute of Irish Studies, 1994)

Ignatieff, Michael, *The Warrior's Honor: Ethnic War and the Modern Conscience* (London: Chatto and Windus, 1998)

Virtual War: Kosovo and Beyond (London: Chatto and Windus, 2000)

Keogh, Dermot and Haltzel, Michael H. (eds), *Northern Ireland and the Politics of Reconciliation* (New York: Woodrow Wilson Center Press and Cambridge University Press, 1993)

Kiberd, Declan, *Inventing Ireland: The Literature of the Modern Nation* (London: Vintage, 1996)

'Romantic Ireland's Dead and Gone', *Times Literary Supplement*, vol. 12 (June 1998)

Kymlicka, Will and Norman, Wayne, 'Citizenship in Culturally Diverse Societies: Issues, Contexts, Concepts', in Will Kymlicka and Wayne Norman (eds), *Citizenship in Diverse Societies* (Oxford: Oxford University Press, 2000)

Liechty, Joseph, 'History and Reconciliation: Frank Wright, Whitley Stokes and the Vortex of Antagonism', in Alan D. Falconer and Joseph Liechty (eds), *Reconciling Memories* (Dublin: Columba Press, 1998)

McCartney, Robert, *Liberty and Authority in Ireland*, Field Day Pamphlet no. 9 (Derry: Field Day, 1985)

MacIntyre, Alasdair, *After Virtue: A Study in Moral Theory* (London: Duckworth, 1981)

McKay, Susan, *Northern Protestants: An Unsettled People* (Belfast: Blackstaff Press, 1999)

McLaughlin, Mitchel, 'The Irish Republican Ideal', in Norman Porter (ed.), *The Republican Ideal: Current Perspectives* (Belfast: Blackstaff Press, 1998)

Machiavelli, Niccolò, *The Discourses*, trans. Leslie J. Walker (Harmondsworth, Middlesex: Penguin, 1970)

Morrow, Duncan, 'Suffering for Righteousness' Sake? Fundamentalist Protestantism and Ulster Politics', in Peter Shirlow and Mark McGovern (eds), *Who are 'The People'? Unionism, Protestantism and Loyalism in Northern Ireland* (London: Pluto Press, 1997)

Nietzsche, Friedrich. *The Will to Power*, trans. Walter Kaufmann and R.J. Hollingdale (New York: Vintage, 1967)

Norval, Aletta S., 'Identity and the (Im)Possibility of Reconciliation: The Work of the Truth and Reconciliation Committee in South Africa', *Constellations*, vol. 5, no. 2 (1998)

Nussbaum, Martha, 'Human Functioning and Social Justice: In Defence of Aristotelian Essentialism', *Political Theory*, vol. 20, no. 2 (May 1992)

O'Brien, Brendan, *The Long War: The IRA & Sinn Féin from Armed Struggle to Peace Talks* (Dublin: O'Brien Press, 1993)

O'Hagan, Des, 'The Concept of Republicanism', in Norman Porter
(ed.), *The Republican Ideal: Current Perspectives* (Belfast: Blackstaff
Press, 1998)

O'Malley, Padraig, *Biting at the Grave: The Irish Hunger Strikes and the
Politics of Despair* (Belfast: Blackstaff Press, 1990)

O'Neill, Shane, 'Pluralist Justice and Its Limits: The Case of Northern
Ireland', *Political Studies*, vol. 42 (1994)

Porter, Norman, *Rethinking Unionism: An Alternative for Northern Ireland*,
new updated edition (Belfast: Blackstaff Press, 1998)

'The Ideas of 1798', in Mary Cullen (ed.), *1798, 200 Years of Resonance:
Essays and Contributions on the History and Relevance of the United
Irishmen and the 1798 Revolution* (Dublin: Elo Press, 1998)

'The Republican Ideal and Its Interpretations', in Norman Porter
(ed.), *The Republican Ideal: Current Perspectives* (Belfast: Blackstaff
Press, 1998)

Rawls, John, *A Theory of Justice* (Oxford: Oxford University Press, 1972)

Political Liberalism (New York: Columbia University Press, 1993)

Rorty, Richard, *Philosophy and the Mirror of Nature* (Princeton, NJ:
Princeton University Press, 1979)

Philosophy and Social Hope (Harmondsworth, Middlesex: Penguin,
1999)

Ruane, Joseph and Todd, Jennifer, 'The Belfast Agreement', in Joseph
Ruane and Jennifer Todd (eds), *After the Good Friday Agreement:
Analysing Political Change in Northern Ireland* (Dublin: University
College Dublin Press, 1999)

Sandel, Michael, *Democracy's Discontent: America in Search of a Public
Philosophy* (Cambridge, Mass.: Harvard University Press, 1996)

Self, Peter, *Rolling Back the Market: Economic Dogma and Political Choice*
(London: Macmillan Press, 2000)

Stewart, A.T.Q., *The Narrow Ground: Patterns of Ulster History* (London:
Faber and Faber, 1977)

The Shape of Irish History (Belfast: Blackstaff Press, 2001)

Taylor, Charles, *Human Agency and Language: Philosophical Papers, 1*
(Cambridge: Cambridge University Press, 1985)

Multiculturalism and the Politics of Recognition (Princeton, NJ: Princeton
University Press, 1992)

'Nationalism and Modernity', in Robert McKim and Jeff McMahan
(eds), *The Morality of Nationalism* (Oxford: Oxford University
Press, 1997)

Todd, Jennifer, 'Nationalism, Republicanism and the Good Friday Agreement', in Joseph Ruane and Jennifer Todd (eds), *After the Good Friday Agreement: Analysing Political Change in Northern Ireland* (Dublin: University College Dublin Press, 1999)

Trimble, David, *To Raise Up a New Northern Ireland: Articles and Speeches 1998–2000* (Belfast: Belfast Press, 2001)

Tully, James, *Strange Multiplicity: Constitutionalism in an Age of Diversity* (Cambridge: Cambridge University Press, 1995)

(ed.), *Philosophy in an Age of Pluralism: The Philosophy of Charles Taylor in Question* (Cambridge: Cambridge University Press, 1994)

Volf, Miroslav, *Exclusion and Embrace: A Theological Exploration of Identity, Otherness, and Reconciliation* (Nashville: Abingdon Press, 1996)

Wittgenstein, Ludwig, *Philosophical Investigations*, trans. G.E.M. Anscombe (Oxford: Blackwell, 1976)

Wright, Frank, 'Reconciling the Histories of Protestant and Catholic in Northern Ireland', in Alan D. Falconer and Joseph Liechty (eds), *Reconciling Memories* (Dublin: Columba Press, 1998)

Young, Iris Marion, *Justice and the Politics of Difference* (Princeton, NJ: Princeton University Press, 1990)

Intersecting Voices: Dilemmas of Gender, Political Philosophy and Policy (Princeton, NJ: Princeton University Press, 1997)

Inclusion and Democracy (Oxford: Oxford University Press, 2000)

INDEX